EARTHLY THINGS

Jim McJunkin

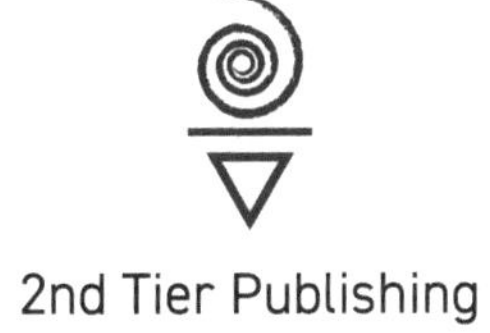

2nd Tier Publishing

Published by:
2nd Tier Publishing
13501 Ranch Road 12, Ste 103
Wimberley, TX 78676

ISBN 978-0-692-88095-1

Edited by Jason Scalise
Book design by Dan Gauthier

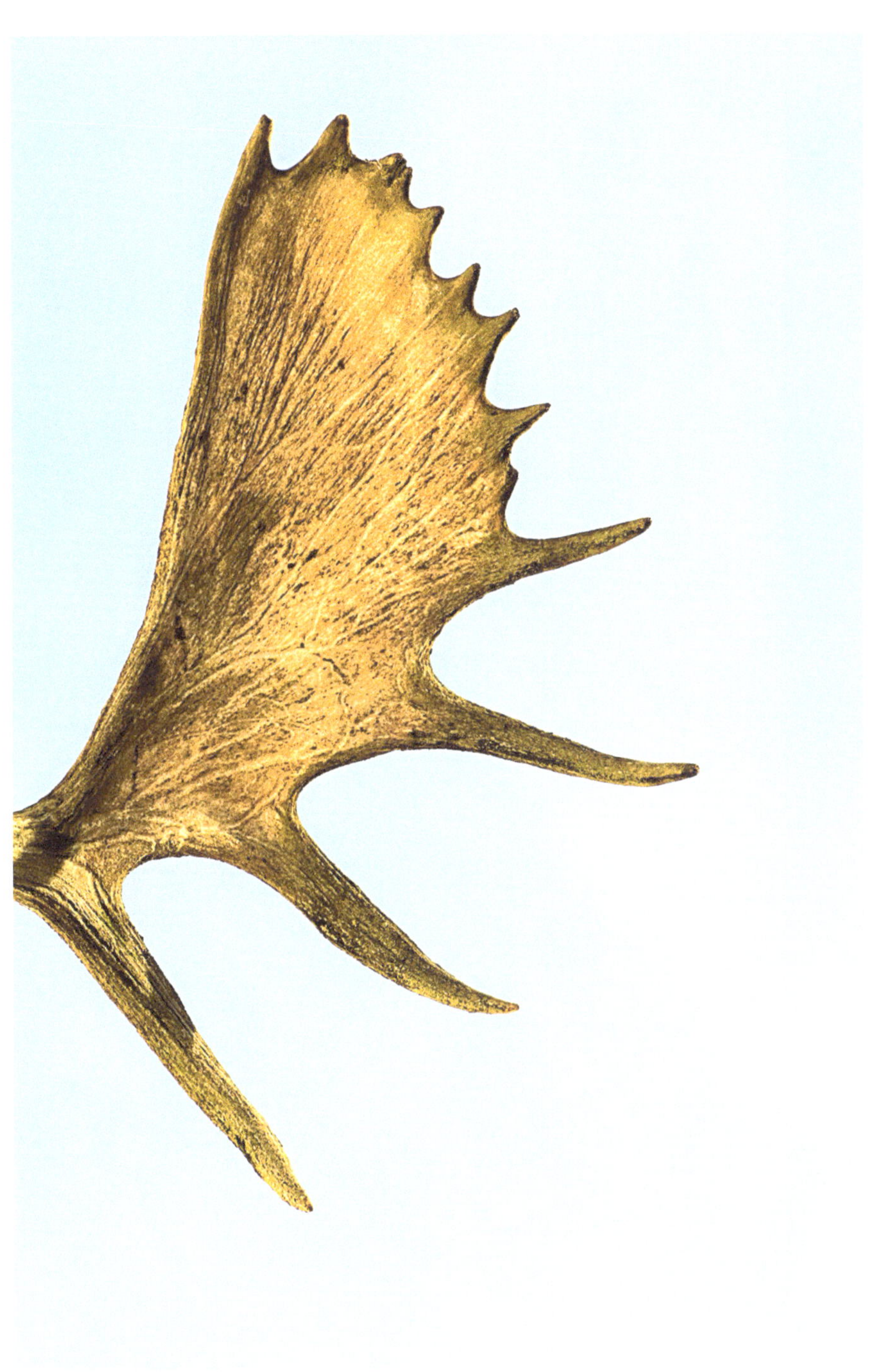

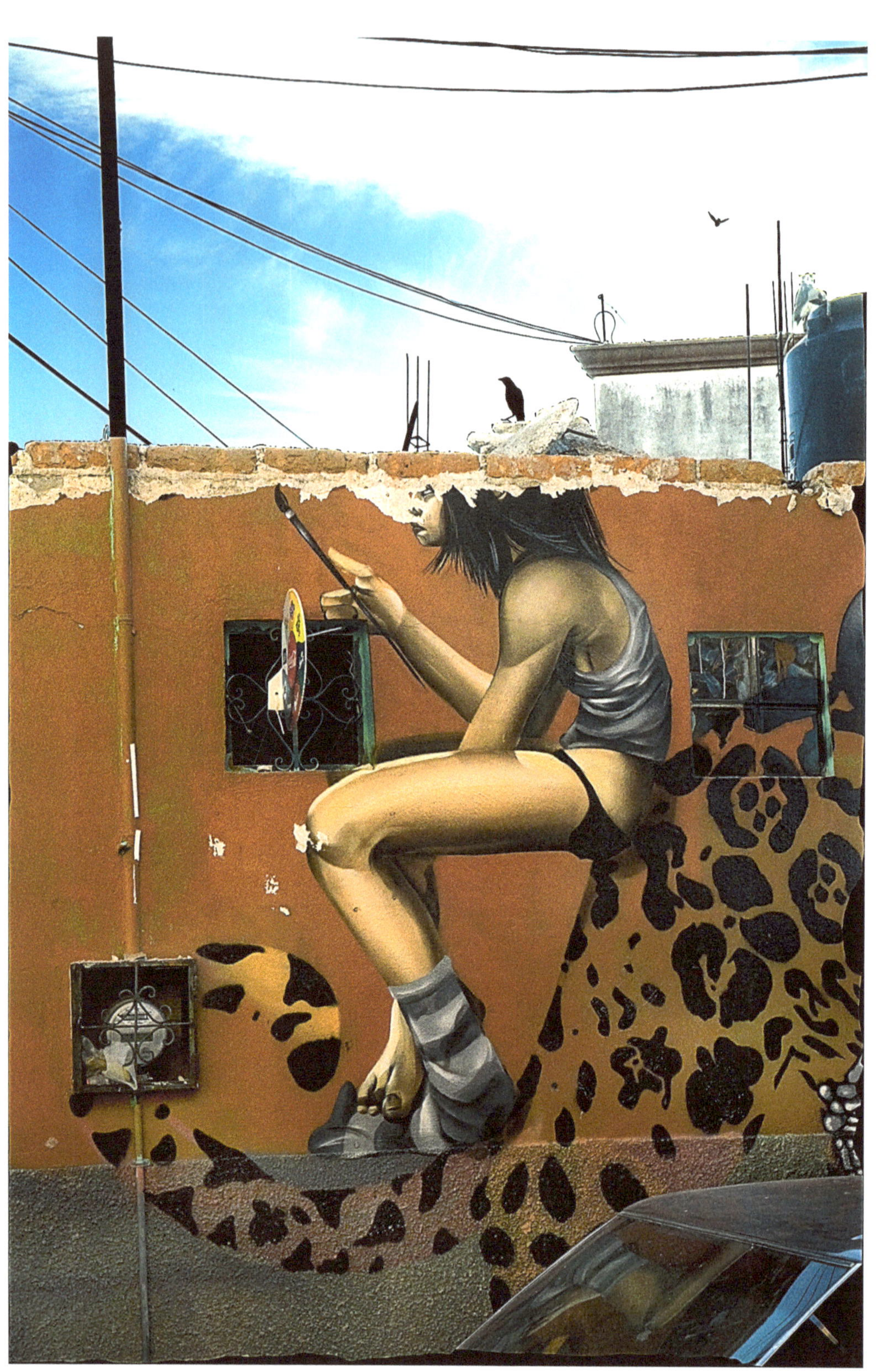

Table of Contents

So Much To See

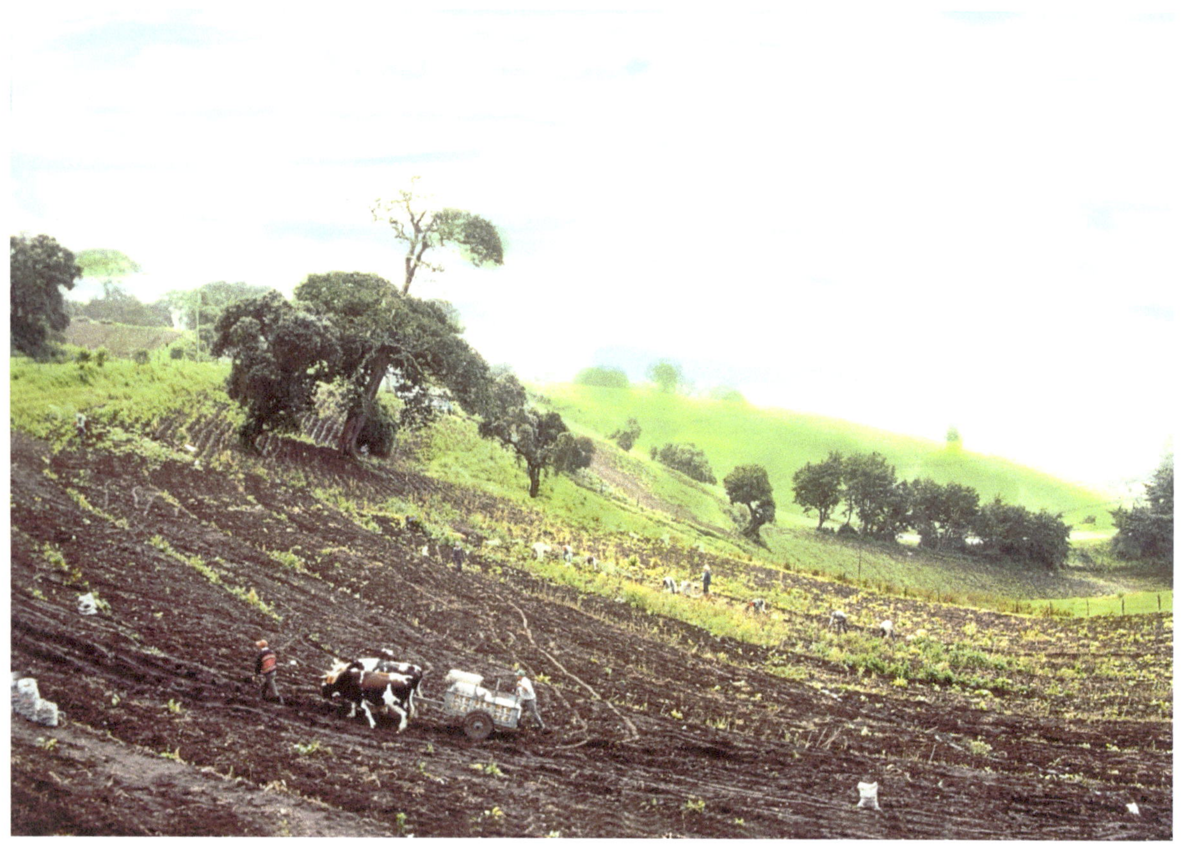

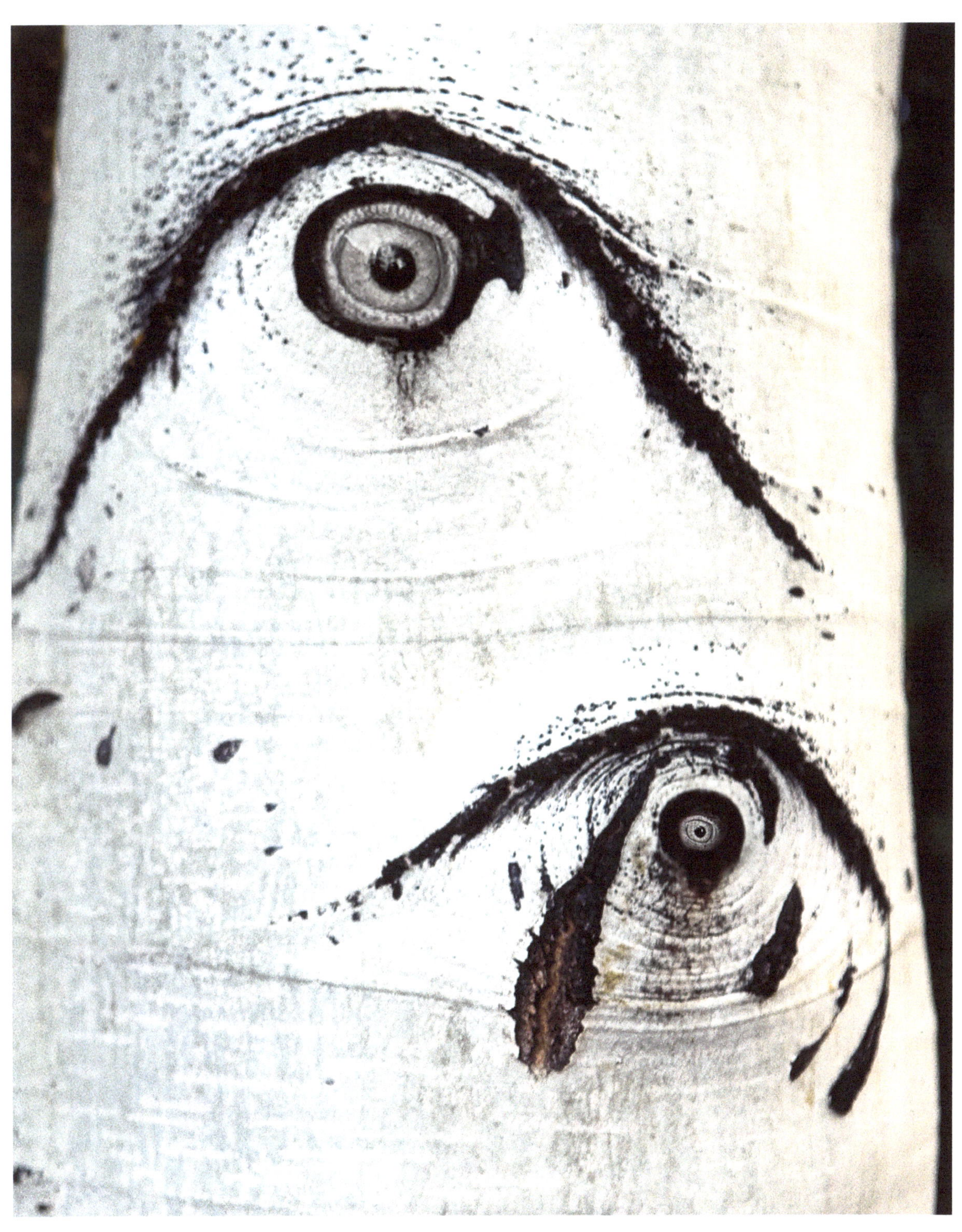

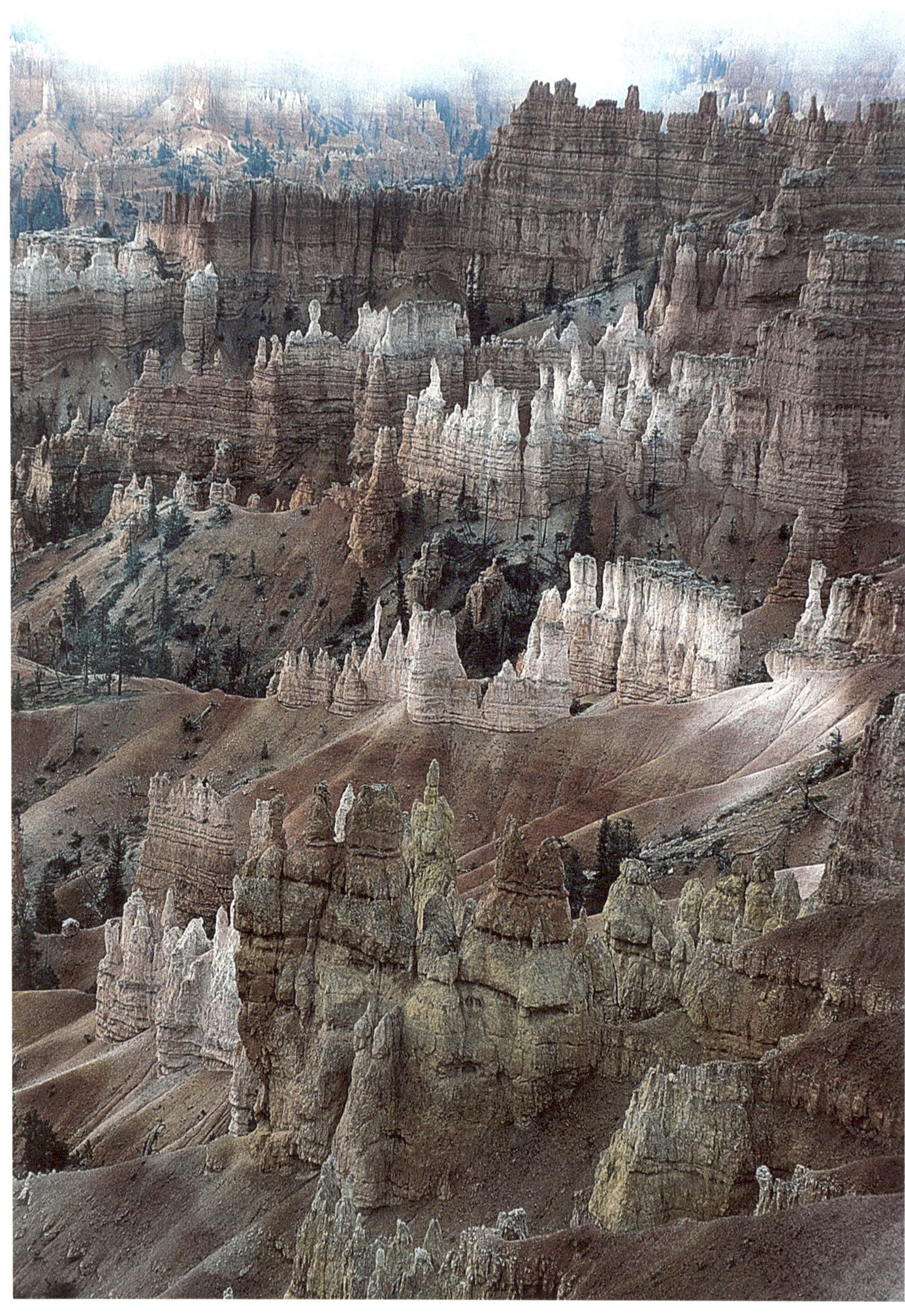

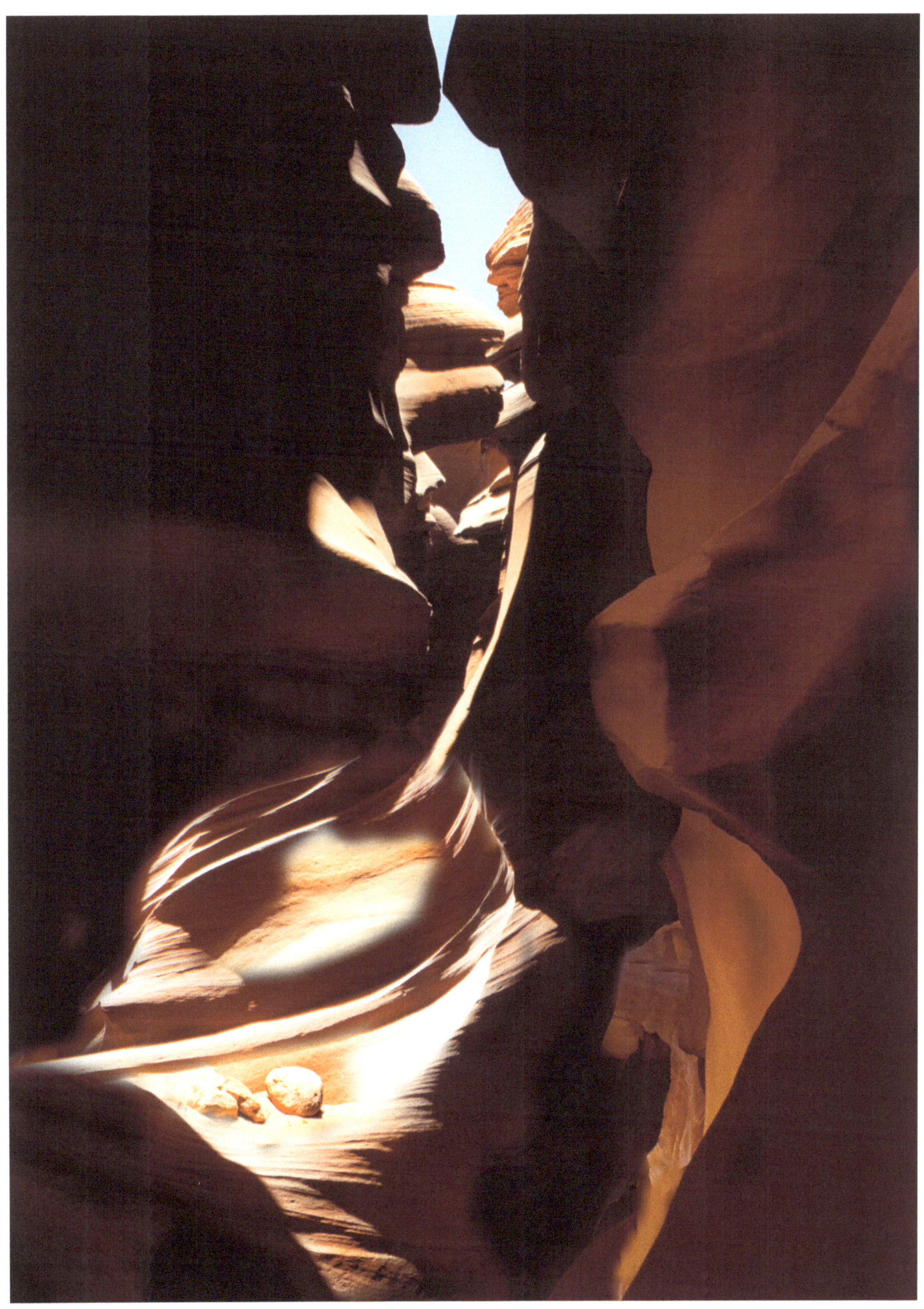

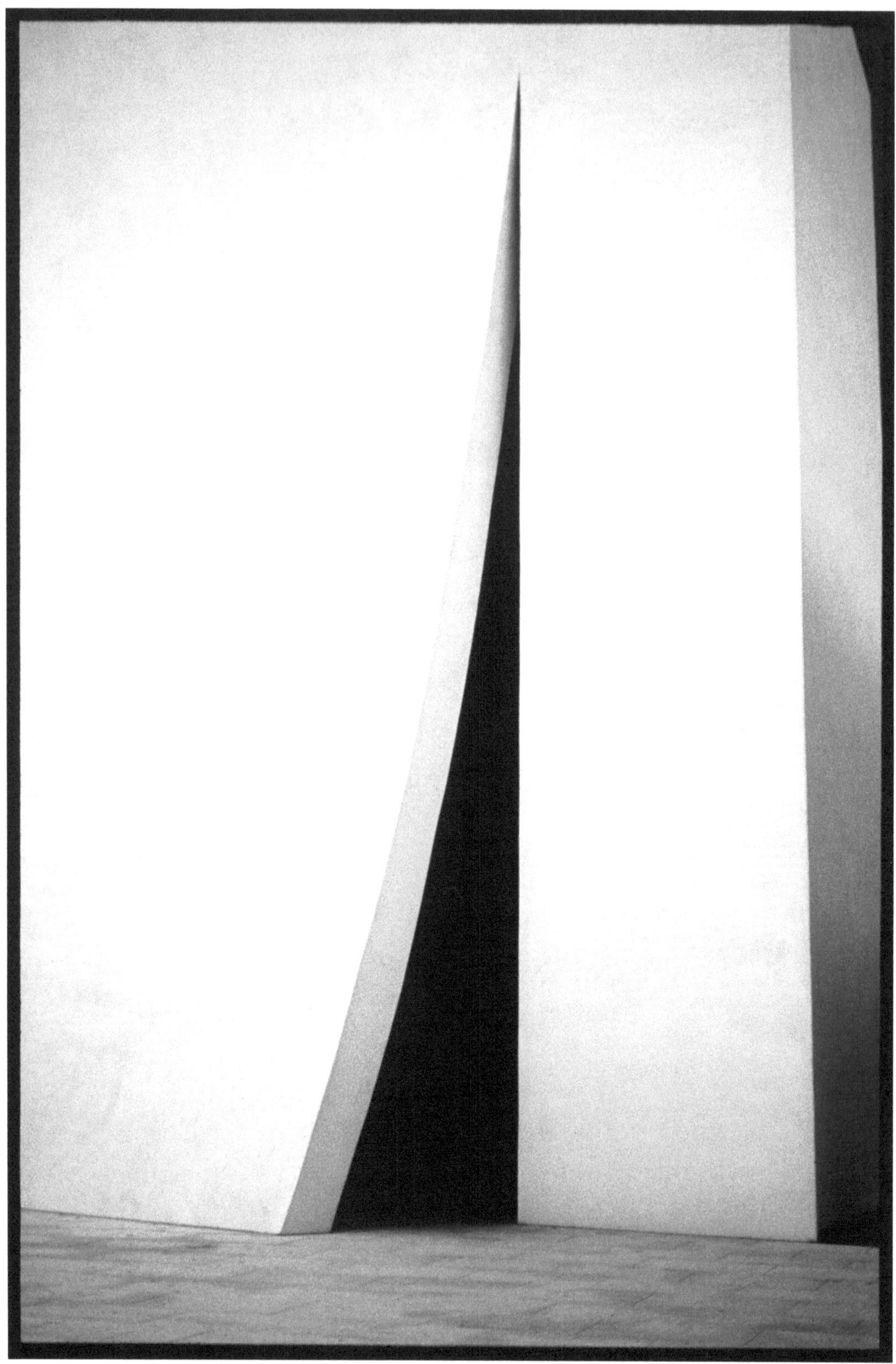

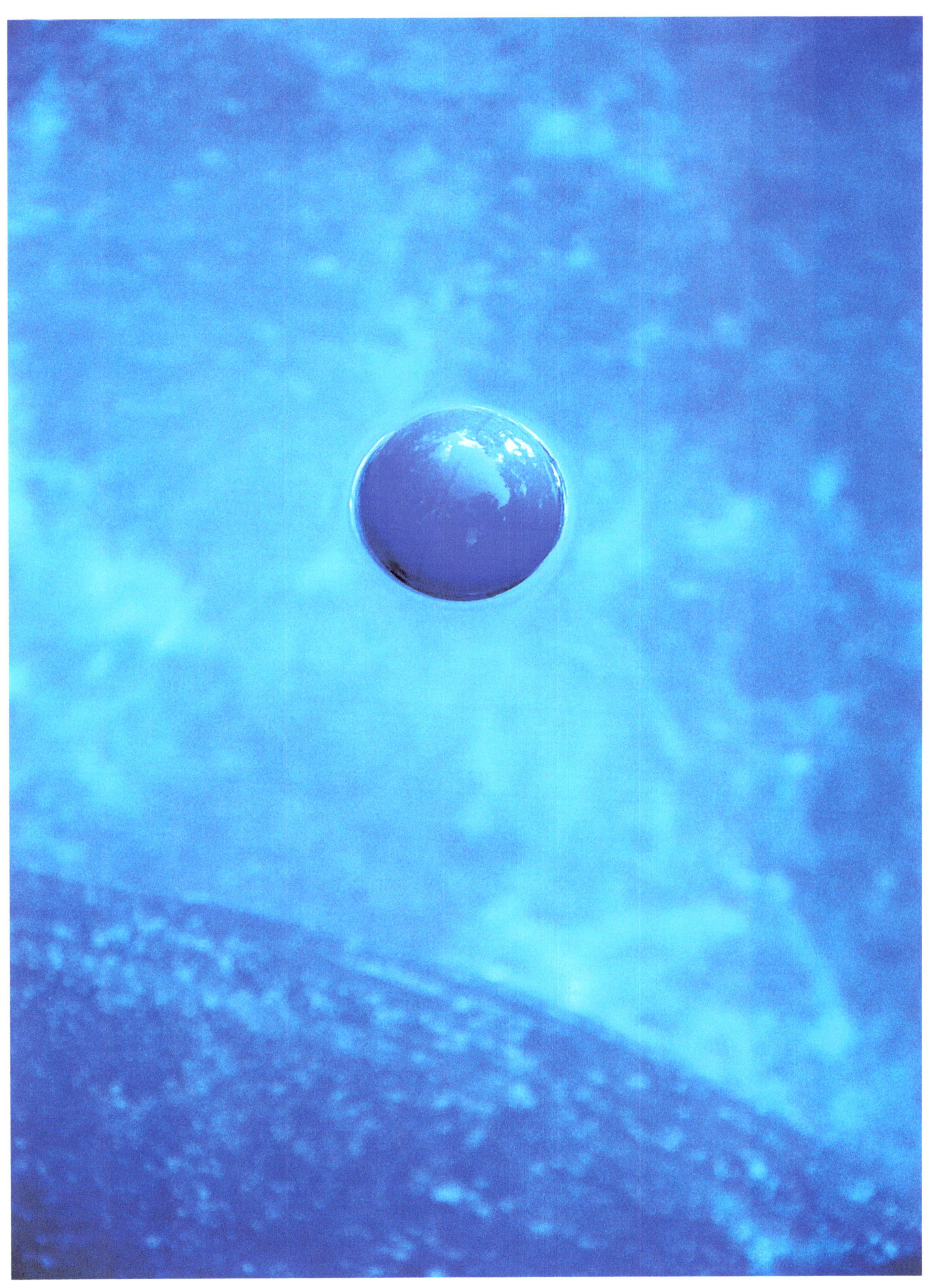

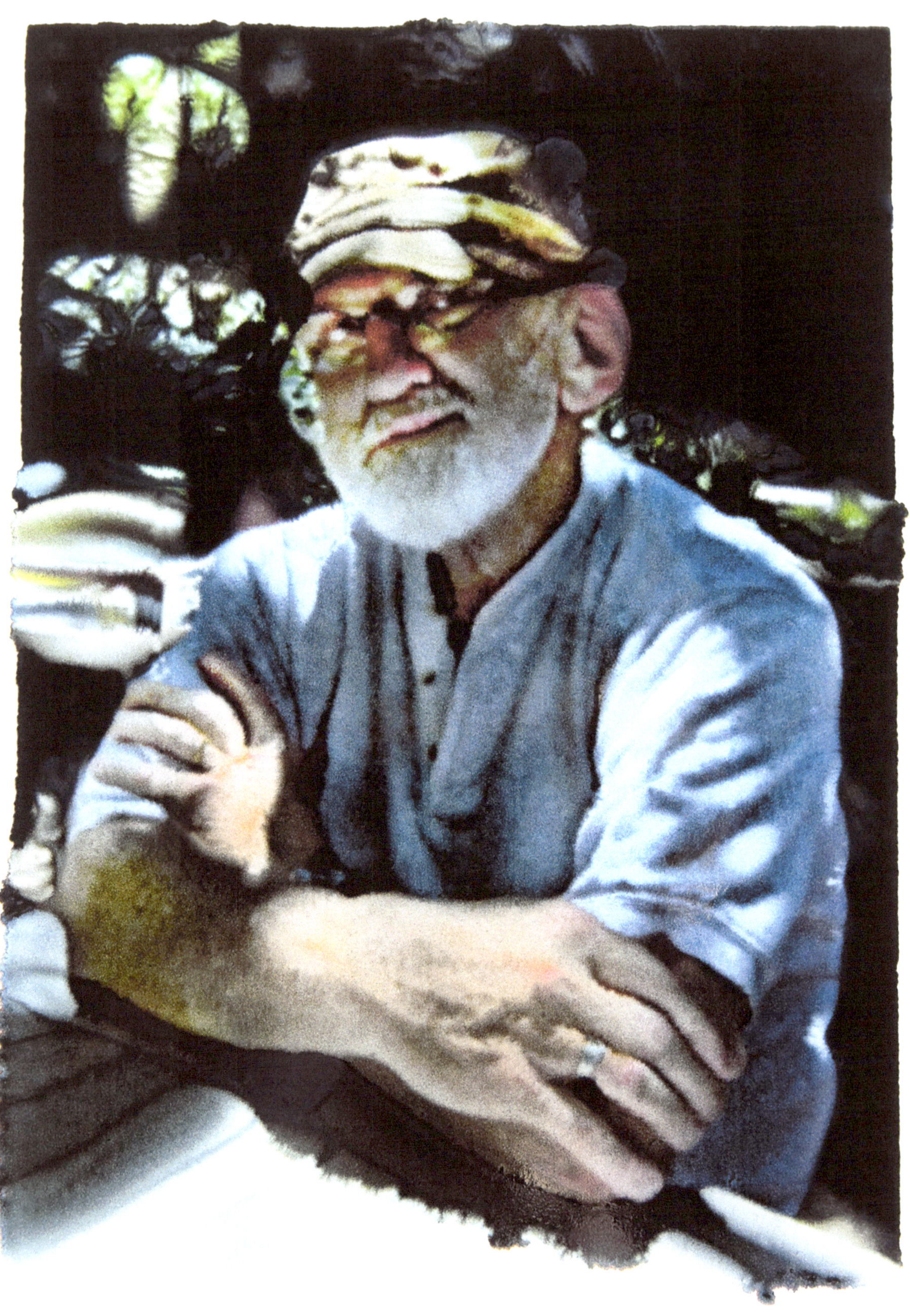

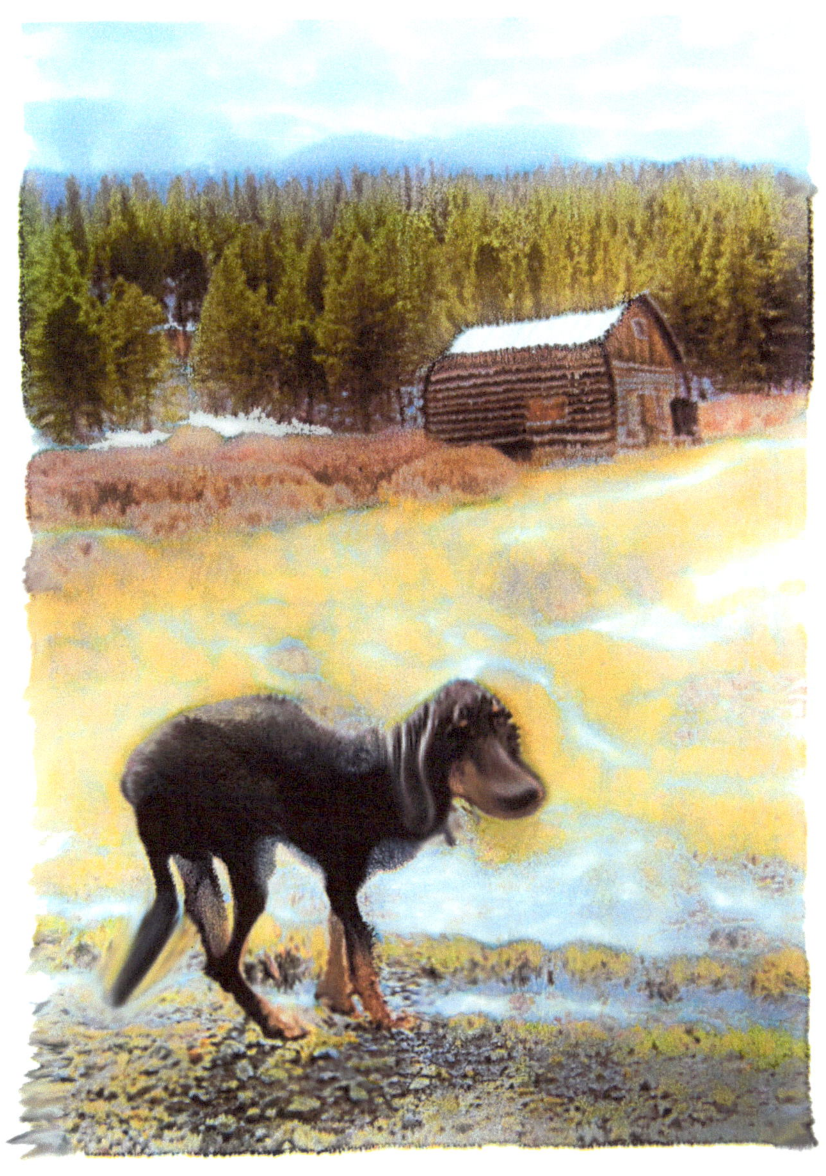

If you come to a fork in the road, take it.

—Yogi Berra

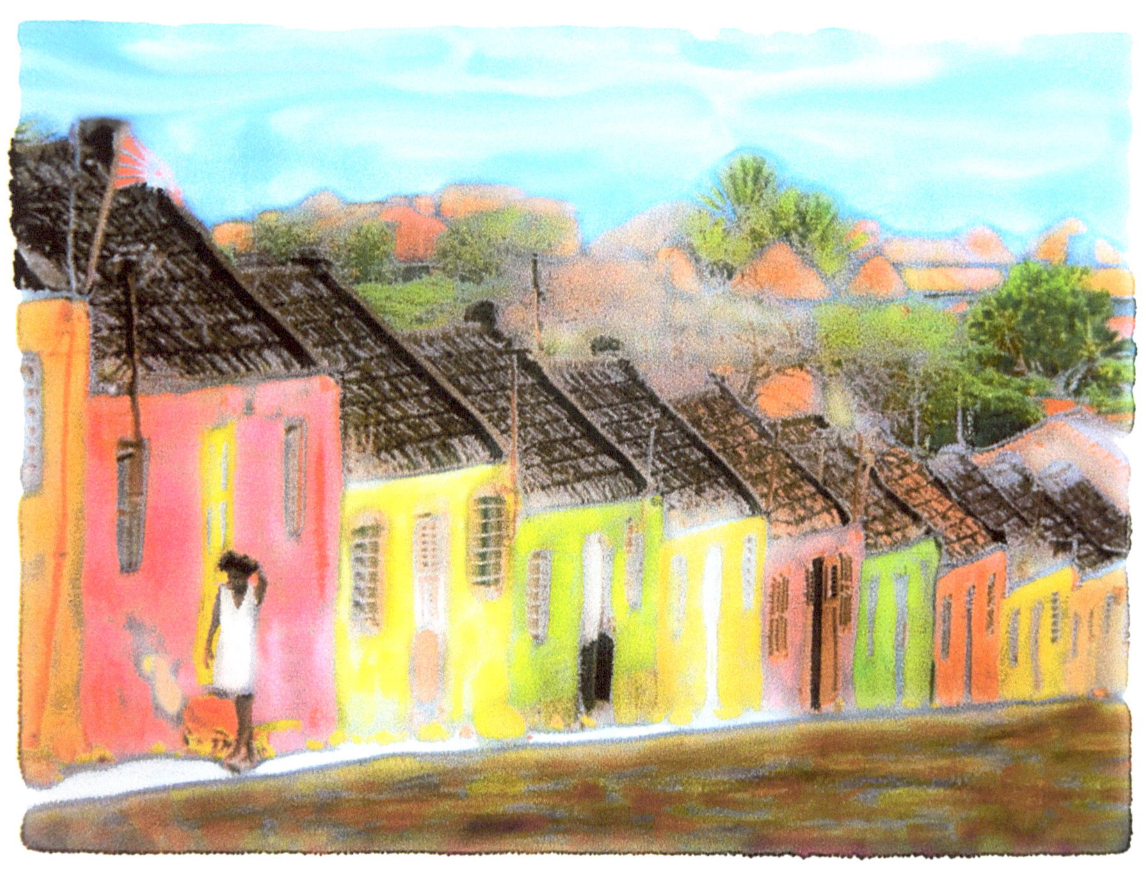

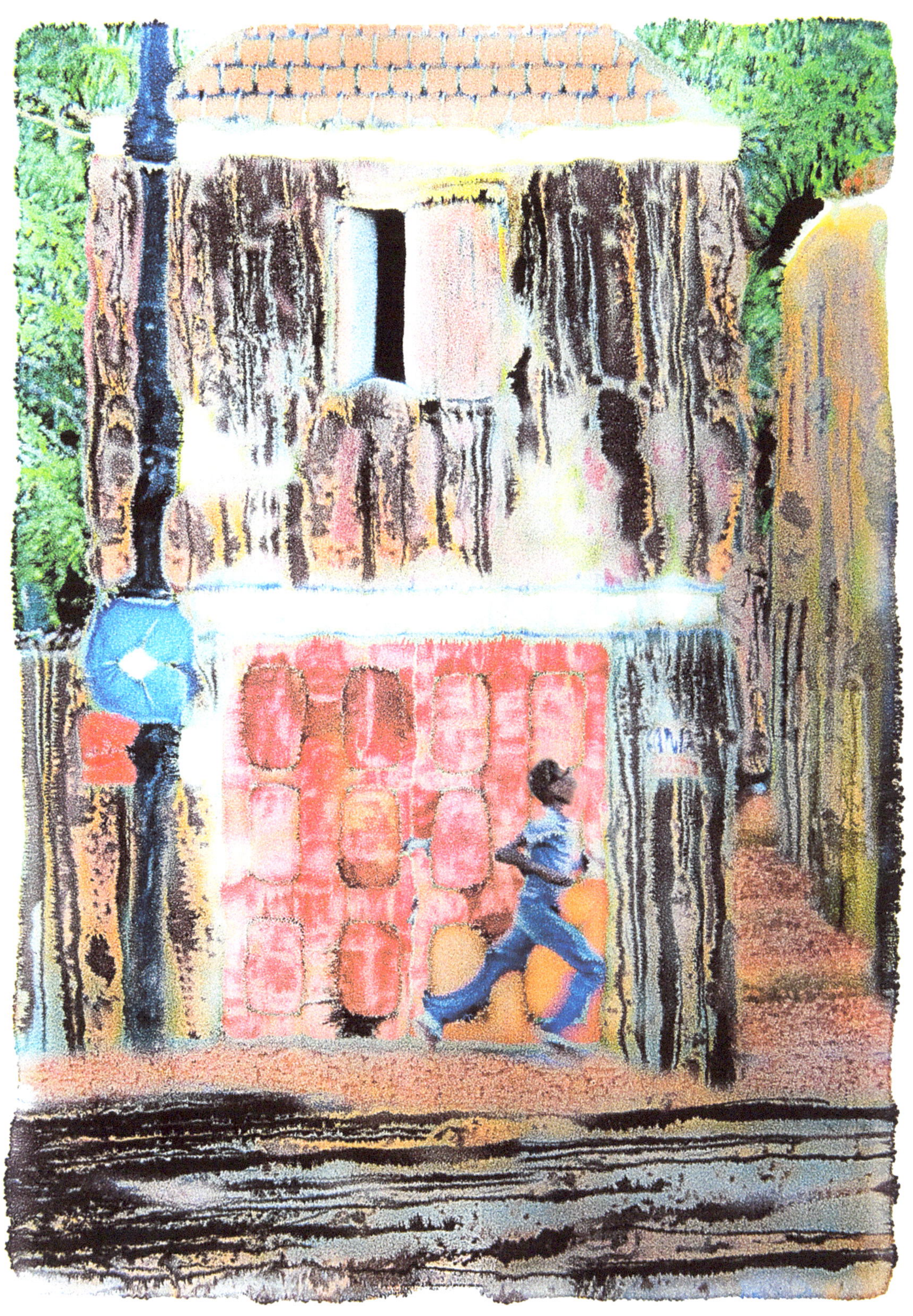

Everybody Has A Story

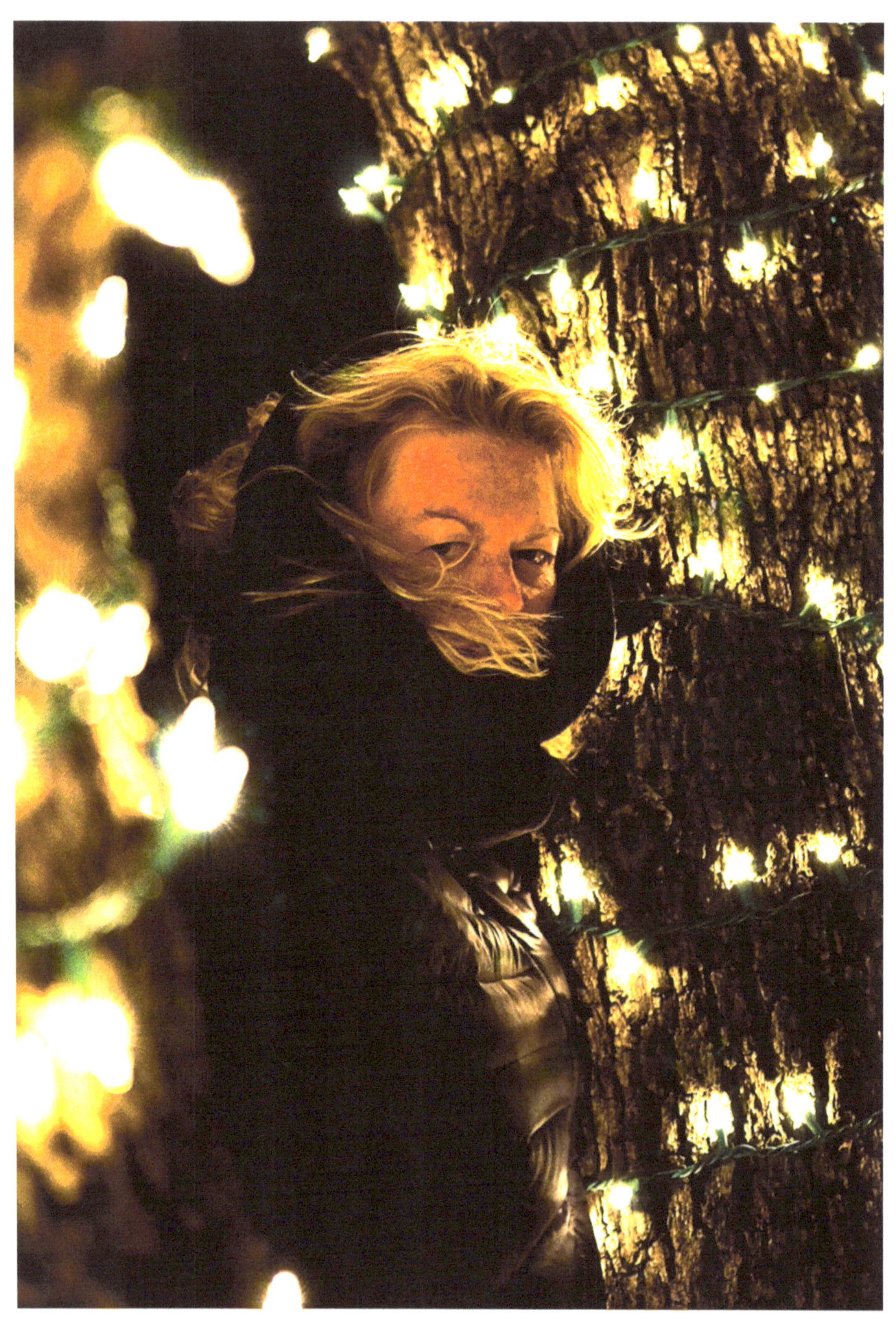

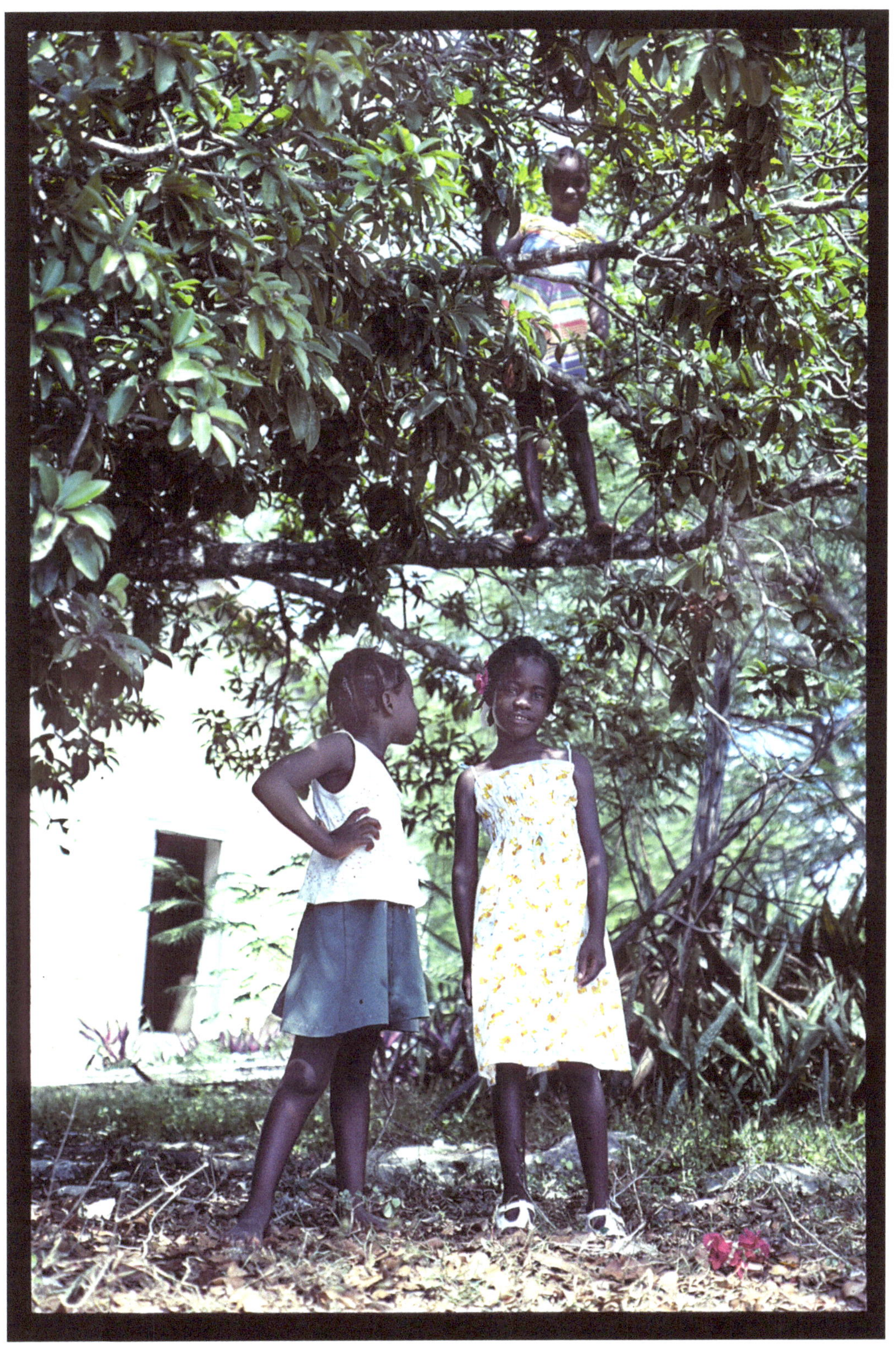

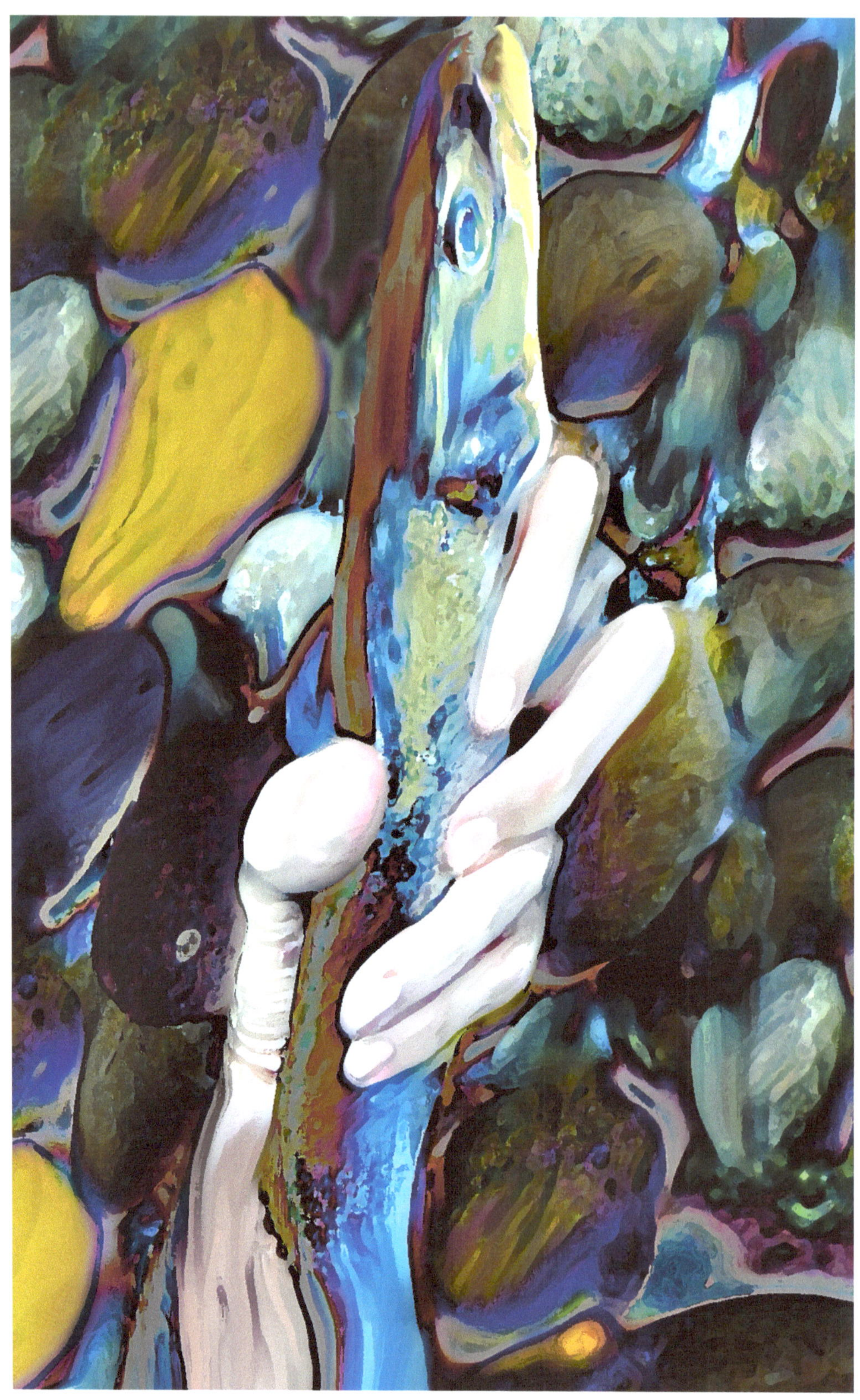

Fish Saga

I

There was a trout that lived on the western slope of the Colorado Rocky Mountains. Lacking the reddish lateral line that denotes the rainbow variety, or most of the characteristics of cutthroat trout, it was more than likely a hybrid. Like the rest of the species, it routinely fed on larval, pupal, and adult forms of aquatic insects. Mayflies were considered fine dining, but terrestrial insects like ants and beetles were welcome tidbits. Its most disgusting culinary choice was fish eggs, and it was not the least bit remorseful if they belonged to another trout. That marine animal and every other fish in the lake ate the offspring of friends and family. When Elliot Welsh told me this story he admitted mentioning these disturbing facts to ease his own guilt. The trout knew even less about humans than Elliot did about fish, and as it turned out, the fish's learning curve ended over fifty years ago while Elliot's continues.

Elliot was camping with a couple of friends, on the shore of a pristine lake, so large you could not see from one end to the other. The reflection of snow-capped mountains shimmered on its surface. It was spring. Pockets of snow still filled shady crevices, and the air turned cold when clouds covered the sun. They had the place to themselves.

Two of the young men were avid fishermen, with enough equipment to supply them all. This was Elliot's first fishing experience, and after an hour or so of casting, and reeling, and listening to discussions about spinners and sinkers, bobbers, and worms, he became certain that fishing would not play a major role in his future. He set the rod and reel down, picked up his camera, and went for a hike.

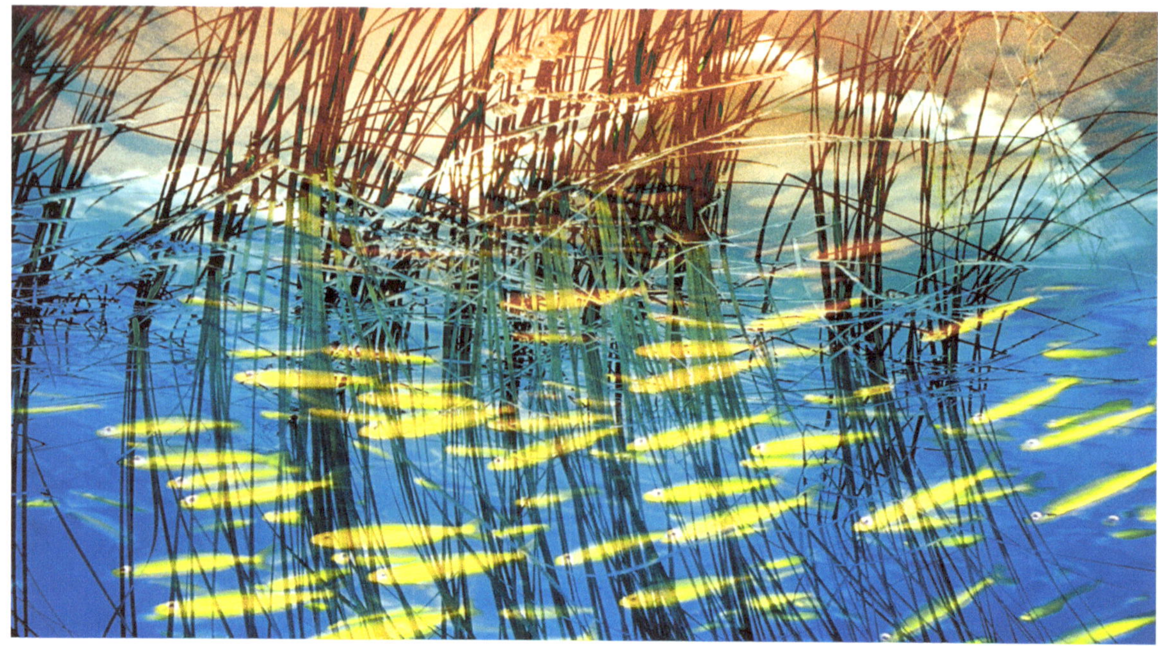

After following the edge of the lake for a couple of hours, Elliot was barely halfway around its perimeter. In a shallow lagoon, he noticed a good-sized trout nibbling at something on the surface. It submerged and swam along the bottom for a minute before returning to the same spot. It seemed as if the fish followed a routine with slight deviation. Elliot stood at the water's edge and snapped a picture as its lips barely rippled the glossy surface. Then he changed optics, refitting the camera with a telephoto lens, and snapped another picture. It was difficult to focus because the lips only broke the surface for a moment before disappearing again, and Elliot decided the fish portrait was a futile gesture. The trout either did not see the young man, or did not care, because the routine continued.

"You're just asking for trouble," Elliot muttered to himself. Then, to his shame, he set the camera down and picked up a rock. When the trout resurfaced, Elliot hit it square in the face. It was a one-in-a-million shot. The fish was no more than fifteen feet away, but the small target size and perfect timing necessary for a direct hit led Elliot to believe there was no chance of injuring it. Actually, there was no process of decision, no weighing of consequences. Elliot just picked up a rock and threw it, like the time when he was a kid and shot a bird off a telephone wire with his BB gun. That had also seemed like an impossible shot until the bird fell to the ground. Elliot remembered picking the creature up and staring at the lifeless body, with its open mouth and vacant eyes, and felt as if he had committed evil. Now he felt like that again.

The trout sank to the bottom of the lagoon, and lay there. The water was crystal clear, and no more than four feet deep, so Elliot could see its image perfectly. He willed the fish to move, shake it off, and swim away, but it was as still as the smooth stones that littered the lagoon bottom. Elliot needed absolution, or some sort of forgiveness that was not going to come from a dead fish.

It can be argued that intention is what differentiates the senseless killing of an innocent creature, and what might be considered an act of survival. Elliot's intention had been to smack a fish in the head with a rock. The fact that he never expected to actually hit his mark was not much of an excuse. He rationalized that postmortem actions play an equal role. Eating the fish would absolve the sin and ease his guilt, so he stripped off his clothes and jumped into the freezing water.

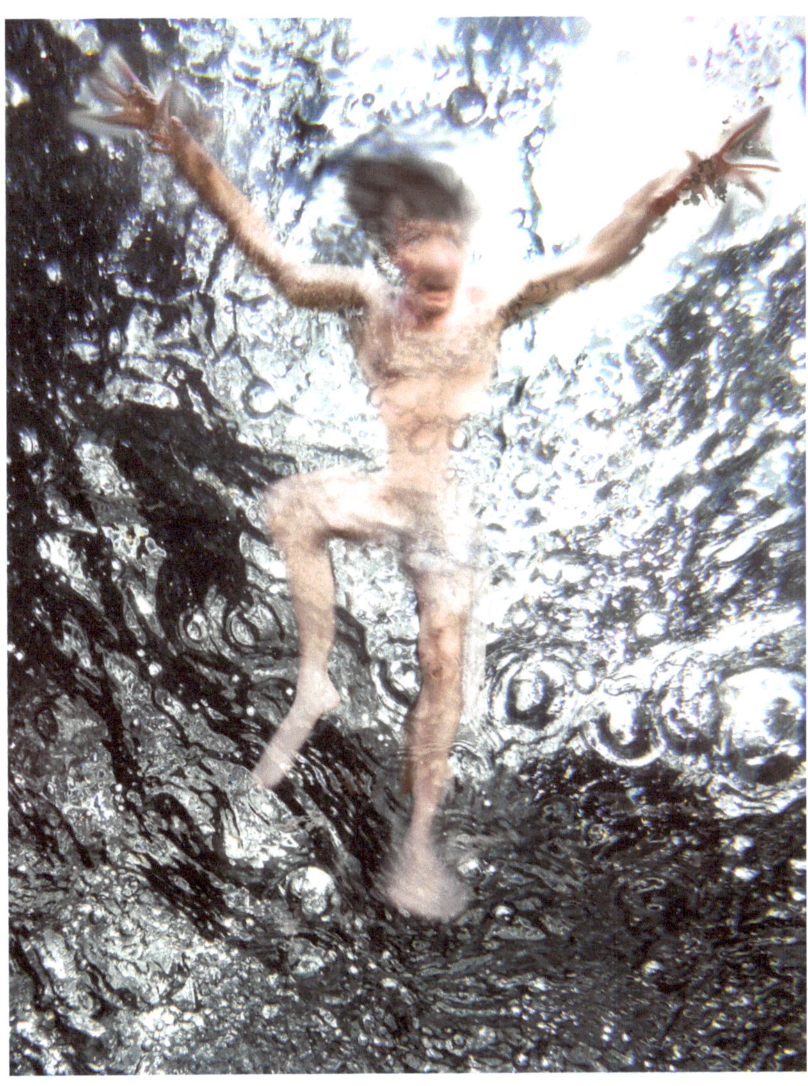

Body extremities like arms, legs, and fingers acquire movement from muscles that react to mental commands. They function in a warm-blooded body temperature range, and tend to contract when that temperature plummets. The brain reacts by going into shock.

The distress that Elliot's body experienced when it entered the freezing water could have been an act of contrition. Painful confusion became the dominant sensation. He tried to gasp, but his lungs refused to accept the offer. Extremities curled inward in a state of premature rigor mortis and his genitals sucked back into his body like a turtle escaping into its shell. Elliot's first instinct was to sink below the surface and lie next to the fish. Luckily, the brain has an emergency generator that neuroscientists call self-preservation.

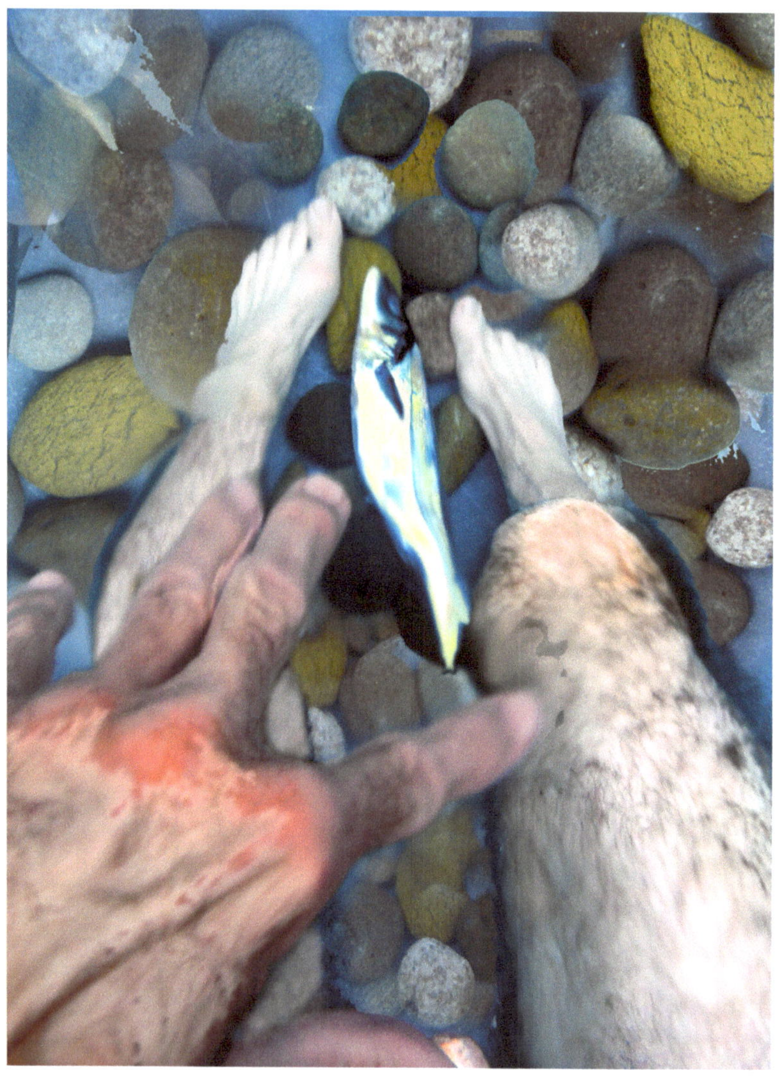

Elliot could see the fish lying near his feet, but the water was just deep enough that in order to scoop it up with his hands, he would have to bend at the knees or waist and submerge his head. That did not seem like a reasonable option so he tried pushing the trout toward the bank with his feet. It was a slow process. Then, through the blurry swirl of water, Elliot thought he saw it move. Again he nudged the fish toward shore, and it twisted to the right. The trout was regaining consciousness, and at that point Elliot could have let it go, but in his mind he could see the rock smacking it square in the face, and he knew it was too injured to survive. The trout would never again be able to swim upright, making perfect ovals. Injured animals die slowly, or are eaten quickly. No doubt aquatic creatures followed the same rules of nature.

Elliot herded the fish toward the bank, ducked his head underwater, and grabbed it. As expected, his brain went into shock. It had only been traumatized when his torso was submerged. This was brain freeze, and the pain that resulted from cranial muscle contraction made body muscle contraction feel good. Elliot resurfaced in a frozen contortion and the trout twisted out of his grasp. Even if the electrical pulses that produced the urge to scream had not iced up en route, the sound itself would have cracked his throat. Through the icy blur Elliot could see the fish just in front of his legs, and he pushed it closer to shore. In an effort to escape, the fish swam up, in front of his hands. Elliot pushed, and spasmodically lifted, and saw it come out of the water, and flip the last couple of feet onto dry land. Elliot slow motion scrambled to the edge and pushed it further inland, then began the agonizing process of clawing his own body up the side of the bank. His muscles and bones felt as if they were being compacted in a pressure vise, and his skin seemed to burn as if his body had burst into flames, and the fire was being extinguished by a million sharp darts.

He lay on the edge of the shore waiting for the pain to subside, and watched the fish flop around, edging closer to the water. There was an urgency to keep it from escaping, and to end its suffering, but Elliot's own body was not yet ready to comply with mental instructions. The fish was asphyxiating in dry air. Elliot forced himself onto his knees, and tried to grab the fish's tail, hoping to slam its head into the ground, but the trout was wet and slimy, and kept twisting out of his grasp.

Their slow dance shifted towards the area where Elliot had discarded his clothes, and on top of the pile were his woolen sox. They were usually reserved for ski attire since they stretched up to his knees, over long underwear, and under blue jeans. This was before the invention of ski pants, or at least before Elliot owned a pair. He managed to maneuver the trout into one of the sox, and grasping the open end, slammed it into the earth until it stopped moving. They lay there together until the sun threatened to sink below the distant snowcapped mountains.

That rainbow trout was the largest fish any of the young men caught during their camping trip, and the fact that his companions said it tasted like old sox did not diminish Elliot's bragging rights. Remorse and shame never entered into the conversation.

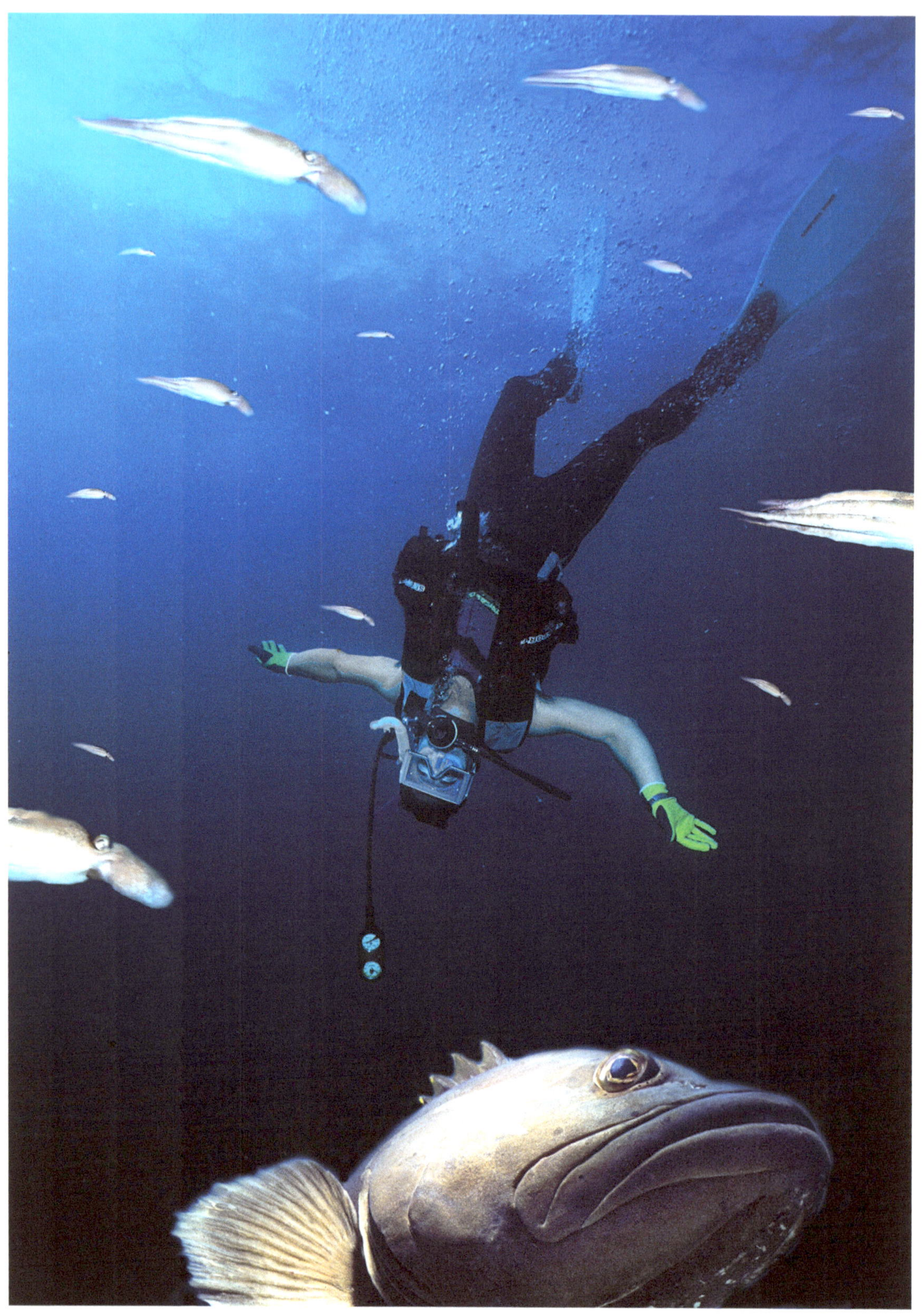

II

Roatan, Honduras

Fast-forward about fifteen years, and Elliot is in a small boat off the coast of Roatan, Honduras, with a guy named Poppy. He is there to scuba dive, and since he is staying in a shack on an isolated part of the island, Poppy and his boat are the only link to the marina where the dive boat is moored. That morning, Poppy did not show up to shuttle Elliot across the bay to catch the dive boat. Elliot has been giving him the silent treatment for a couple of hours, but the beer Poppy brought to compensate for his tardiness has taken effect, and Elliot has almost forgotten to act upset.

The boat is barely large enough to hold the two of them. Poppy is manning the trolling motor, and Elliot is in control of the fishing line. This is his second fishing experience. Poppy's fishing gear consists of a wad of fishing line that he found and pieced together, wrapped around an empty plastic bottle. There is a hook that he also found, with a chunk of meat on it trailing aft, and leeward. Something tugs on the line, shaking Elliot out of his reverie, and then tugs again, even harder.

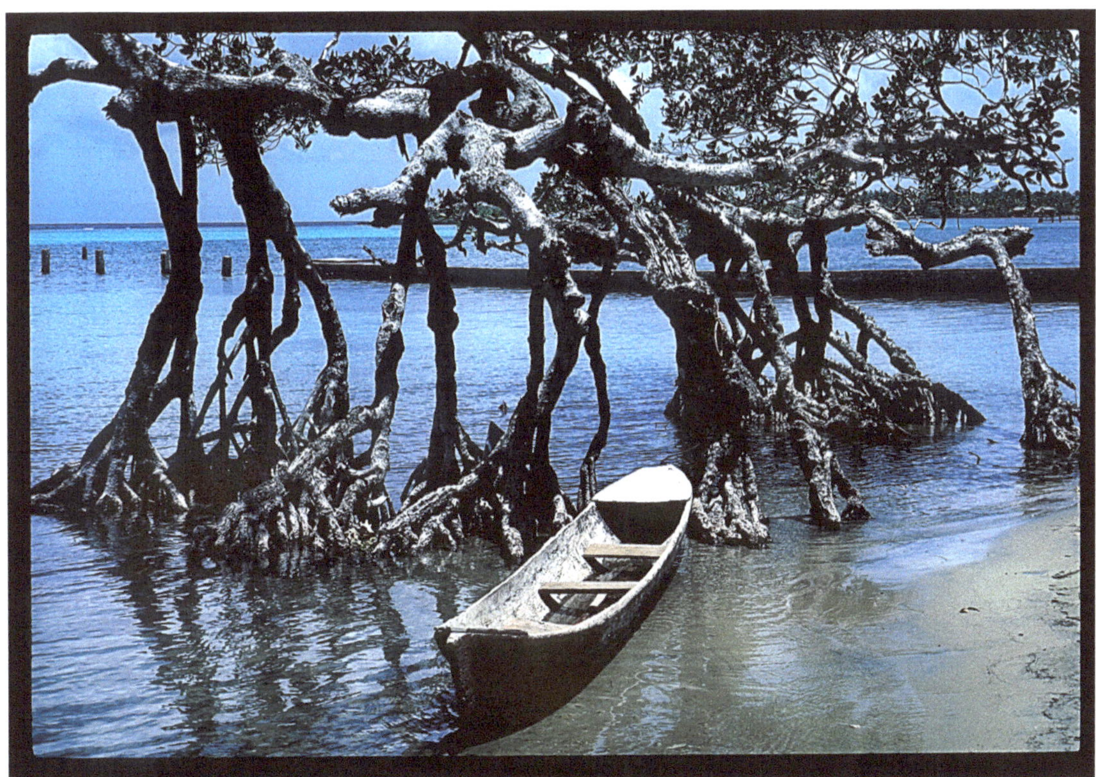

"Sink the hook, Mon," Poppy yells. Elliot pulls hard on the bottle, and can tell they've caught something big. "Reel her in, Mon," Poppy yells, and Elliot begins rolling up the slack, pulling and rolling, pulling and rolling until there is almost as much line around the bottle as there was when he dropped the hook into the water.

Elliot is leaning over the top of the boat with his legs braced against the sides to keep from falling out, and he can see the fish just below the surface, long and sleek. He gives the bottle another pull, and the fish surfaces close to his face. It's a barracuda that consists almost entirely of teeth, sharp and snapping. Elliot jumps back, almost dropping the bottle, and the fish slides back into the water.

"Hold him up, Mon, and I'll whack him," Poppy yells, and Elliot can see he is holding the paddle above his head. Until that moment, Elliot had not questioned Poppy's fishing technique. It had seemed so unorthodox that the thought of actually catching a fish seemed unlikely. Now, the thought of pulling the barracuda aboard seemed suicidal. "Pull him up, Mon. I can't whack him dere."

Against his better judgment, Elliott took up enough slack to pull the fish's head out of the water. He was on his knees, leaning against the far side of the narrow boat. The line was taut, the 'cudas head held firm against the outside edge of the boat, and Poppy smacked at him with a glancing blow that just seemed to upset the fish.

"Hold him good, Mon," Poppy yelled. Elliot held him good, even though his back felt as though it might break, and Poppy hit the fish against the side of the head again. Fearing he was about to lose his grip, Elliot leaned back and gave it one last upward pull, and the line went slack as the barracuda flew into the boat.

Poppy and Elliot crammed themselves into either end. Elliot braced his bare feet on top of either side of the boat, and pushed his butt off the seat with his hands. Poppy did the same. The barracuda slid and twisted between them, mouth agape, trying to lunge and maim, but unable to thrust his body as he would in water.

Poppy managed to readjust his position enough to continue wacking at the barracuda, not so much injuring the fish as infuriating him.

It became a battle of attrition, and the only reason the humans won is because they were air-breathing mammals. Eventually, the barracuda became so tired that Poppy was able to sink a knife into him. They both knew Elliot had pulled the barracuda into the boat prematurely, but to his credit, Poppy never brought it up. "Dem 'cudas can sure put up a fight," was all he said.

Later, when Elliot asked Poppy how to prepare the fish, he said the most important thing is to cut out a few chunks of meat, preferably from various sections, and feed them to the chickens. "Watch dem chickens till dey either keep standing up, or fall down dead. Den you know if you can eat da fish."

They did that together, and the chickens continued standing and pecking, so Elliot and Poppy enjoyed a dinner of fried barracuda and beer.

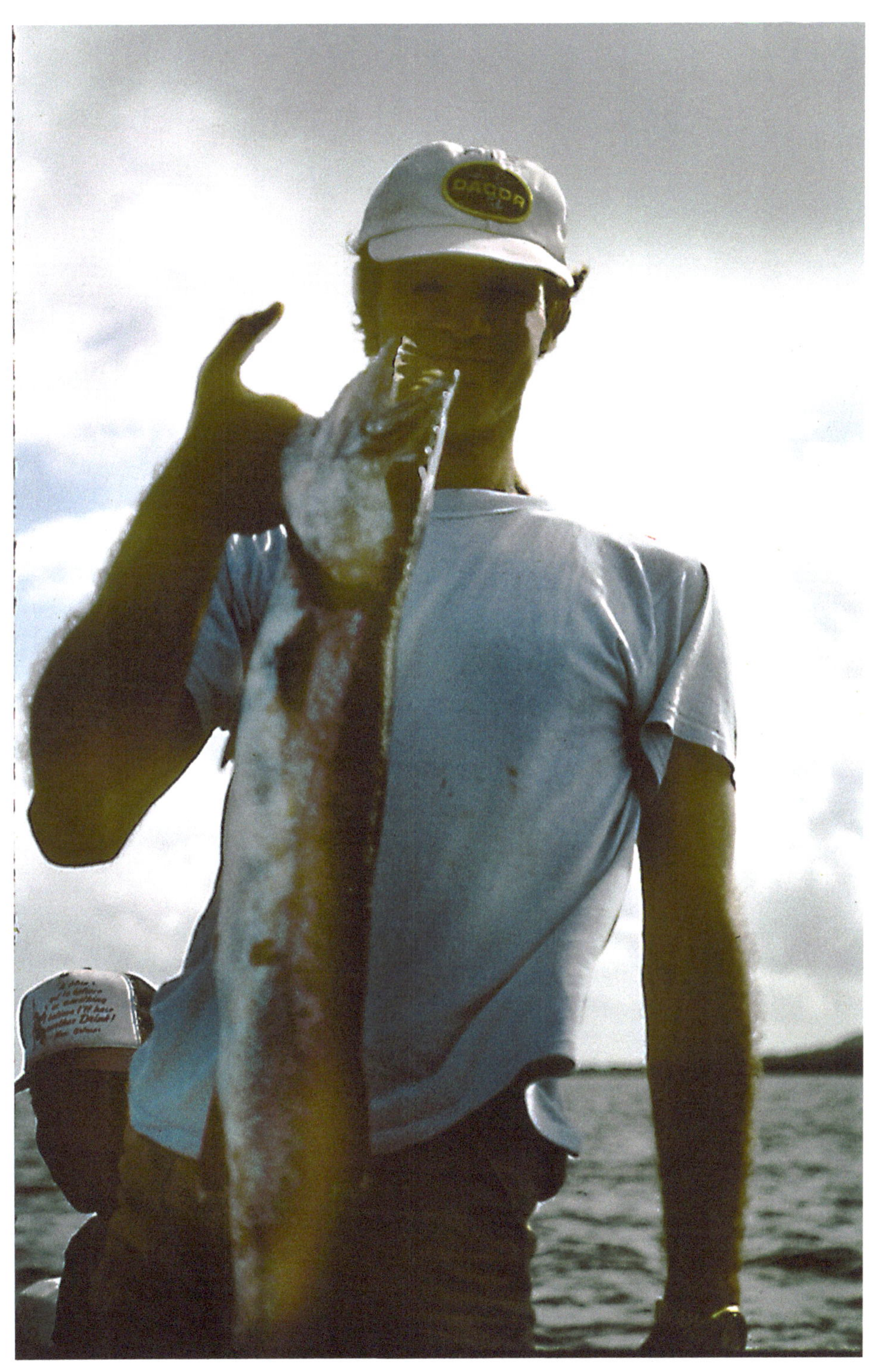

III

Aruba

Almost three years after that, Elliot was in Aruba. It was his last evening on the island, having spent the previous few days scuba diving around its submerged wrecks and reefs.

He decided to treat himself to one last seafood dinner, and drove his rented jeep a short distance down the main road that followed the coastline. He could have walked, but the plan was to drive further out of town after dinner. There was a deserted stretch of beach that Elliot wanted to visit one last time. It was a perfect spot to stare at the blackness of the ocean, and listen to waves lapping at the sand.

At the restaurant he ordered a beer, and the barracuda entrée. About three bites into his dinner, Elliot knew something was wrong. His body began to ache, and his equilibrium had him listing to the right. Elliot pushed himself out of the chair, knocking the beer off the table, and stumbled towards the door. He had to get outside. Aside from the pain and dizziness, that was all he could comprehend. People were staring. The cashier was saying something, a concerned look on her face. Elliot pushed his way past her and out the door. Fresh air did not help the situation, but it meant he was closer to where he could lay down.

From that point Elliot can only recall brief images of what happened. Driving towards the motel at about 5 MPH, two wheels in the gutter, and a grinding noise as the rims scraped against concrete. Knocking over a table in the bar that he had to pass through to get to his room. A large man with a shaved head who looked like he might kill him hovering overhead, and Elliot thinking that would be OK. Trying to insert his key in the door. Falling into bed, and feeling as if every place his skin touched sheets or pillow hurt a hundred times worse than the rest of his body, which felt as if every bone had been crushed into fragments. Thinking he was going to die. Then he passed out.

The next morning Elliot woke up feeling fine, made it to the airport in time to pay for some minor bodywork on the rental jeep, and flew back to the States.

Staring at clouds through the airplane window he kept thinking about how the restaurant had neglected to feed chunks of his barracuda to the chickens. Then Elliot remembered the rainbow trout and began to wonder about karma, and fish retribution.

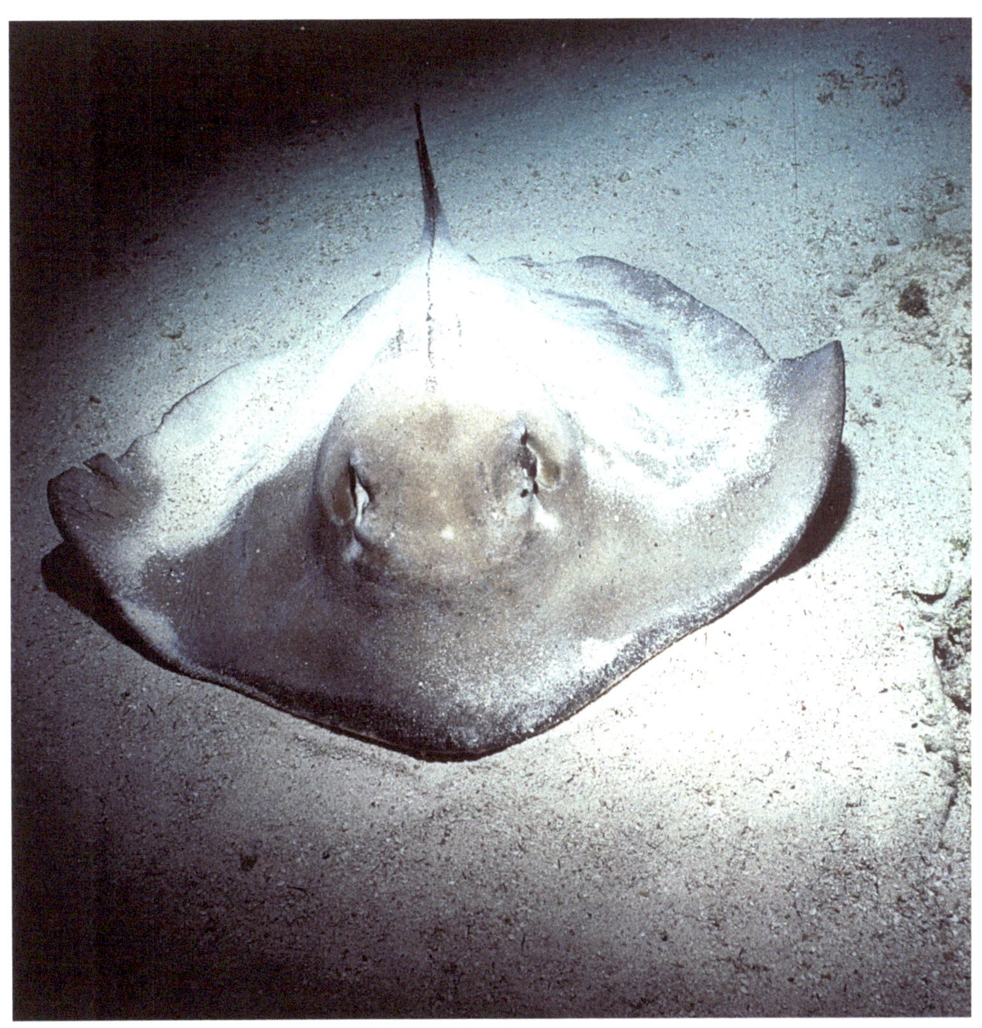

A Crooked Road

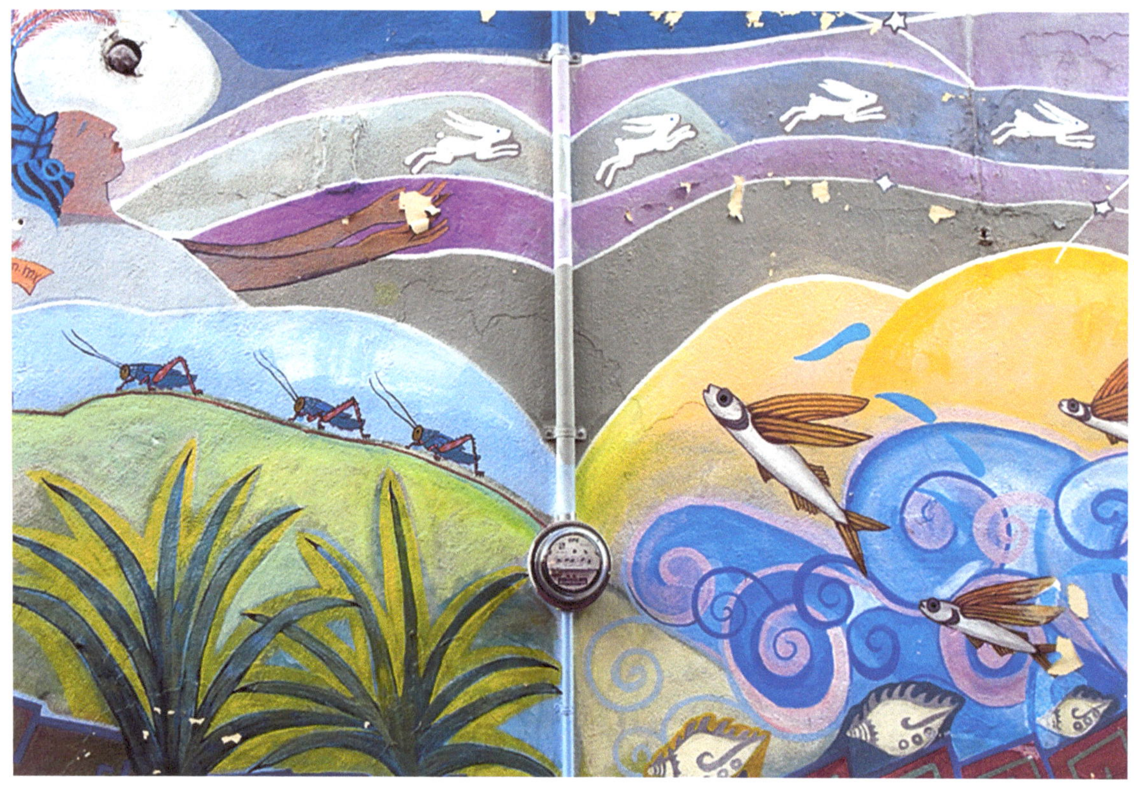

Life is a crooked road. Distance is measured in time rather than miles, and there are detours and miscalculations that can enhance the journey, or cut it short. We begin at different times, from various locations, and experience what we encounter from different viewpoints. Life is a crowded place, with an expanding amount of earthly things to encounter.

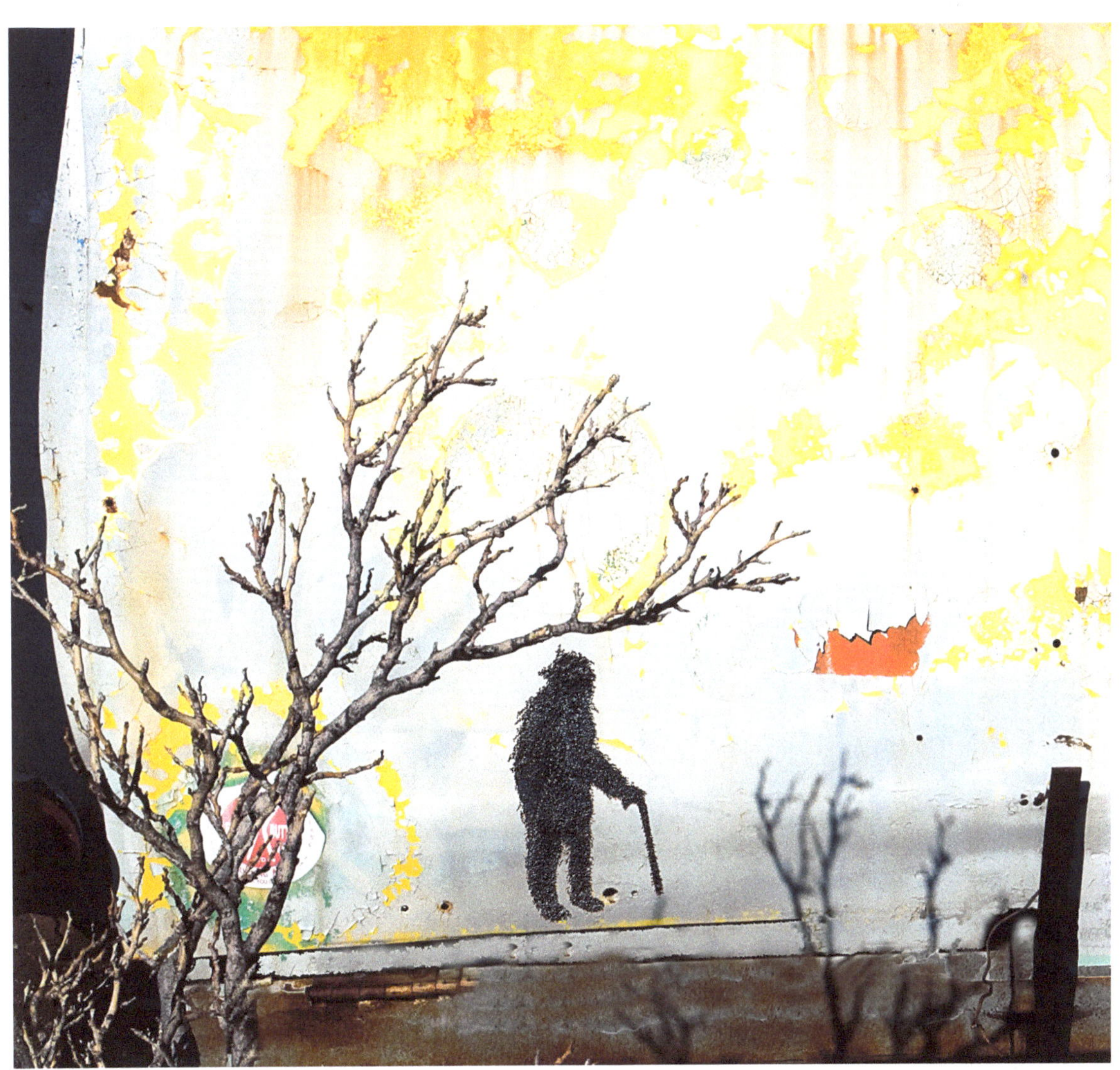

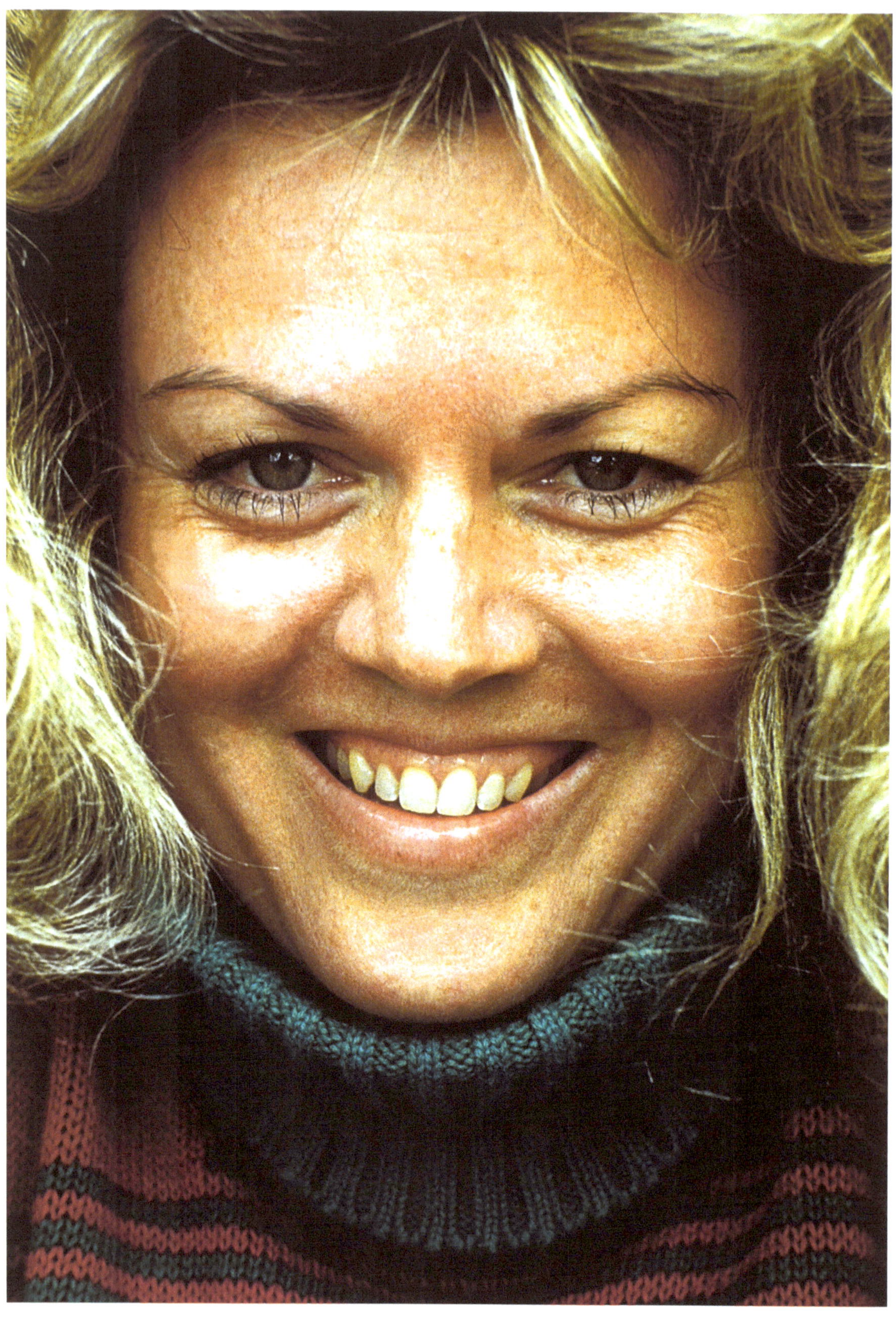

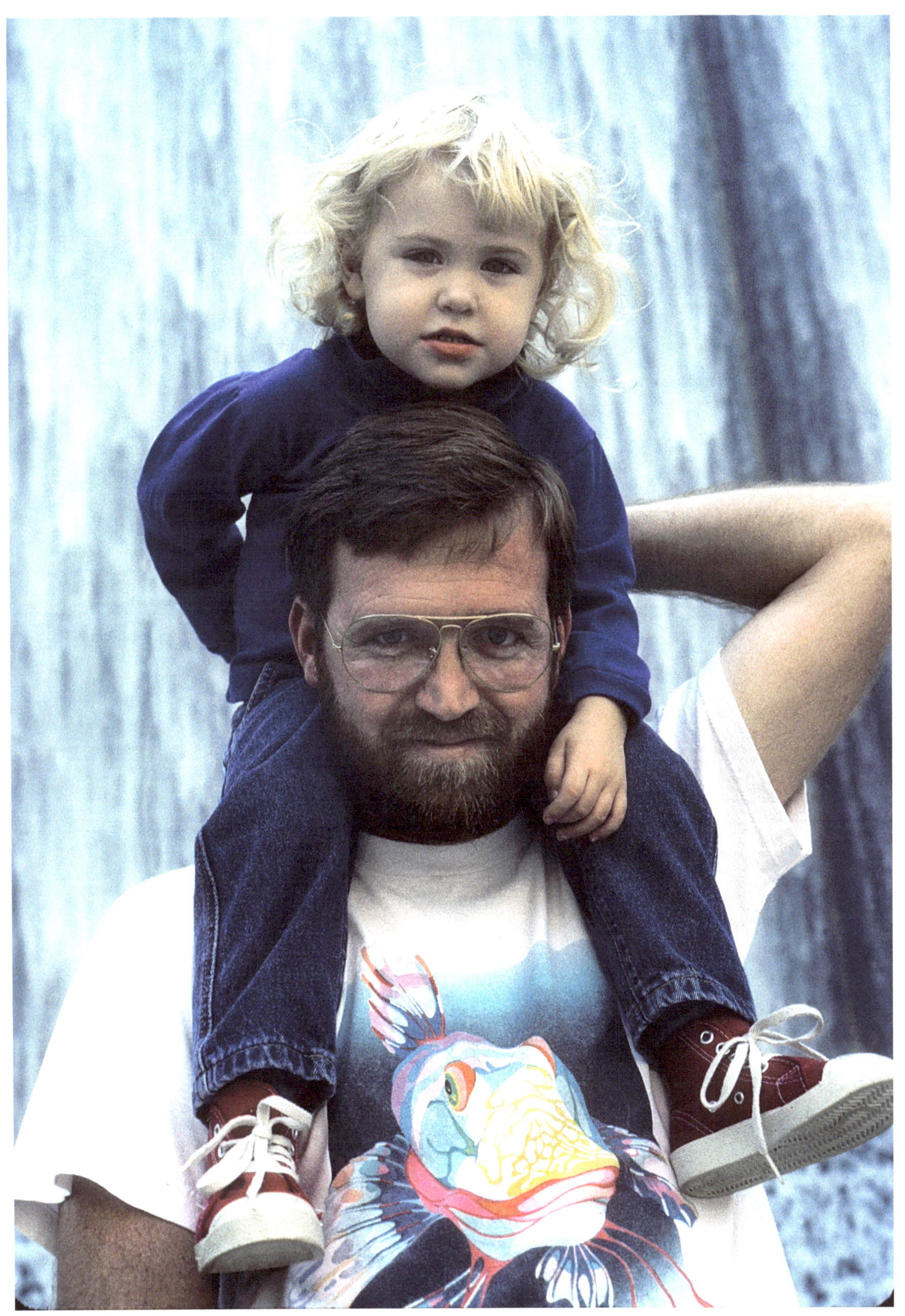

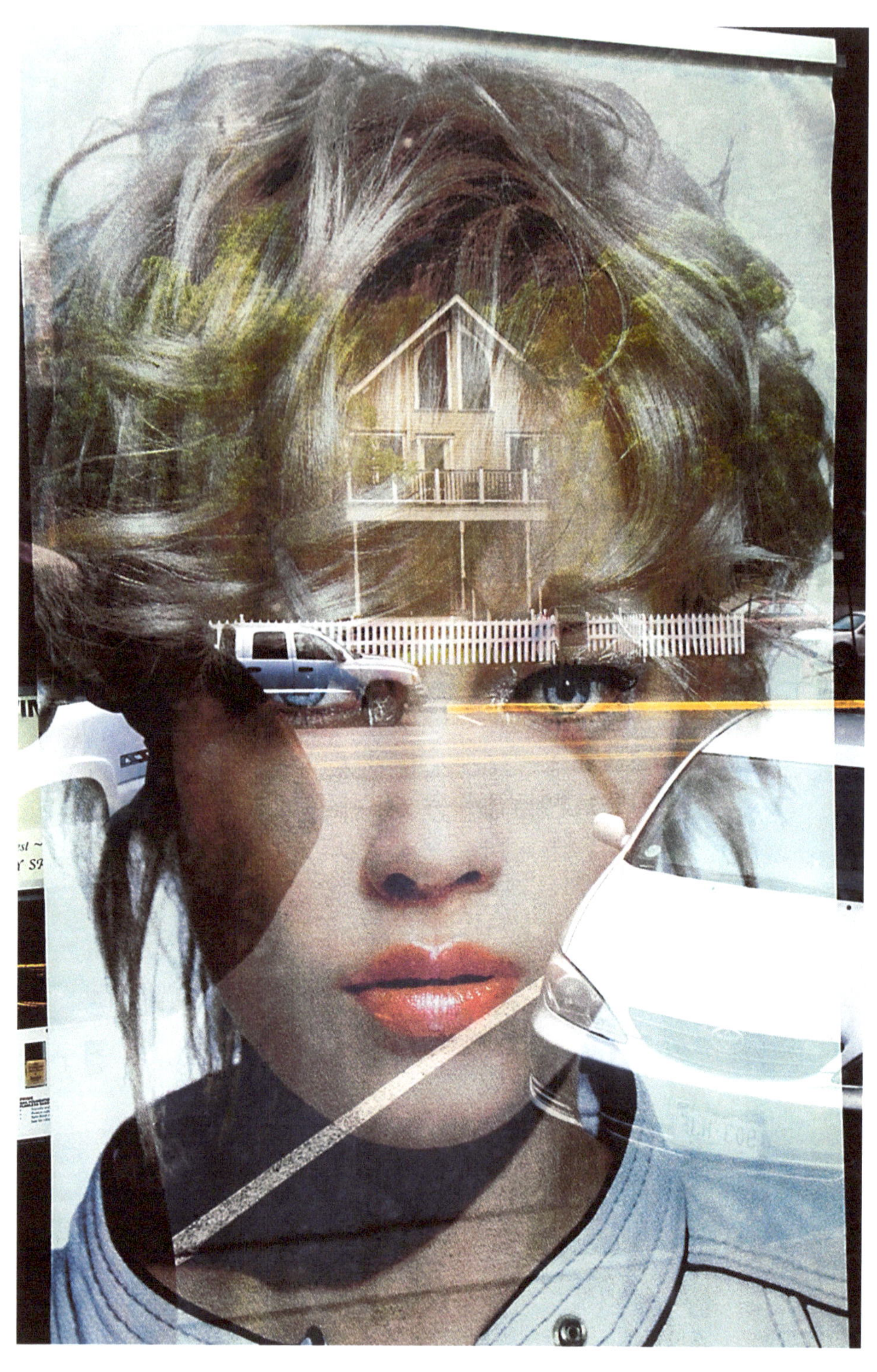

Life begins at the end of your comfort zone.
—Neale Donald Walsch

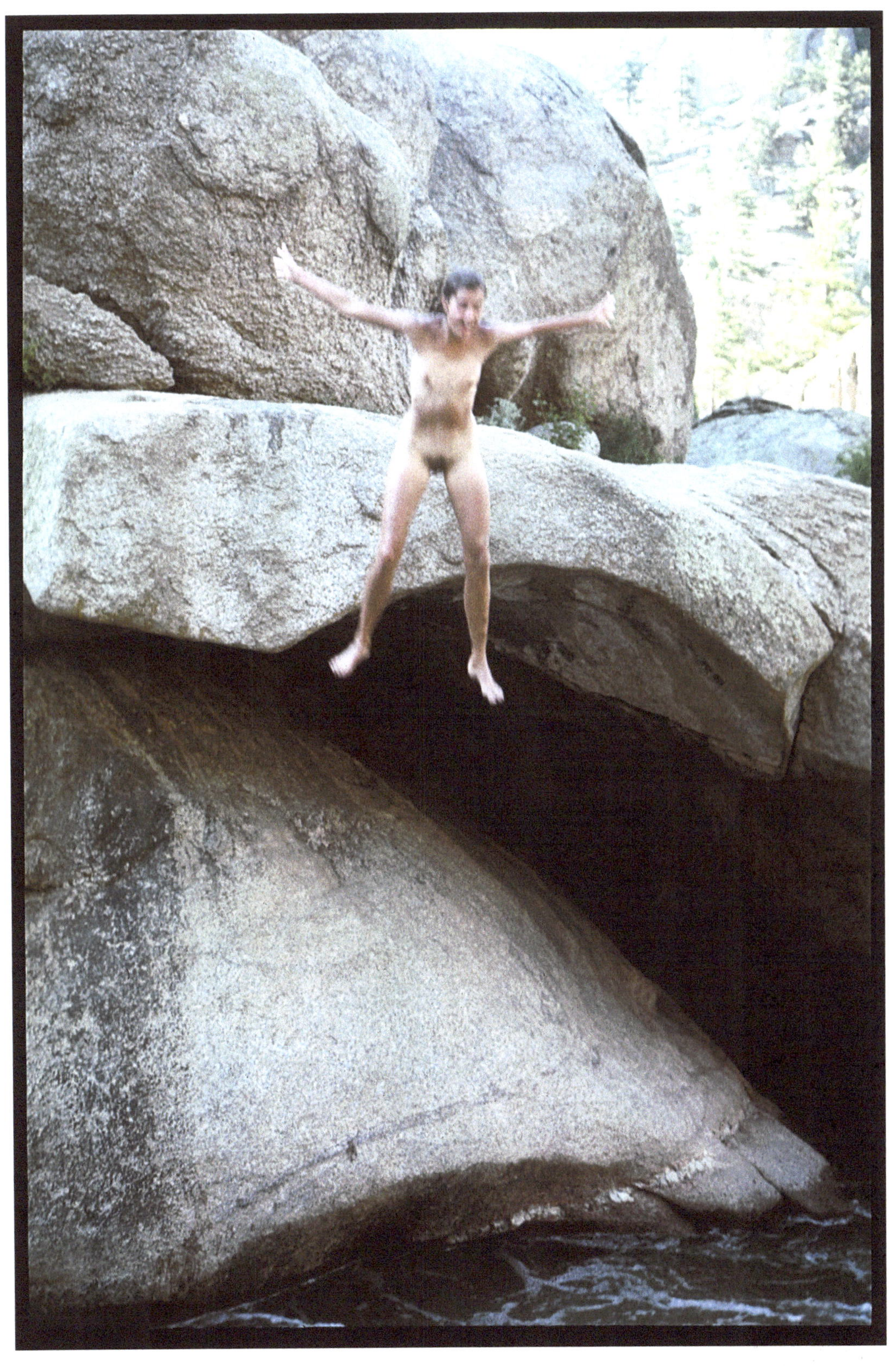

San Miguel de Allende

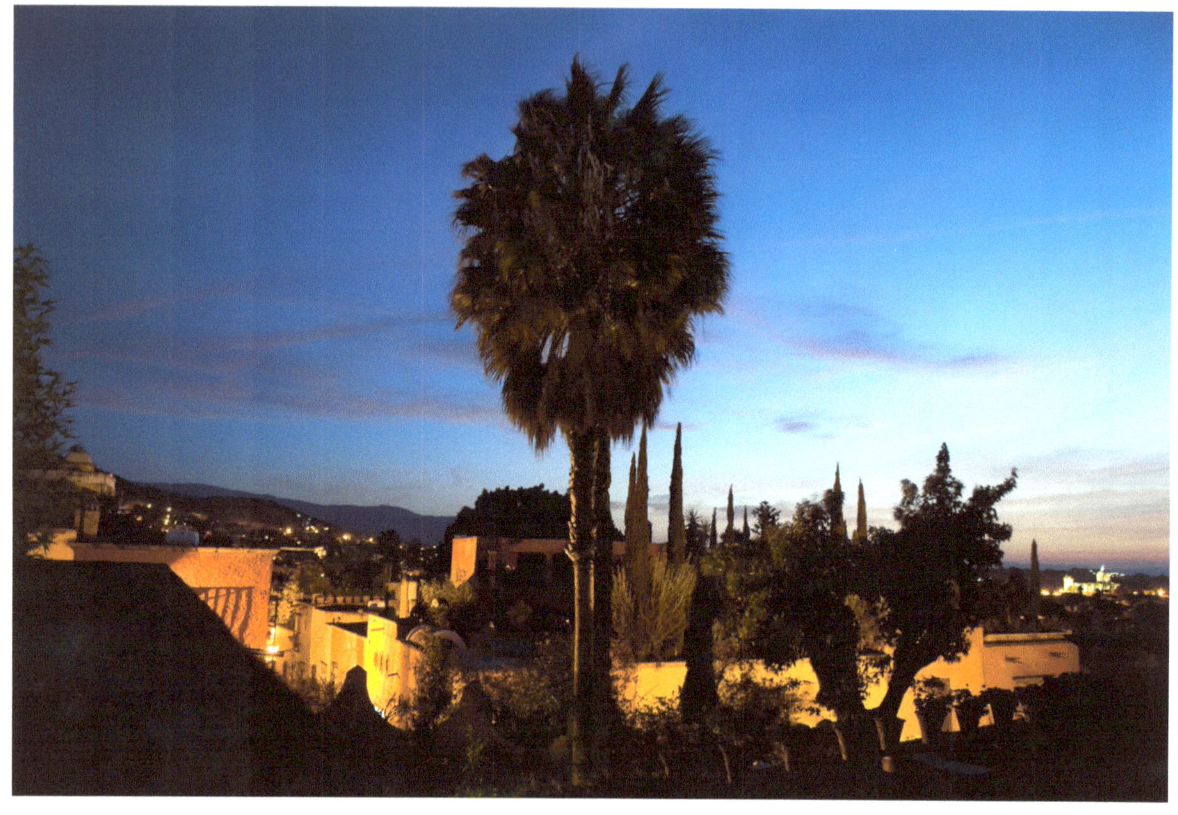

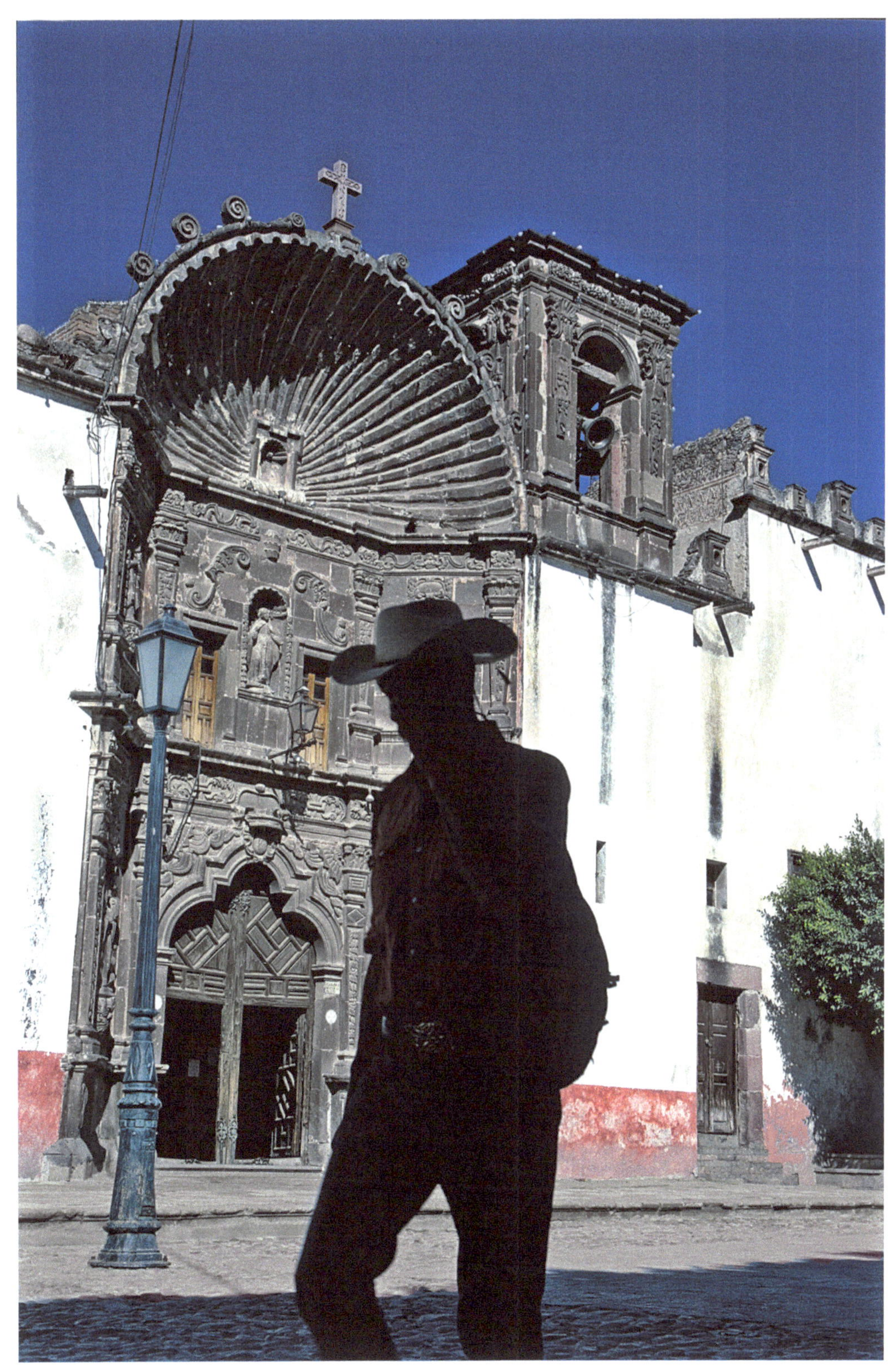

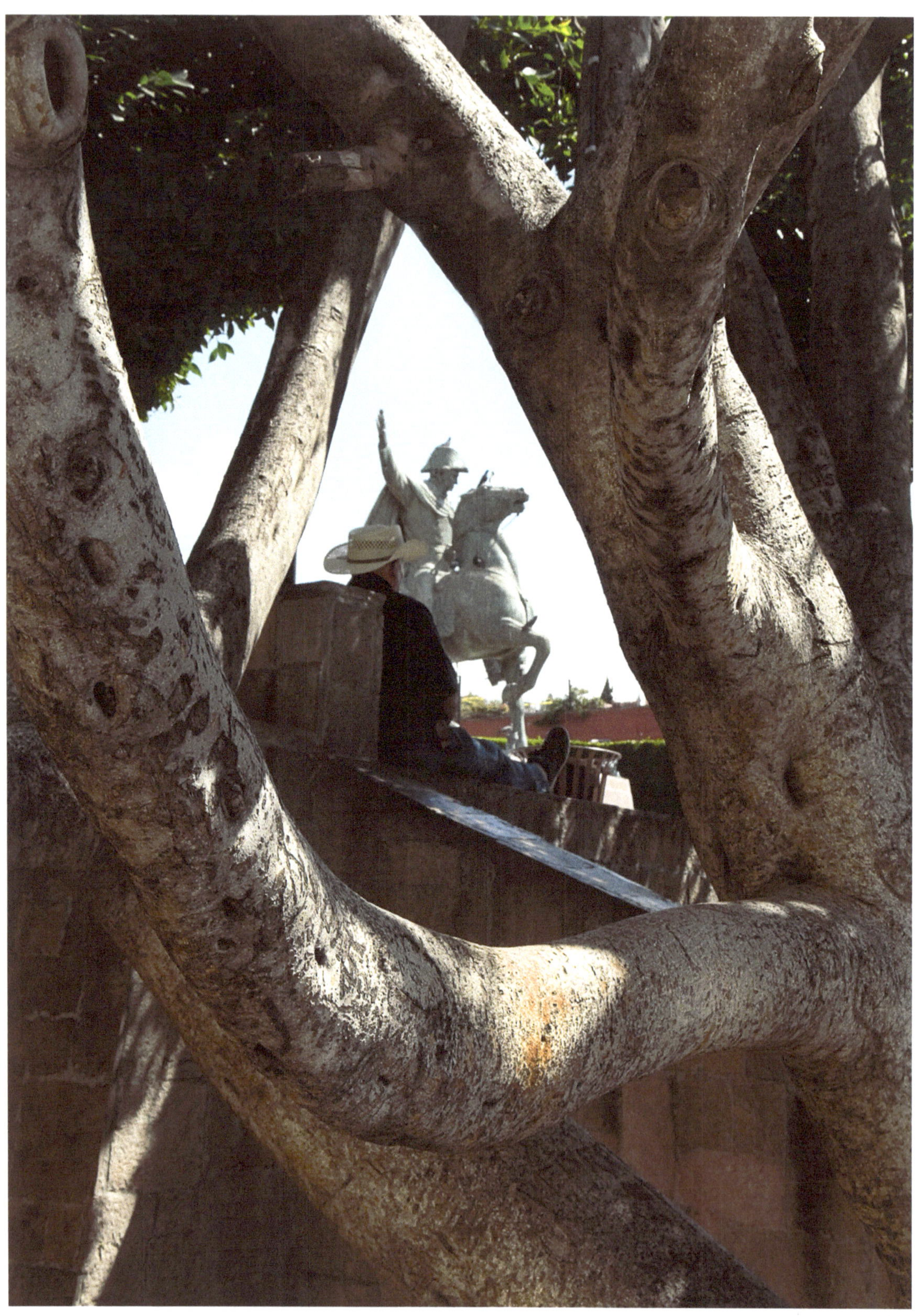

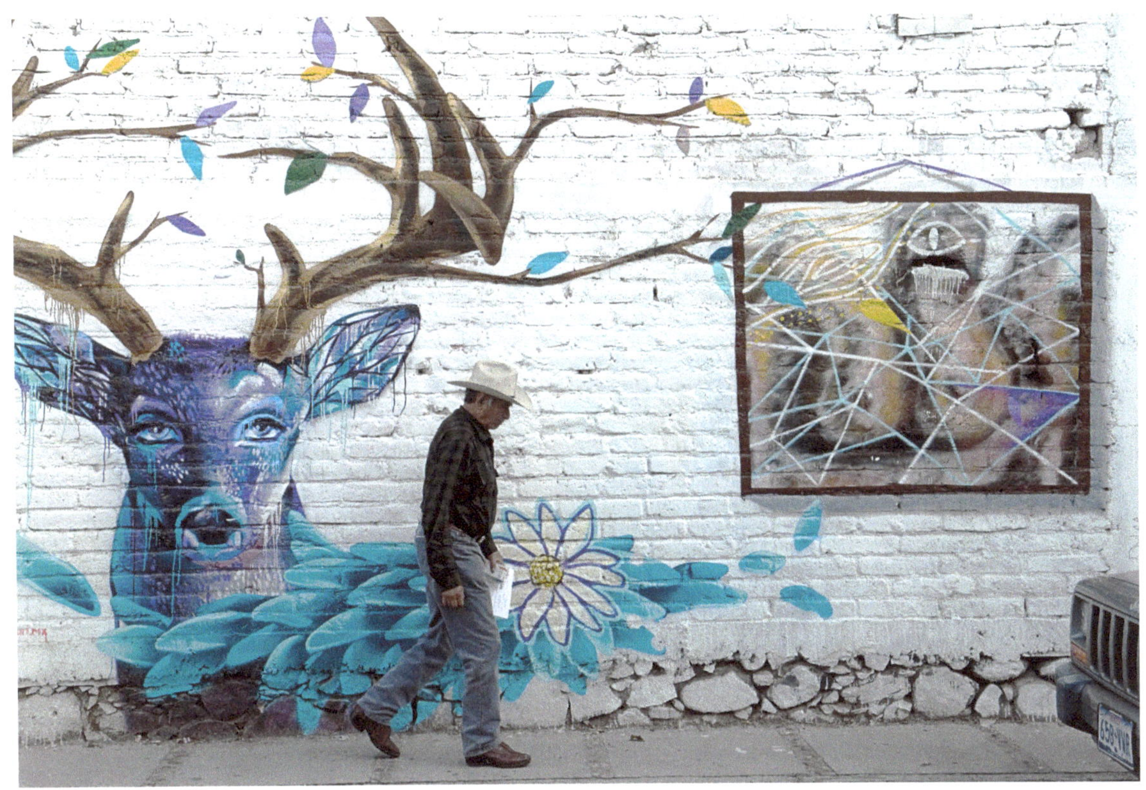

This is not the barrio of my youth, and the pueblo that supported my neighborhood has grown into a city. It is full of gringos now, the very people I swam the river to do commerce with. They came south while I was building their homes in the north. The ironies of this life never cease.

San Miguel was an elegant city in the time of my great-great-grandfather. The magnificent Parroquia de San Miguel Arcangel had already sprouted out of the soil to become one of Mexico's finest cathedrals. The streets around it were cobbled and spread up the hill, past grand haciendas, around el jardin, and down to the lower barrios where our family has lived for so many generations.

By the time my great-grandfather was born, the silver mine in Guanajuato had played out, and San Miguel was no longer on the road to anywhere. It was almost a ghost town when my father was born, but after World War II, the art institute opened, and gringos came to learn Mexican art, and to escape the polio fears north of the border.

I was born in 1956, and by the time I was fourteen there were so many North Americans in San Miguel, I had learned to speak English better than anybody in my family. By the time the hippies came, la ciudad was an artist colony, but my family were not artists. We have always been farmers and laborers, and Papa said even though North America is coming to Mexico, we have to go north to earn money to bring back home.

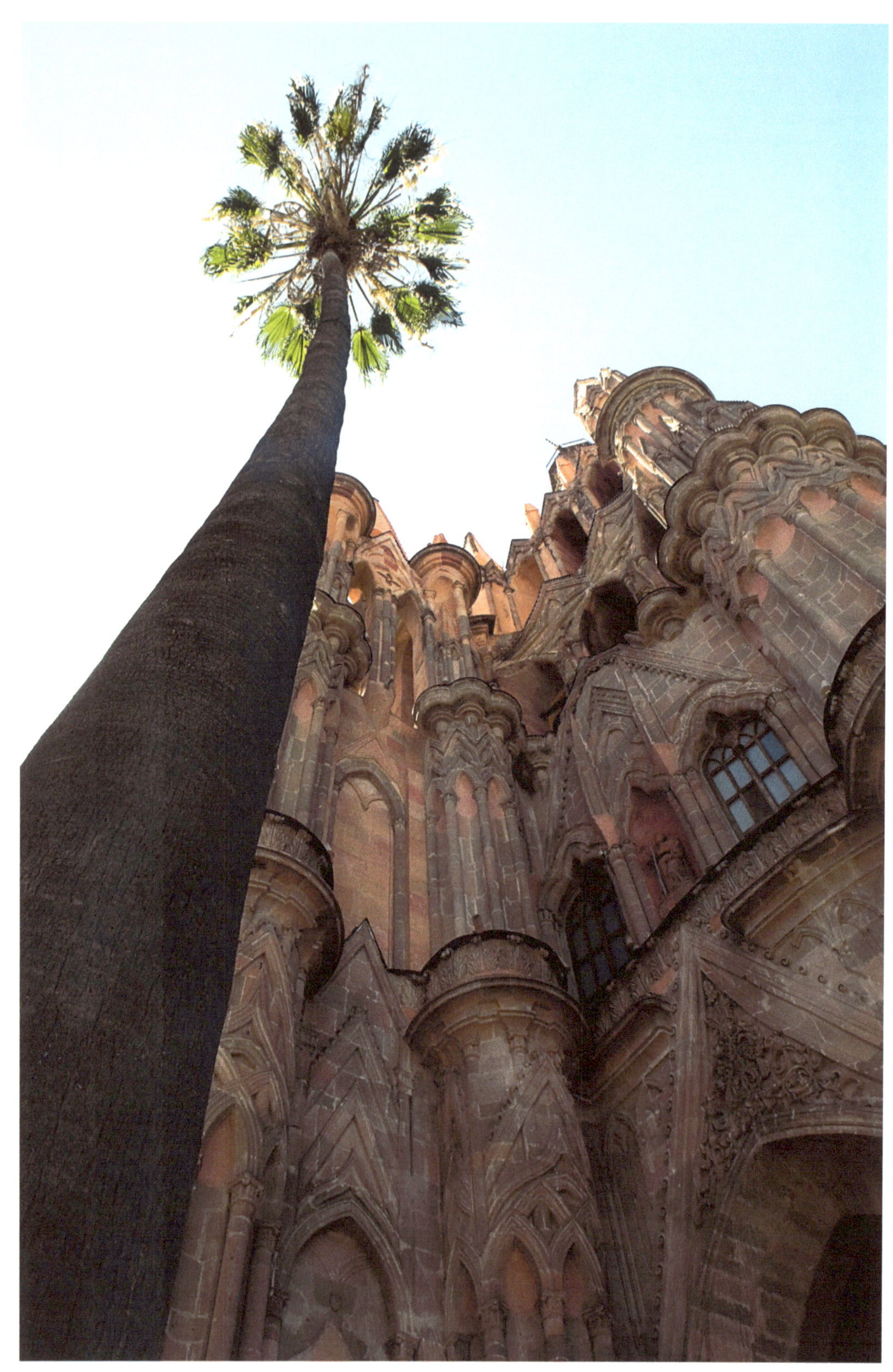

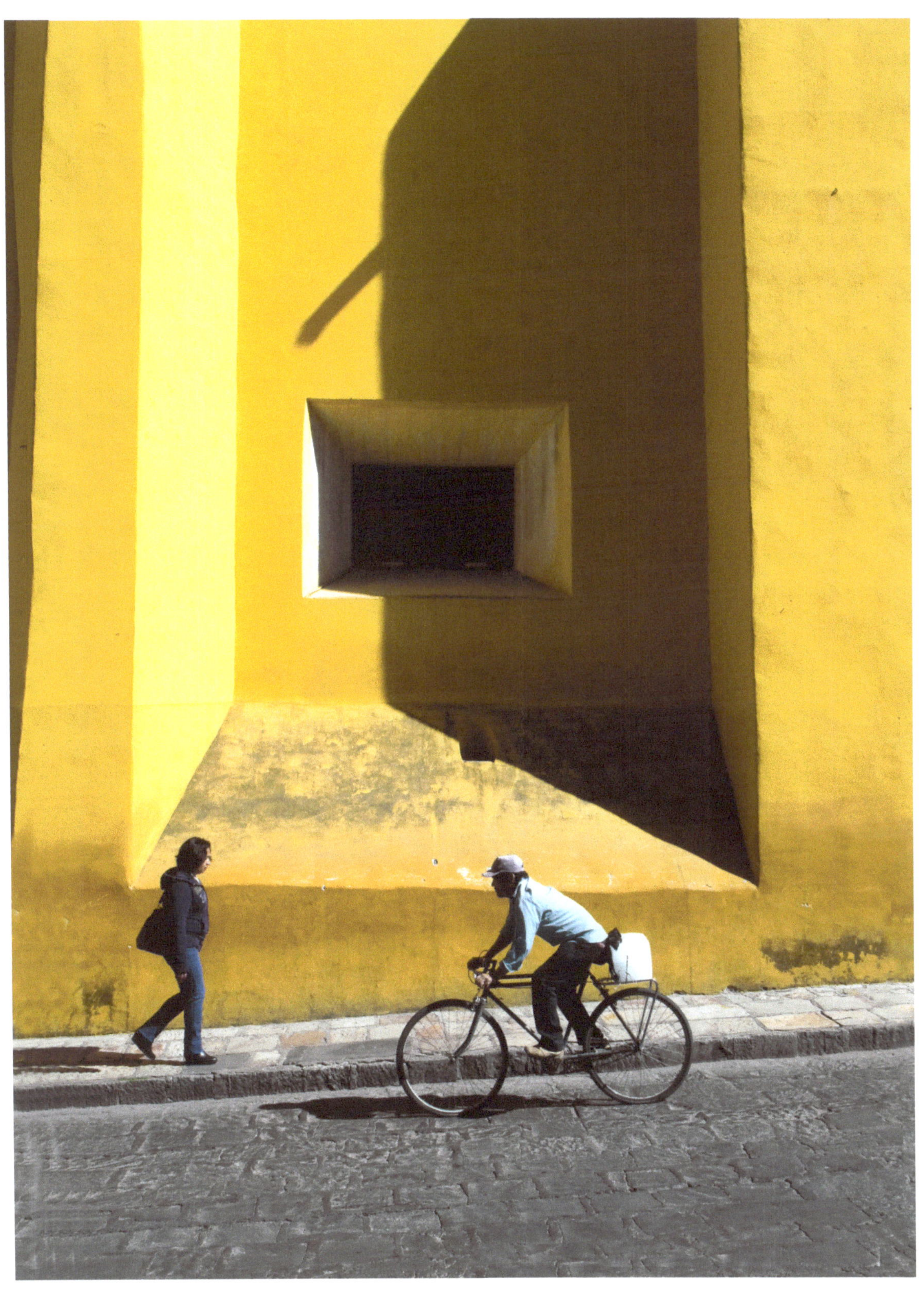

Papa and I crossed the river when I was fourteen years old. It took more than a week to get there because we walked most of the way. He said we could not take the bus because we had to save our money for food. I complained and he said to save my whining for the other side. Papa said it would make us stronger for when we got to Texas, and he was right about that. He was still young enough to out-walk me back then.

We swam the river by ourselves because Papa did not trust anybody. He told me stories about how people paid the money to coyotes to go to Austin or San Antonio and were robbed.

We walked into Texas for three weeks before ever talking to another person. We were careful because we were afraid. Papa did not want to get deported before he could earn some money.

After the first week our tortillas and water were gone. We came to an old trailer and Papa said we would have to ask for water and food. It was empty of people and Papa broke in the door while I hid in an arroyo. He came back with jugs of water and cans of food. We ate pork and beans, and Chef Boyardee, and crackers that mice had chewed on. We got diarrhea, which is not good when your body needs to keep the water that pours out your ass. We stayed in the arroyo for two days because we were too weak to walk. No people came to the trailer and we went back for more water and food to take with us. We took Chicken of the Sea and orange Jell-O. Papa said we should pay the people back some day, but we never did. They would probably shoot us.

After three weeks in Texas we saw some Mexicans digging plants from the desert. They were from Guanajuato, and worked for a man who sold the plants to people who were too lazy to dig for themselves. They told the man about us and he hired us to dig. Papa made good money because he could dig up so many plants without cutting the root. I made money too, but not so much. We had plenty to eat, and el jefe left water for us in the desert.

We worked for el jefe for five weeks and Papa said we could make more money in Austin or San Antonio. We never went that far, but we walked to the city of Johnson, where the President of the United States was born. We worked construction for so many months I don't remember, and made more money than Papa thought we could. At first I just carried tools and lumber, but then I began to learn to build houses.

One day Papa said he wanted to go home. We took the bus, but Immigration caught us near the border. They let us go because we were going home. Papa and I laughed about that after we got back to Mexico.

Papa never left Mexico again, but I crossed the river many times and never got caught. Once, Immigration almost caught me on a flatbed train, but I hid in a big tire. It was the kind of tires they use for big construction machines, and there were too many tires for them to look in all of them. They looked in the front tires, and the back tires, but I was in the middle, where it was difficult to get to. Plenty of Mexicans get caught, and some leave their bones in the desert, but I was always careful.

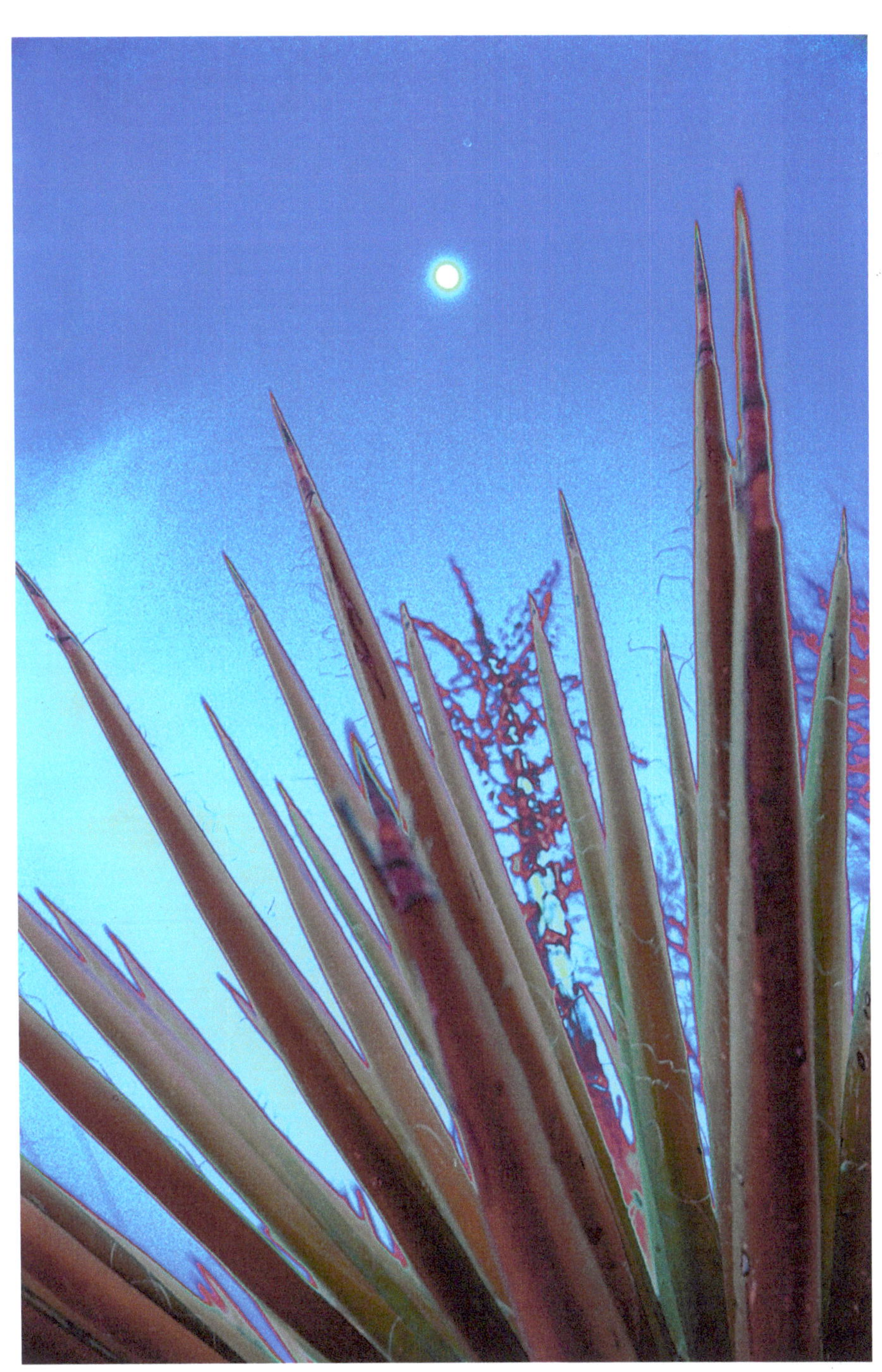

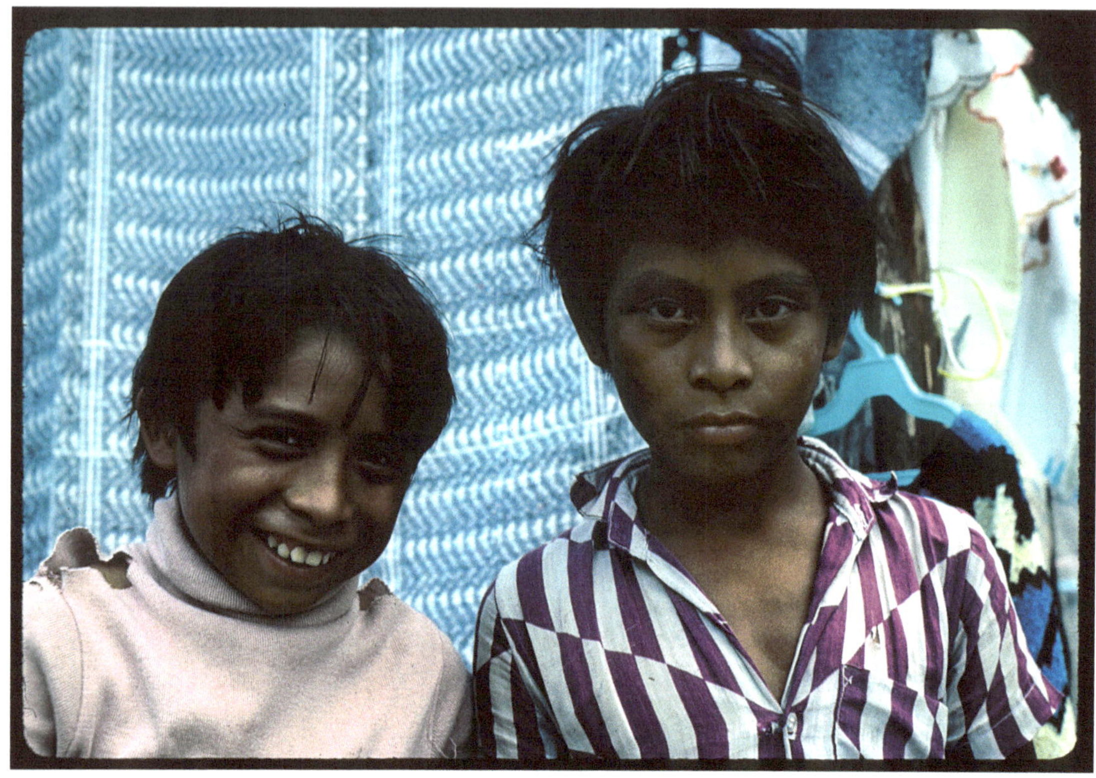

Maybe I never saw the glory of San Miguel because by the time I was born, the city was crumbling, and life was hard. Papa lost his job when the cotton factory shut down. That is when he said we had to cross the border to make money. Now the cotton factory is an art gallery. Stores that were closed for lack of paying customers have reopened. People have enough money to stay in San Miguel. Unlike much of Mexico, they seldom send their sons across the river anymore. We have a Wal-Mart now.

Sections of la ciudad are locked into the time warp of my youth. The great white shade tents of the people's market still billow in the wind, and the same sounds and smells emanate from within. Most of the people have ancestral faces, but there are also hybrids, and incomprehensible languages. There are still pigs and chickens in the barrios, and every once in a while a burro wanders into the city. This is the same place with a different feel, and I have to remind myself that it is better this way.

The place seems nicer now. The dirt streets have been cobbled, and some of the cobblestones have been paved. The crumbling haciendas have been restored, and la ciudad has become an artistic haven for all cultures and currencies. It is good that the city went to art. It is our heritage, woven into the fabric of our lives like the fine threads of Mama's favorite rebozo. It was part of my childhood and I never realized it.

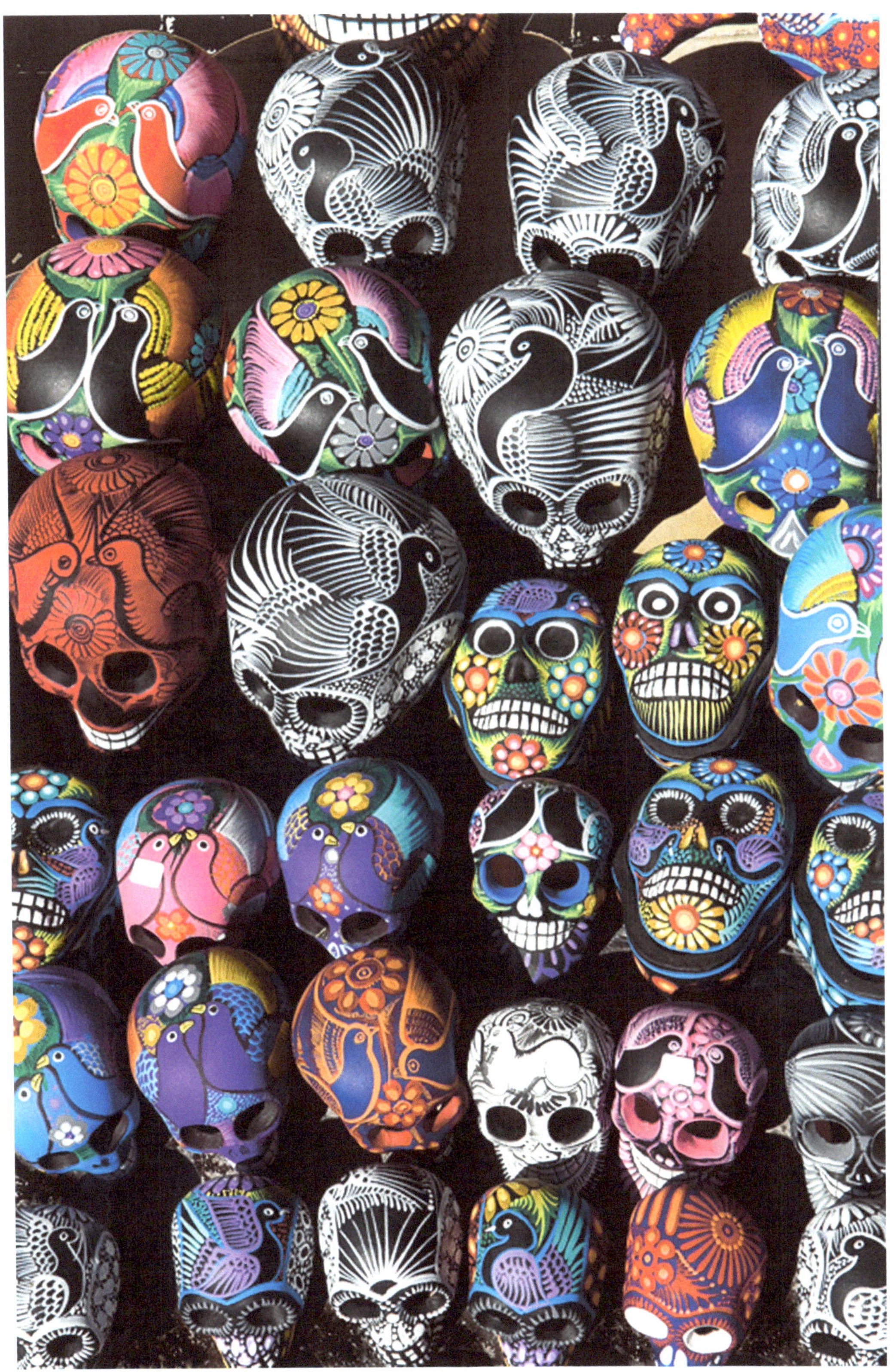

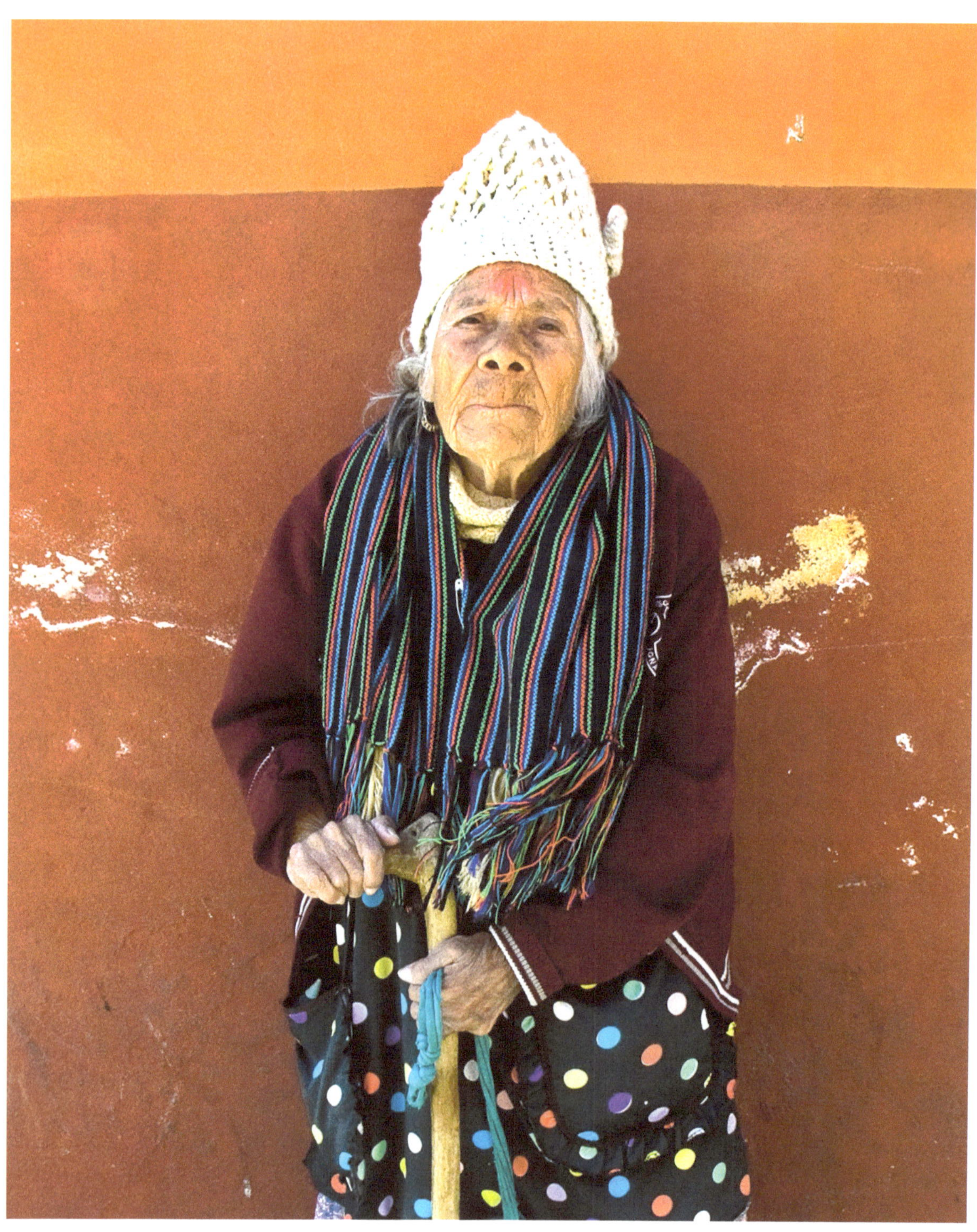

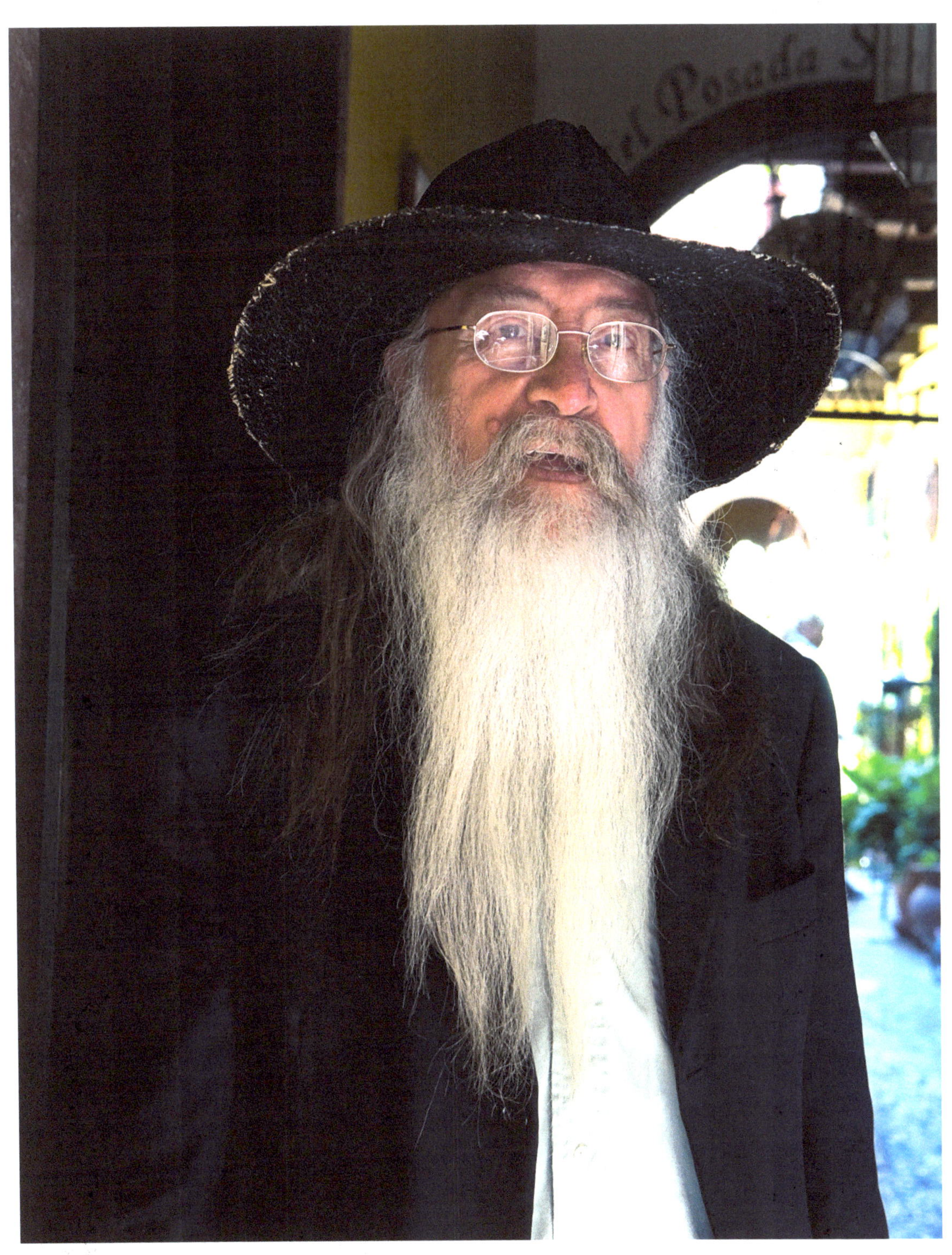
Posada

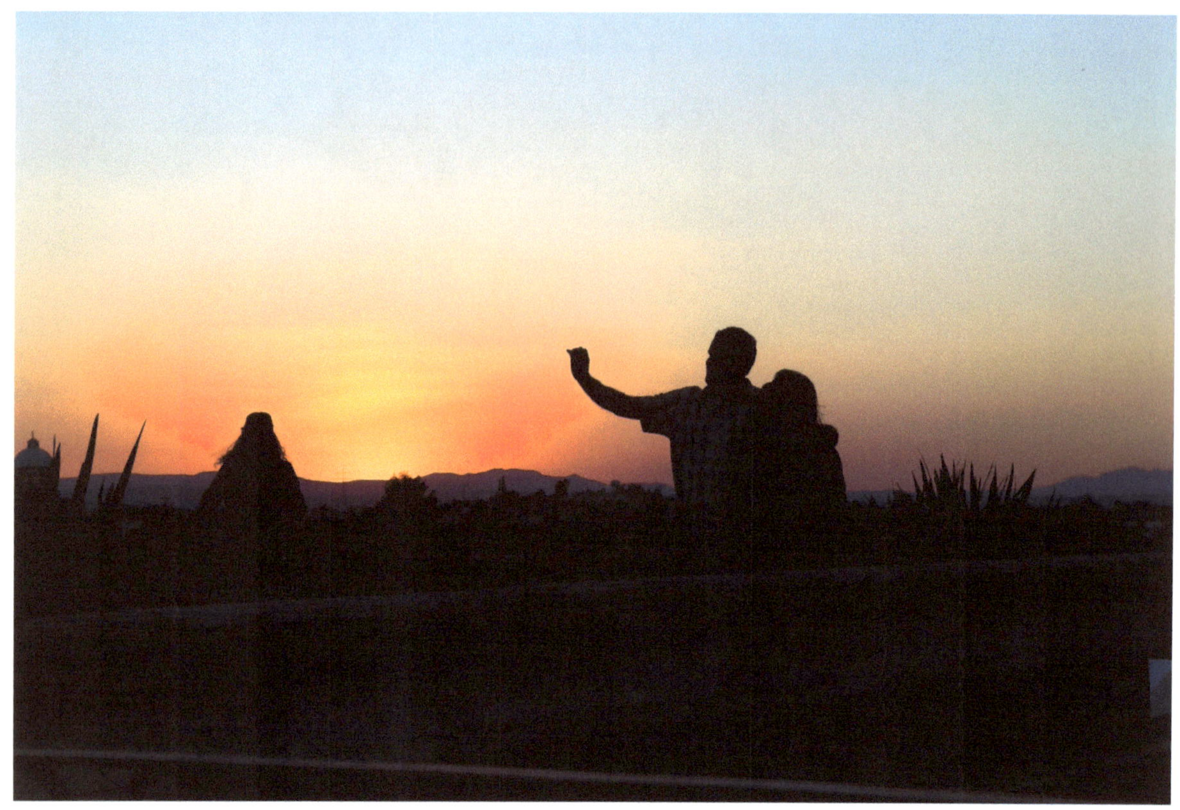

I have returned to this place as many times as I have left it, which is almost as many fingers as I have on both hands. I lost two fingers to a circular saw near Austin, Texas. I also learned what most Mexicans around San Miguel consider impeccable English. I am a skilled carpenter who earned enough money north of the border to return home, and invest in a construction company.

Much has changed in veinte anos. I have children on both sides of the border. Madre is dead, and Padre is ready to join her in heaven. As my body grows old, my mind grows into something more than it was. It thinks about what my eyes have seen in all of the places I have been, and it considers the past and the future. That is how I know what to do and how to feel. I am usually very decisive. I say, "This is what I think about that, and so this is what I will do."

I stand in the place I stood as a boy and think about all these things, and I think, "This is where I will stay forever." Still, this is not the barrio it used to be."

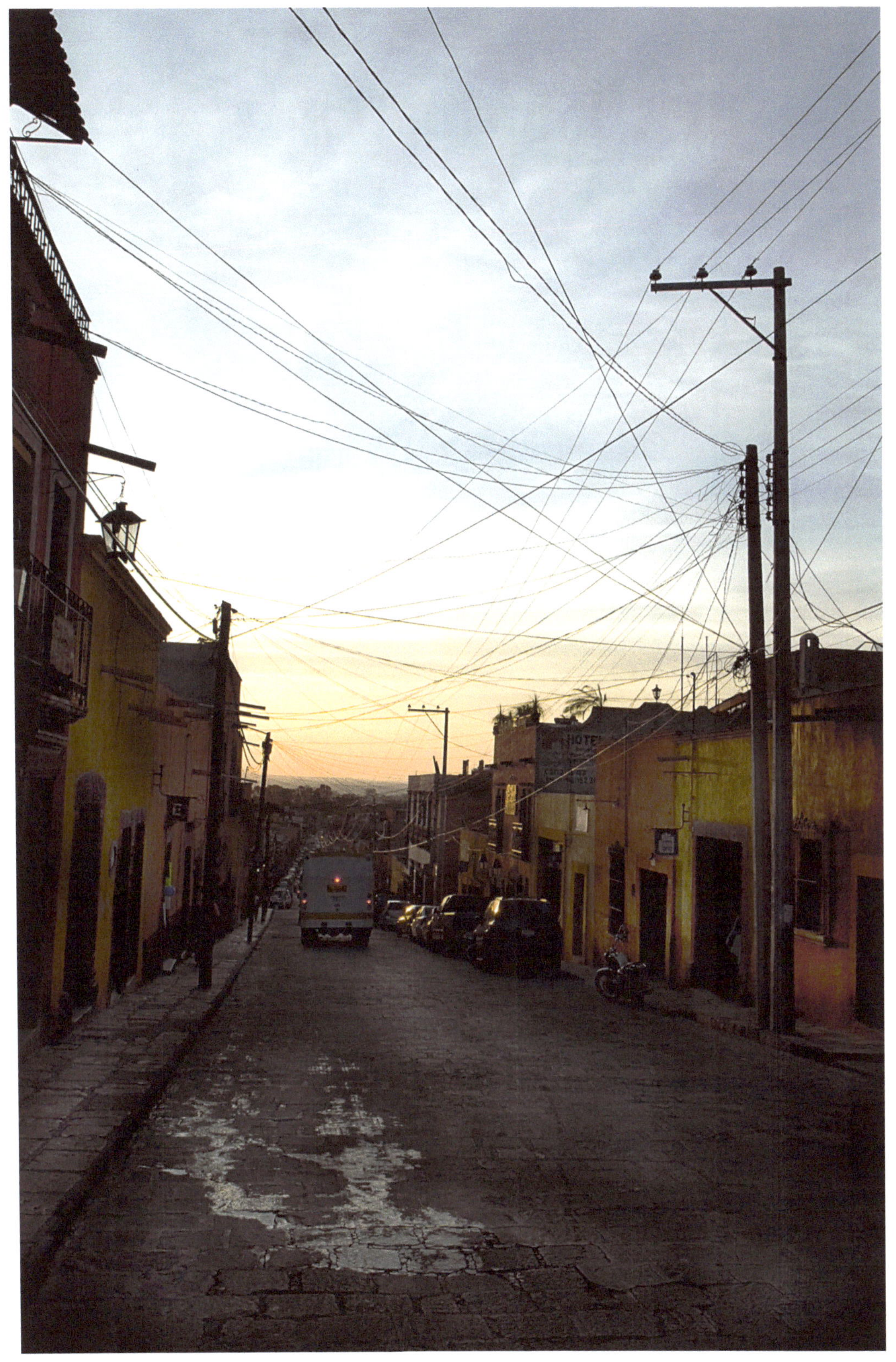

Information

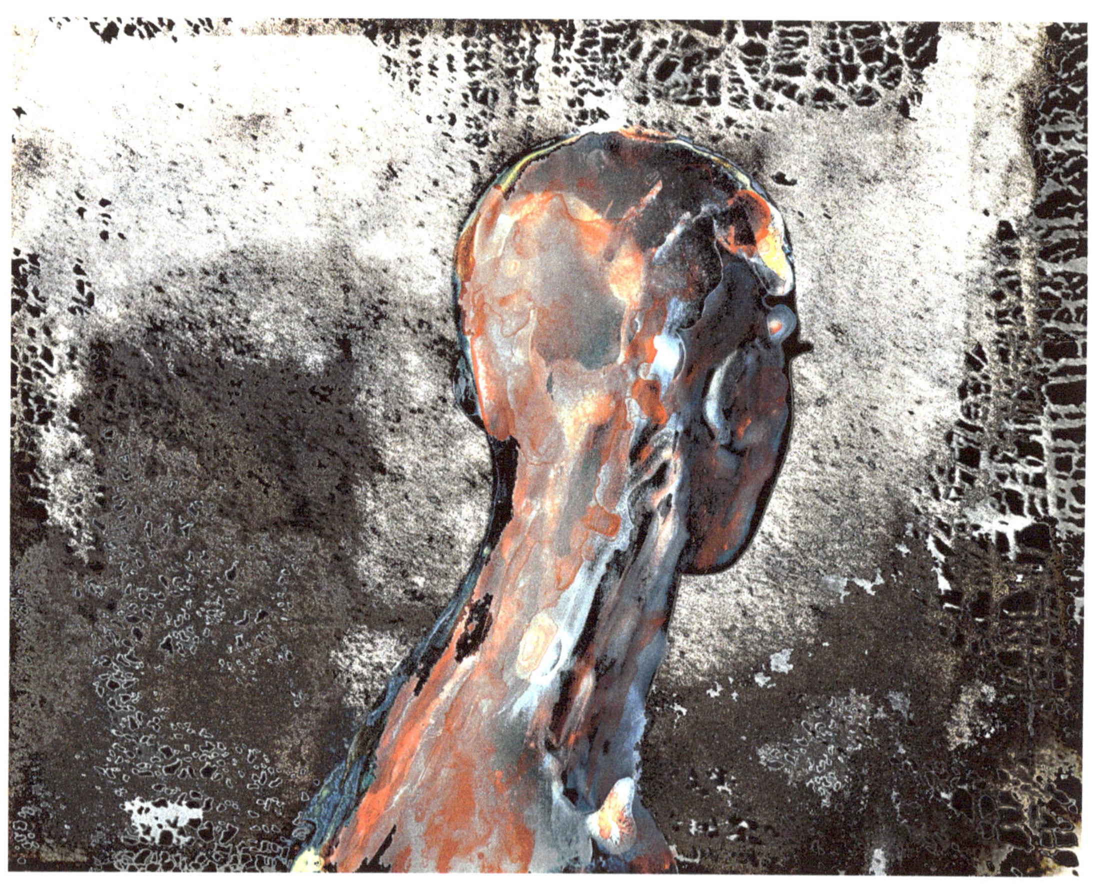

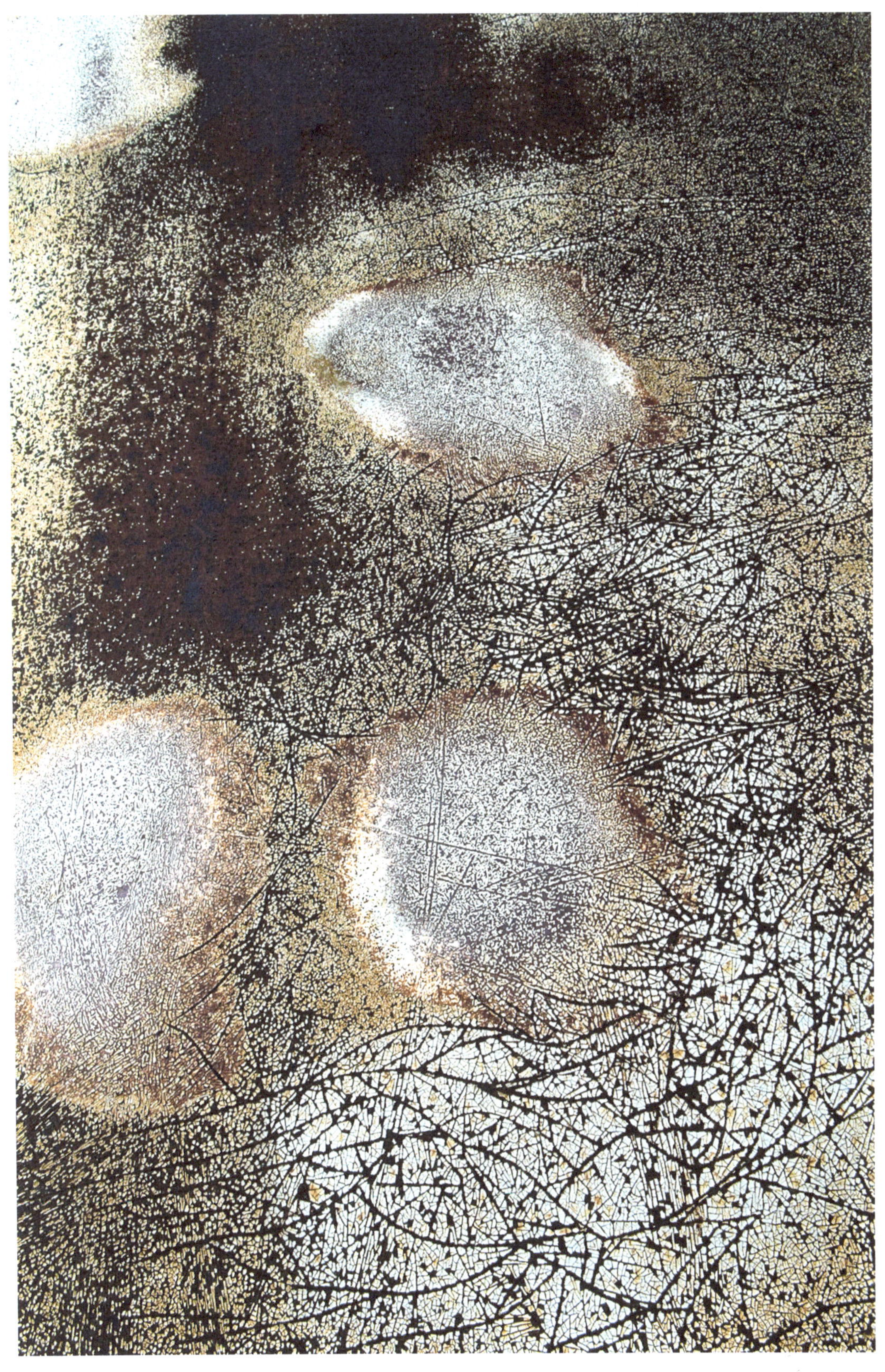

The earth has been cruising through our solar system for about four and a half billion years and was barren of life for almost all of that time. Humans have only been around for approximately two hundred thousand years, so the time lapse from the very first brain wave to the present is relatively short. There must have been an extraordinary amount of brain activity just to get the muscle in shape, but when it finally kicked into gear it quickly made up for those years of inactivity.

Not every thought produces an idea, but after it finally happened for the first time, nature no longer had a lock on what one might encounter in this world. Baskets and spears paved the way for hydroelectric dams and atom bombs. At this point in history, thoughts and ideas are flying by like meteors and space junk, and like eggs and sperm, an idea only has to land in the proper place to grow exponentially.

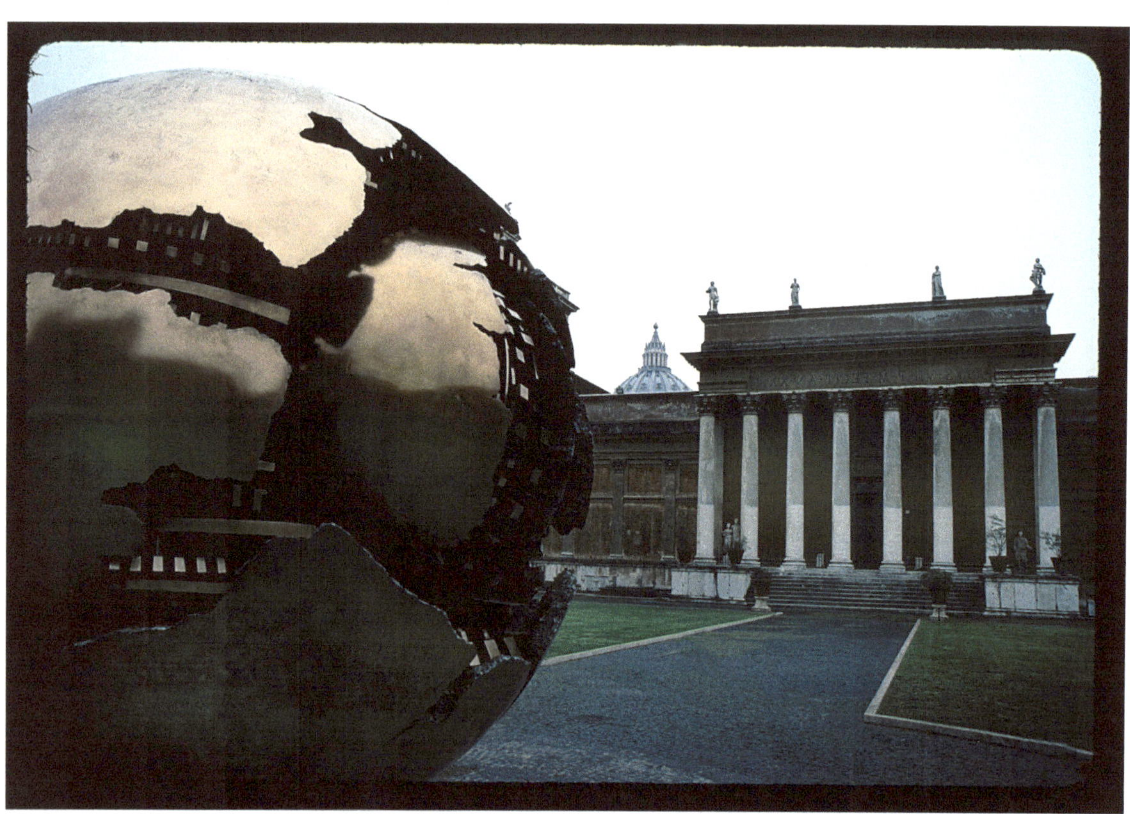

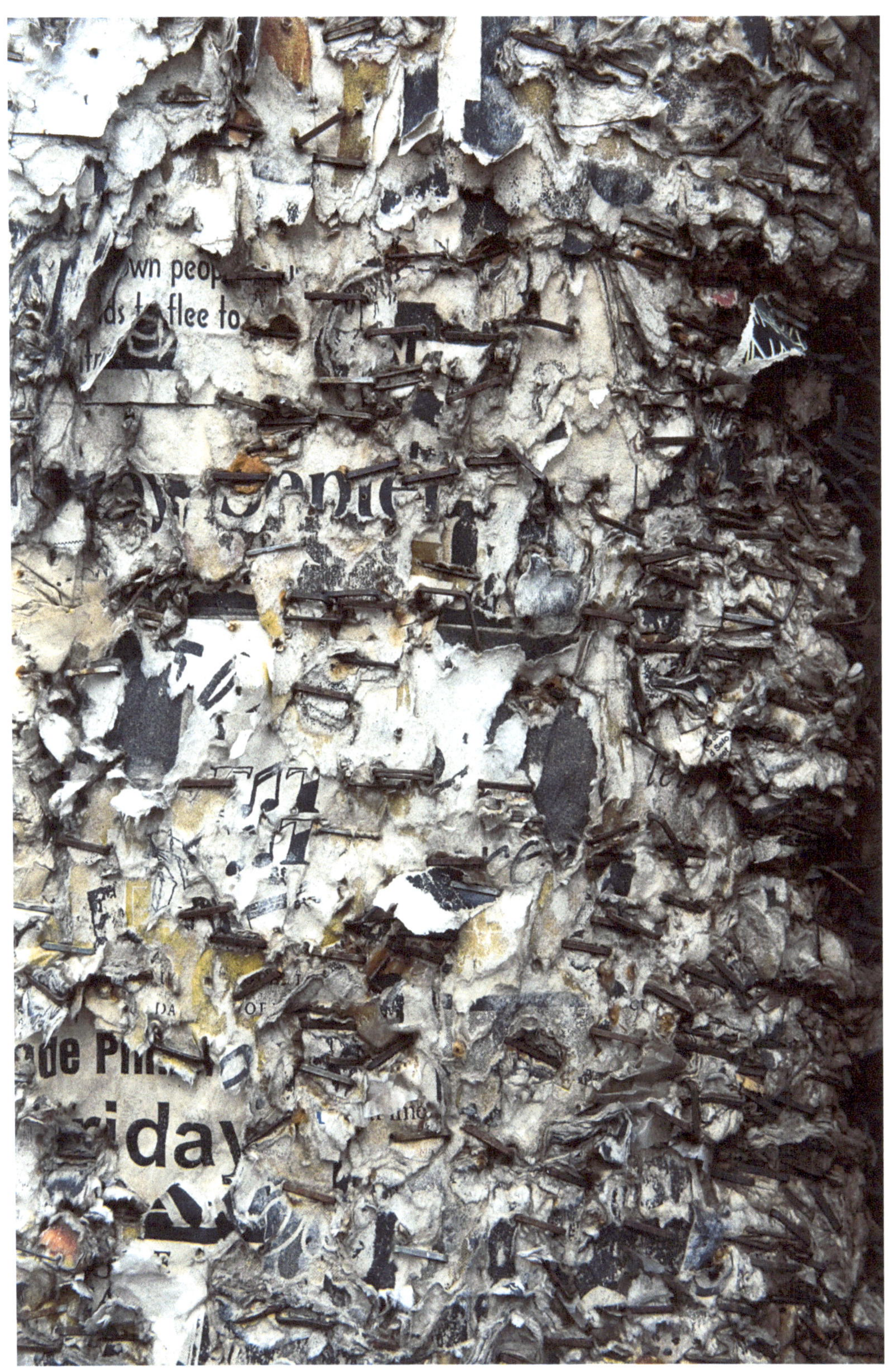
flee to

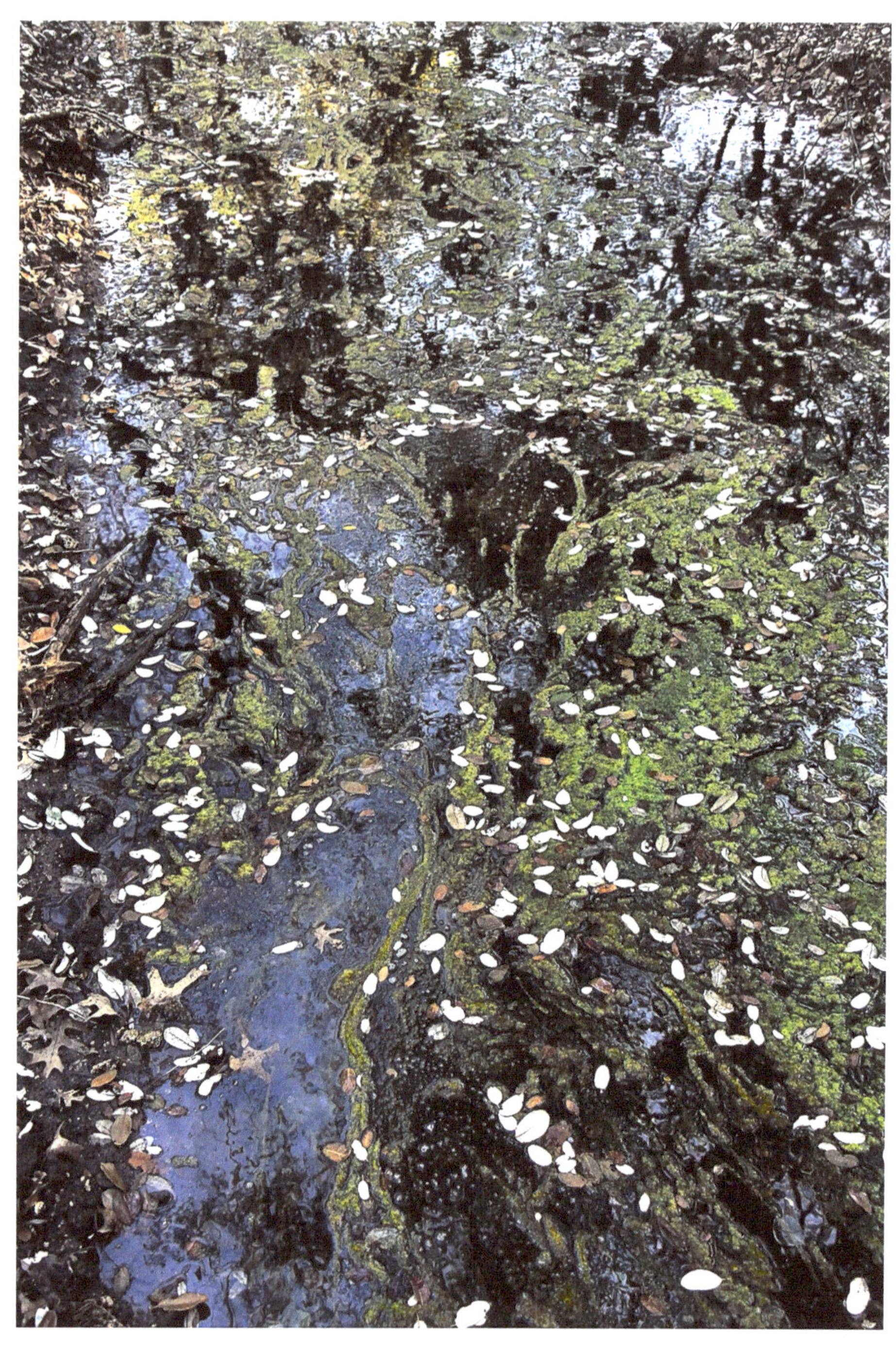

Life's ambition is to succeed.

—Anonymous

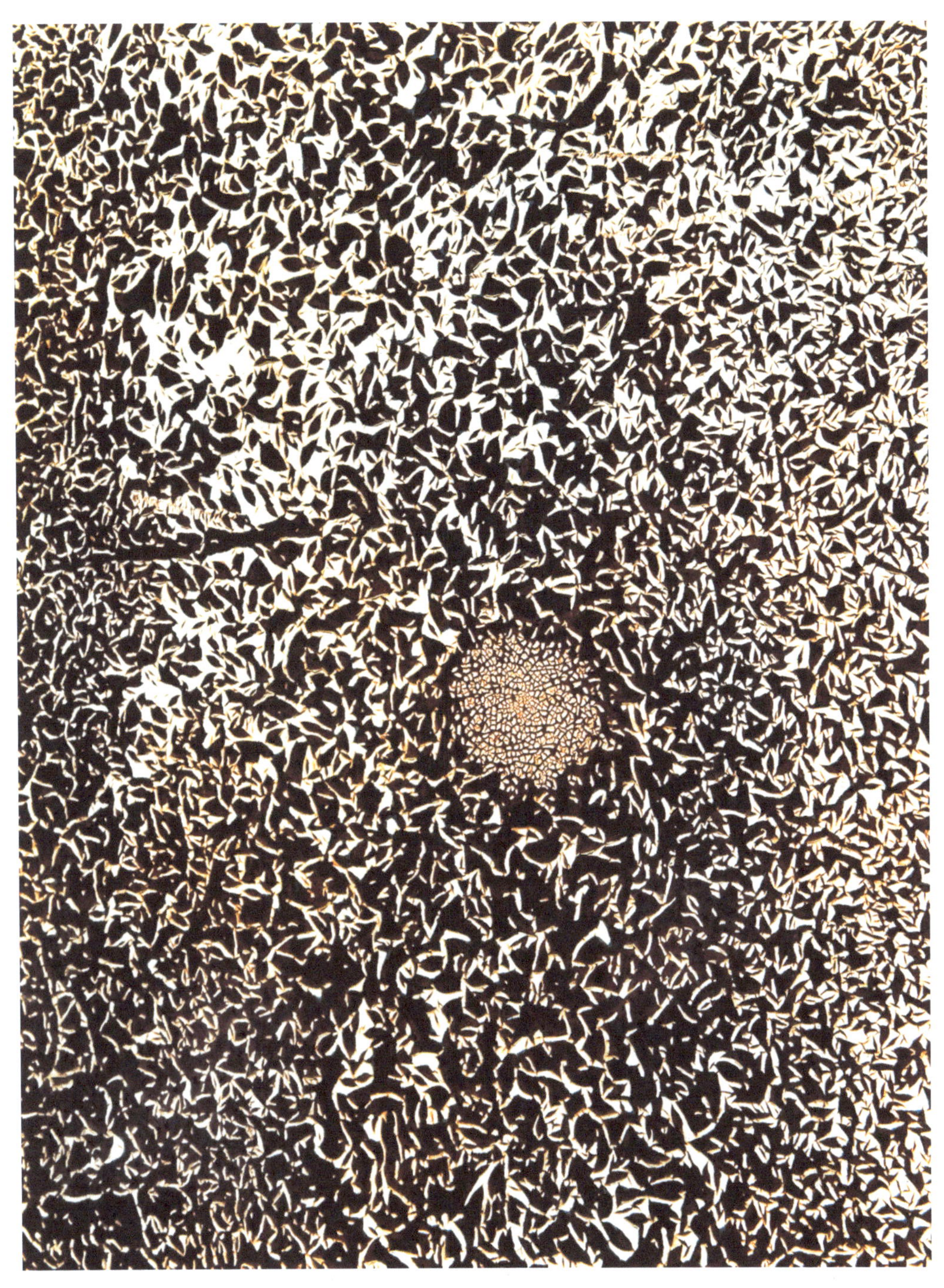

Get your sperm away from my egg.

—Anonymous

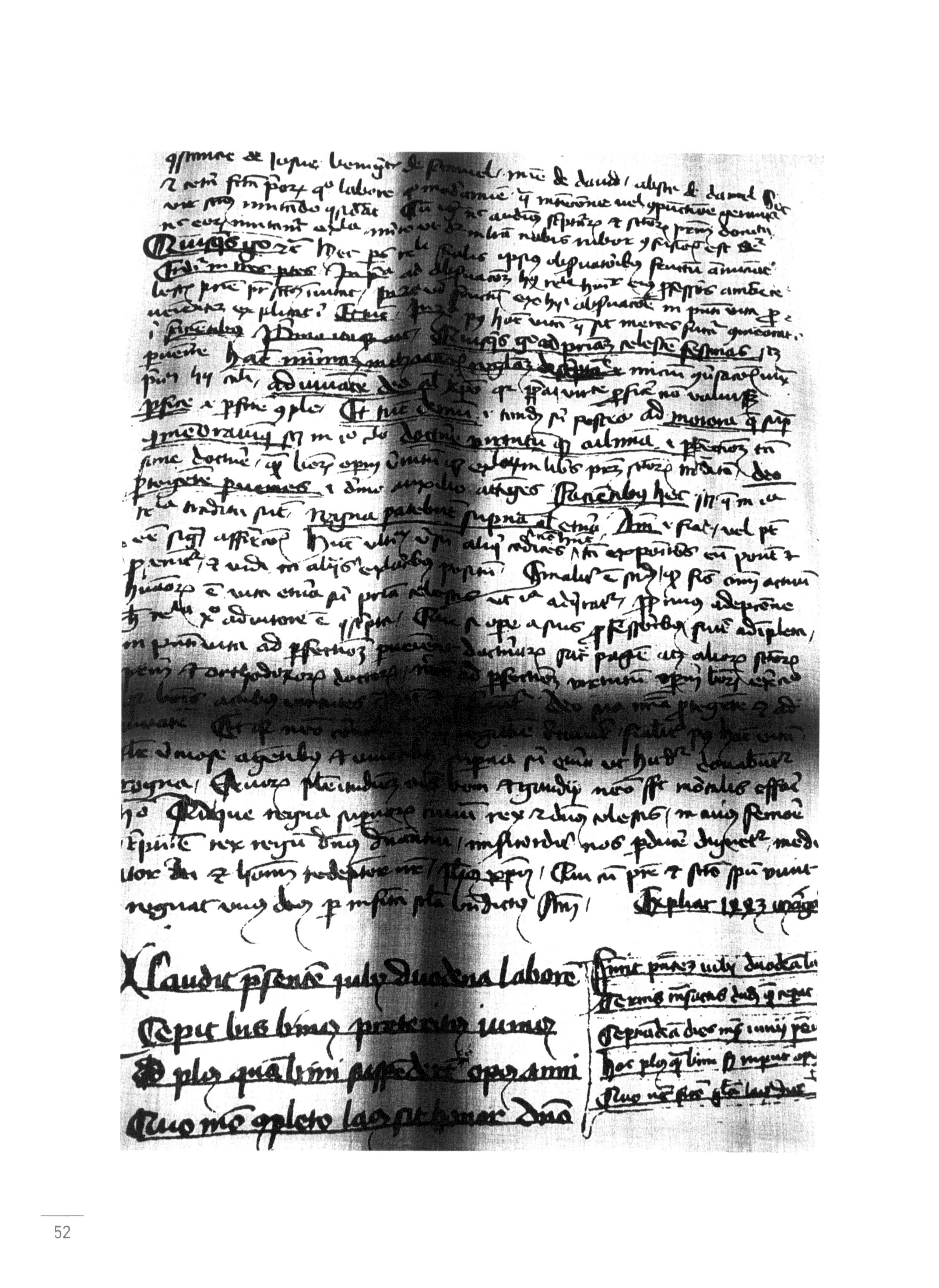

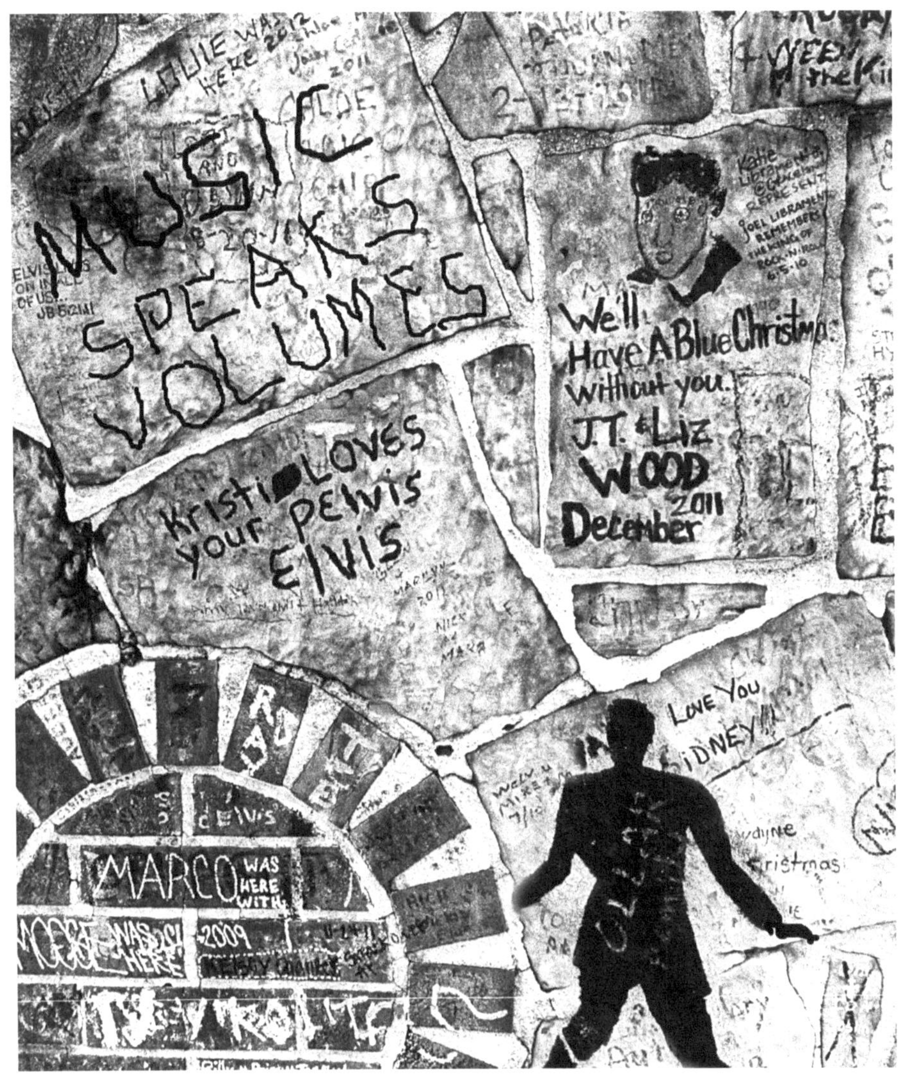

Thinkers and doers do not always come in the same human package, so the ability to convey an idea was a very big deal. Shared information was a major milestone. Language in the form of gestures, pictures and spoken words eventually led to data transferred by light pulses and reconfigured into auditory and visual information.

Brain activity created a thought that was passed along as information. More ideas produced more information, clutter and misinformation. Those building blocks of the creative process enabled the production of more substantial elements like toys, cities, highways and paraphernalia.

One only has to walk outside and look to the sky to see nature. The first idea created a competition between mankind and the natural world, and the human footprint is still just an expanding speck on our globe.

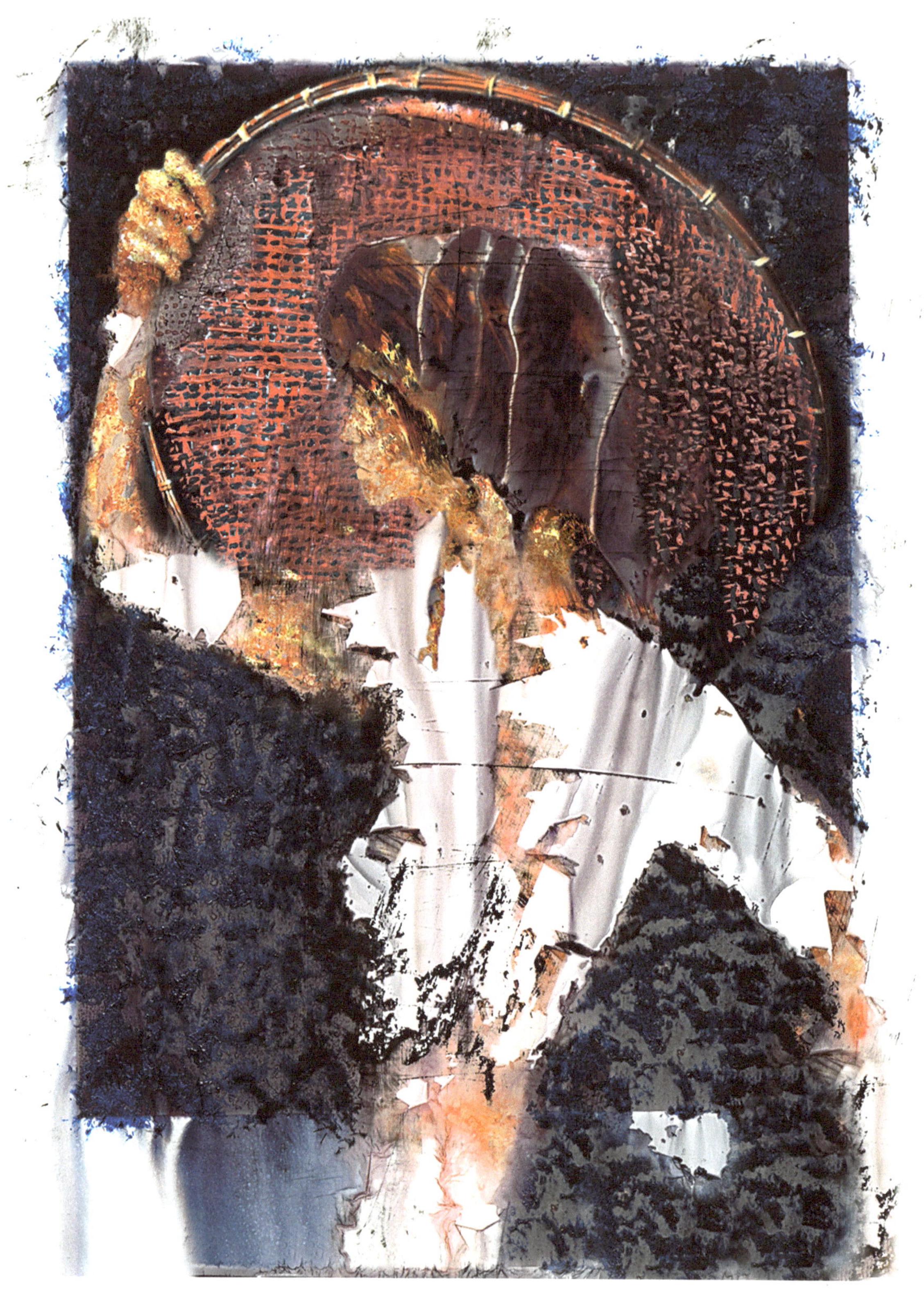

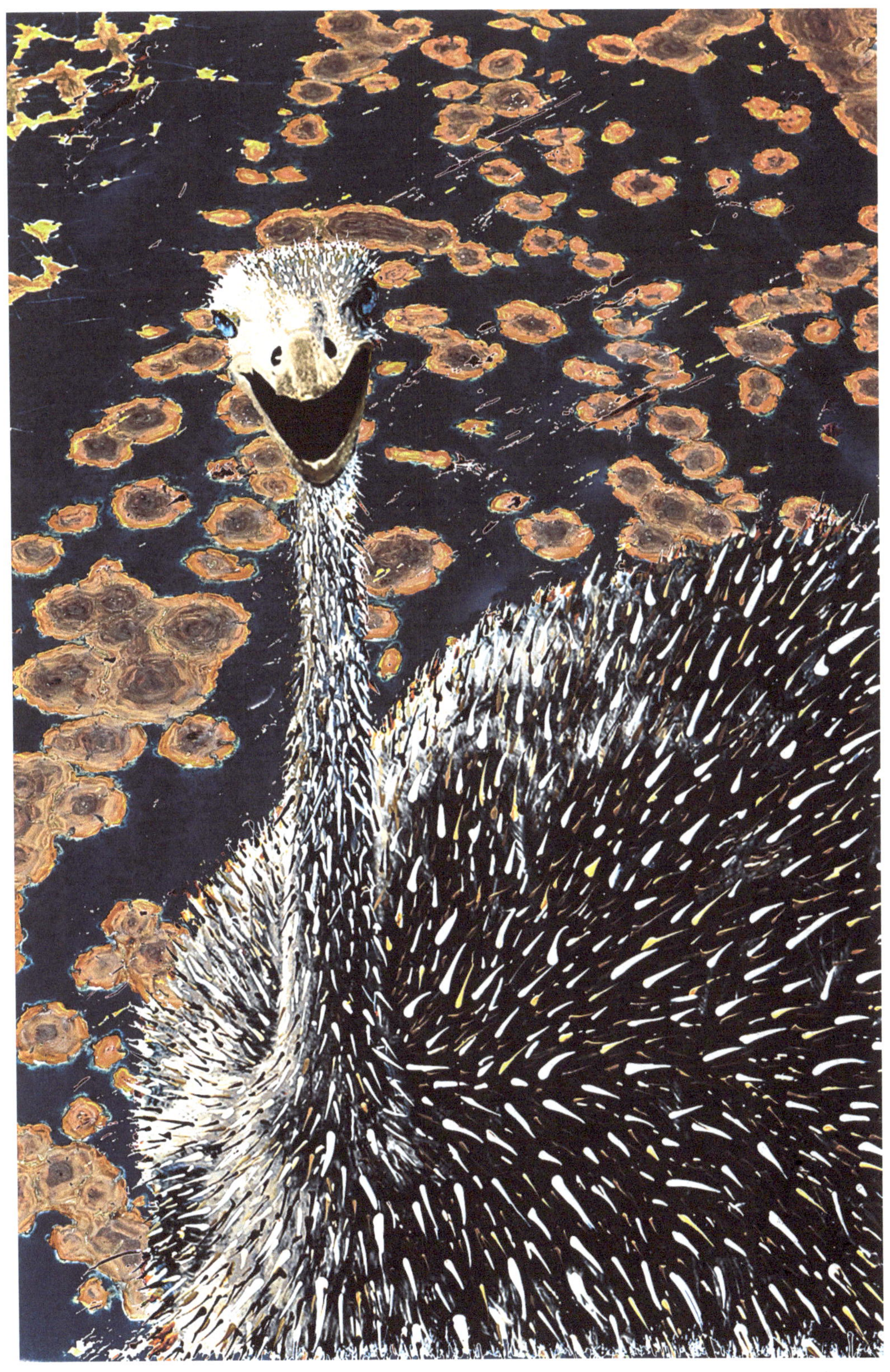

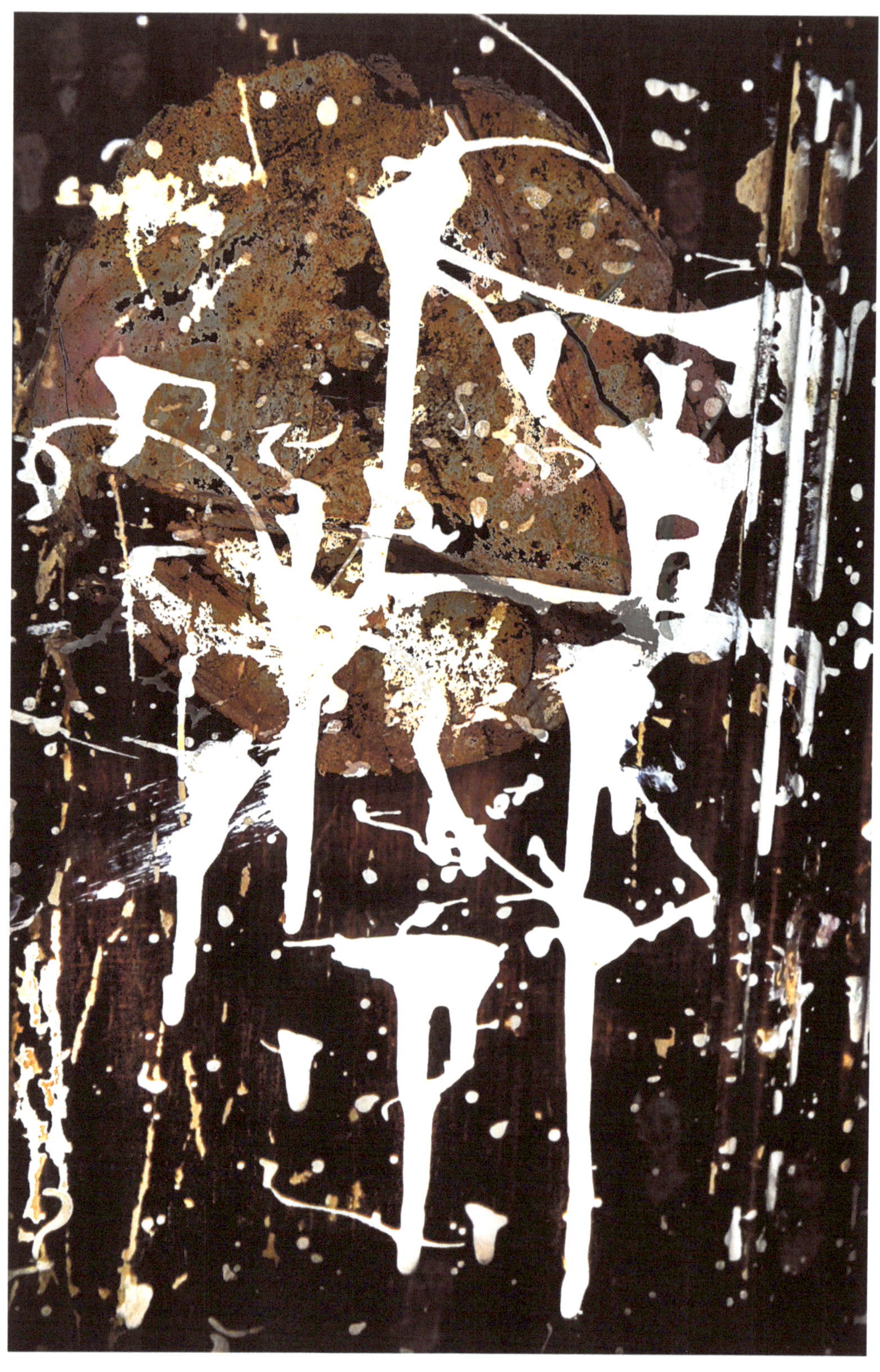

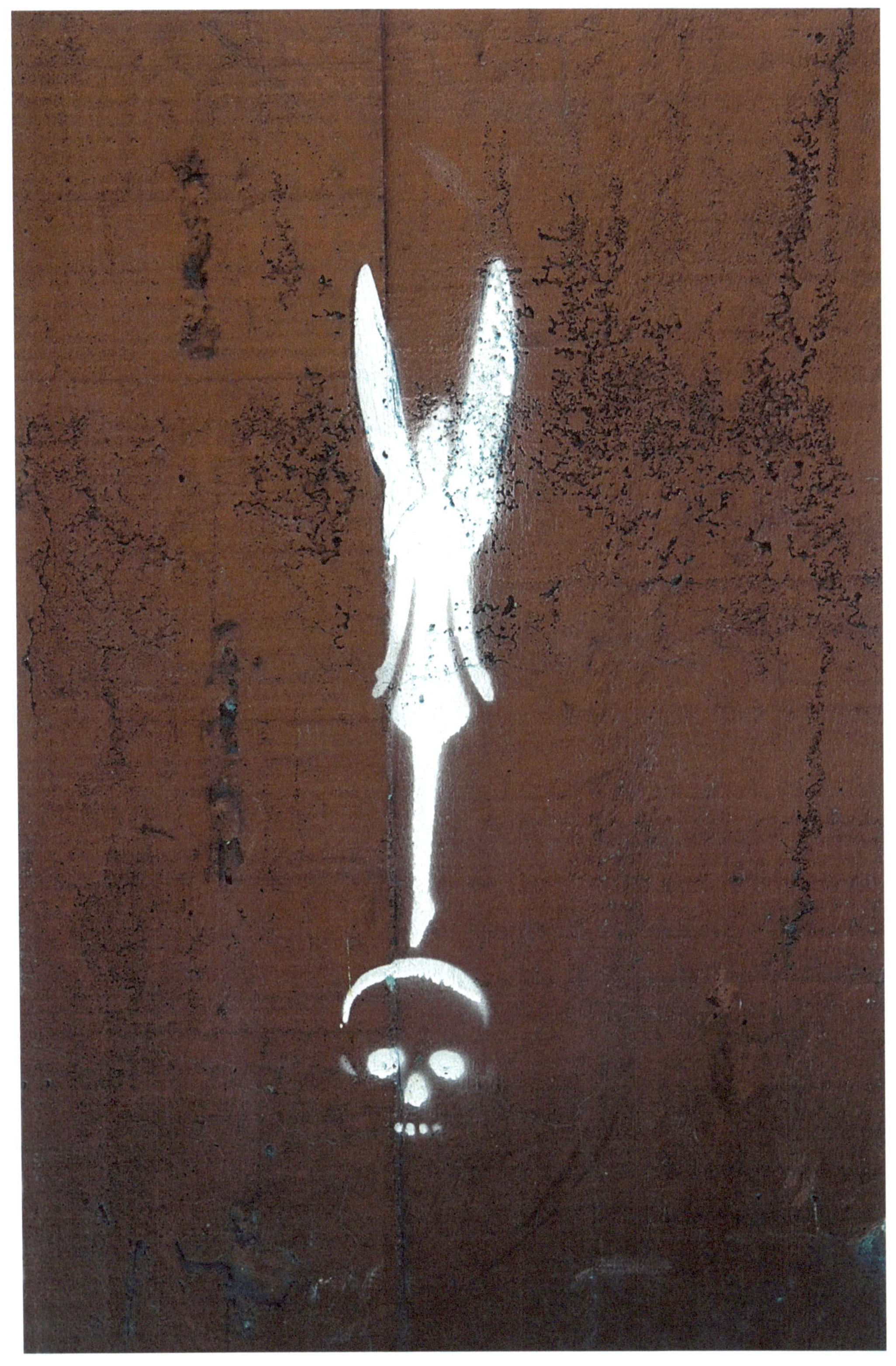

Give Me Shelter

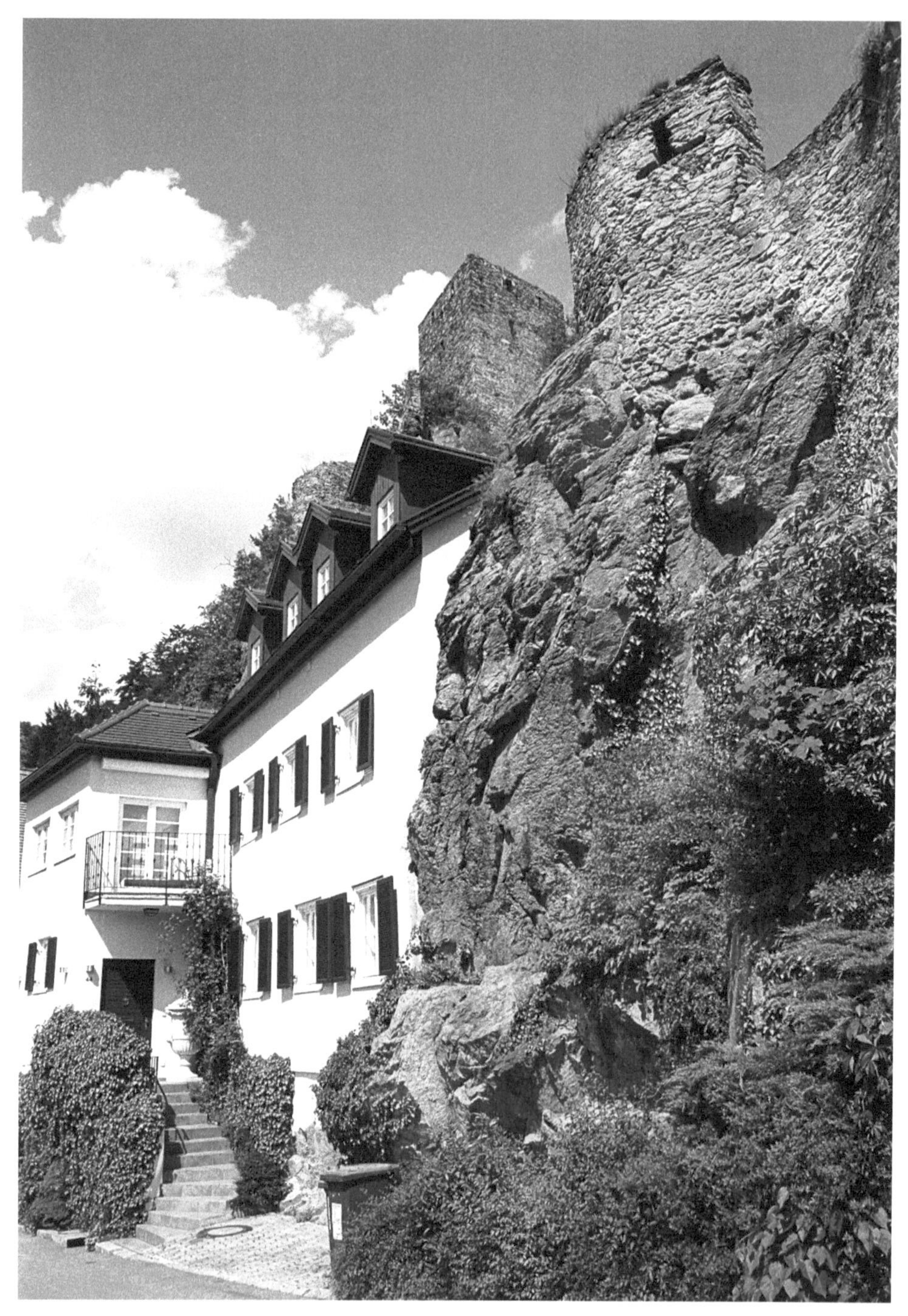

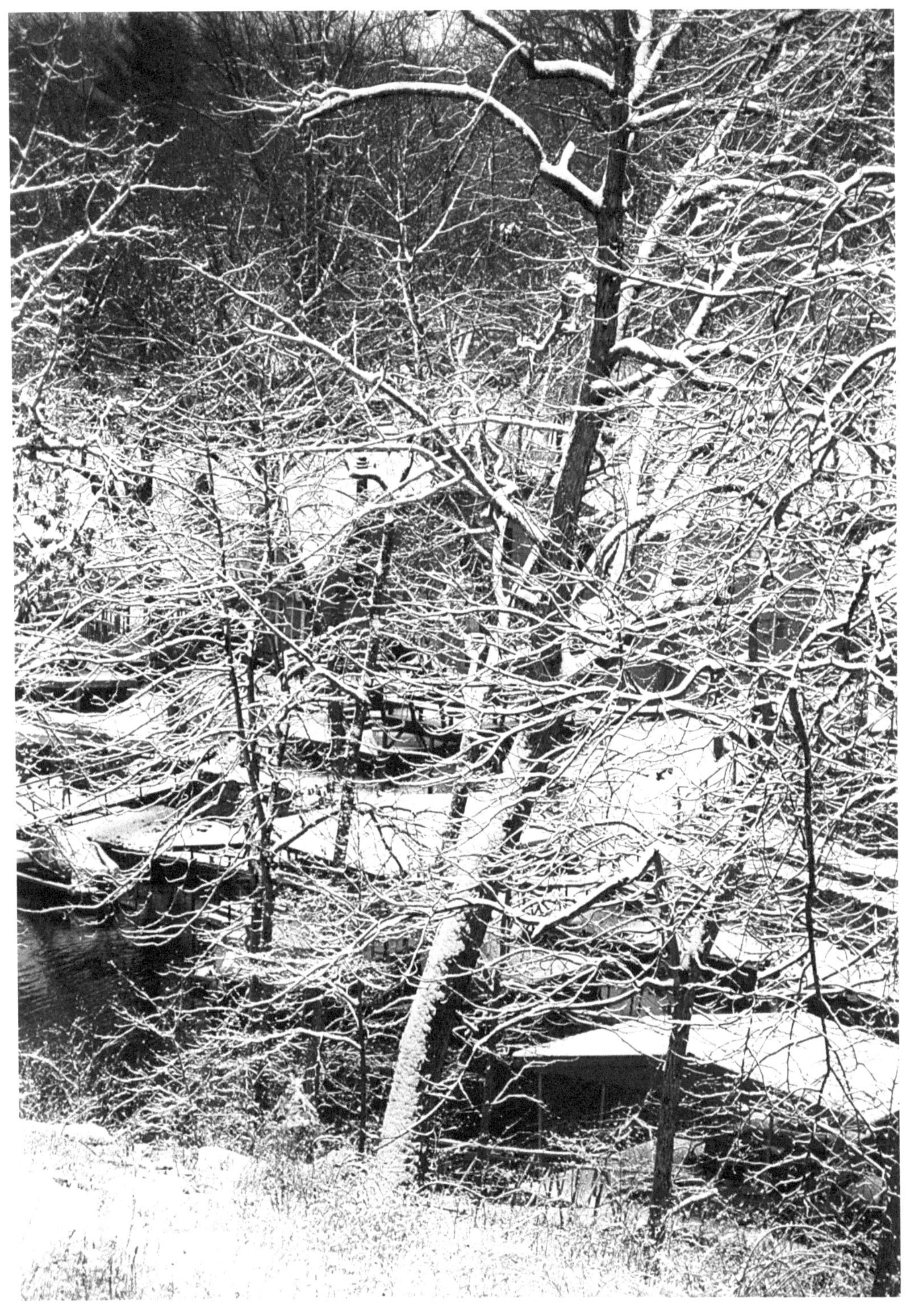

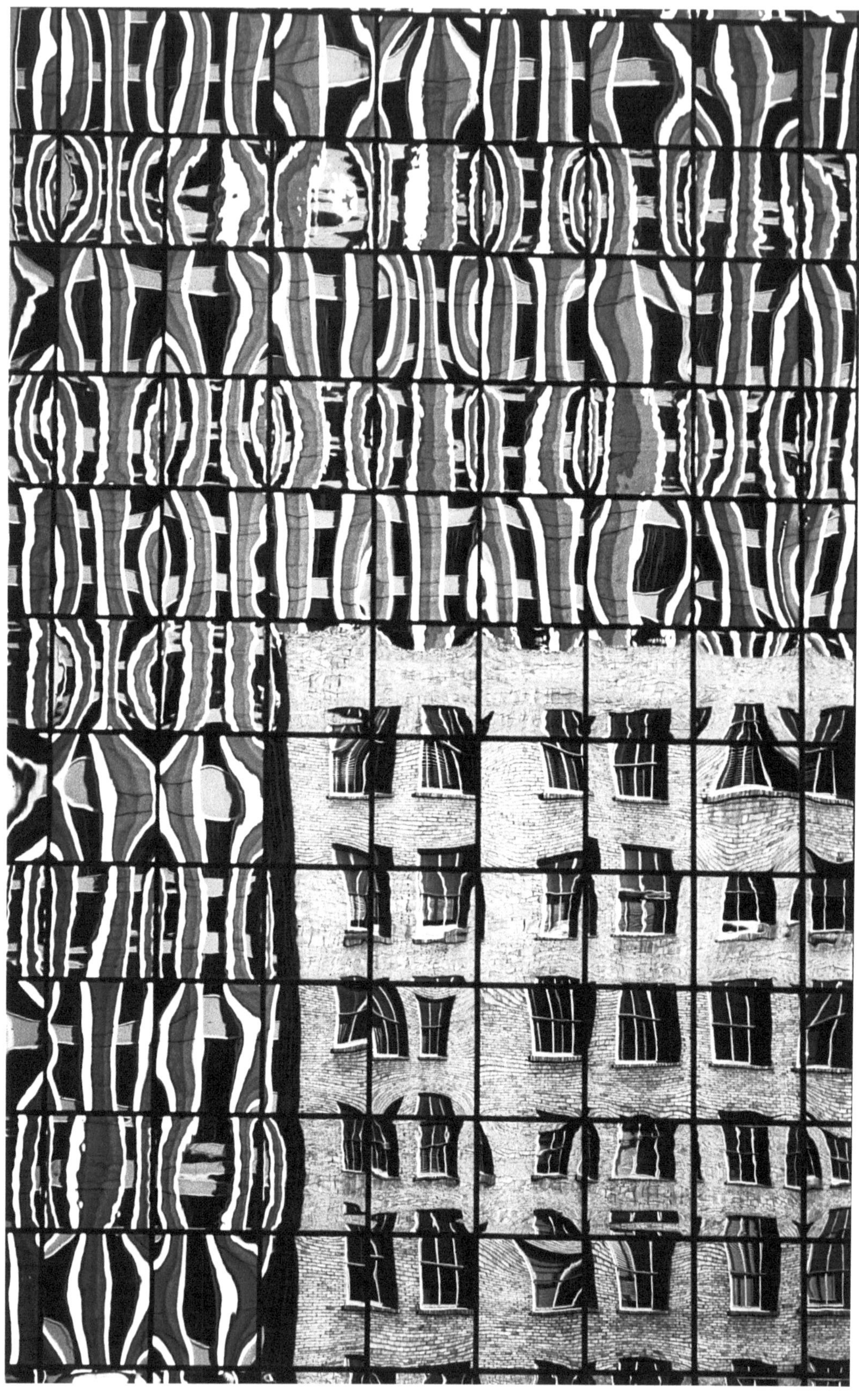

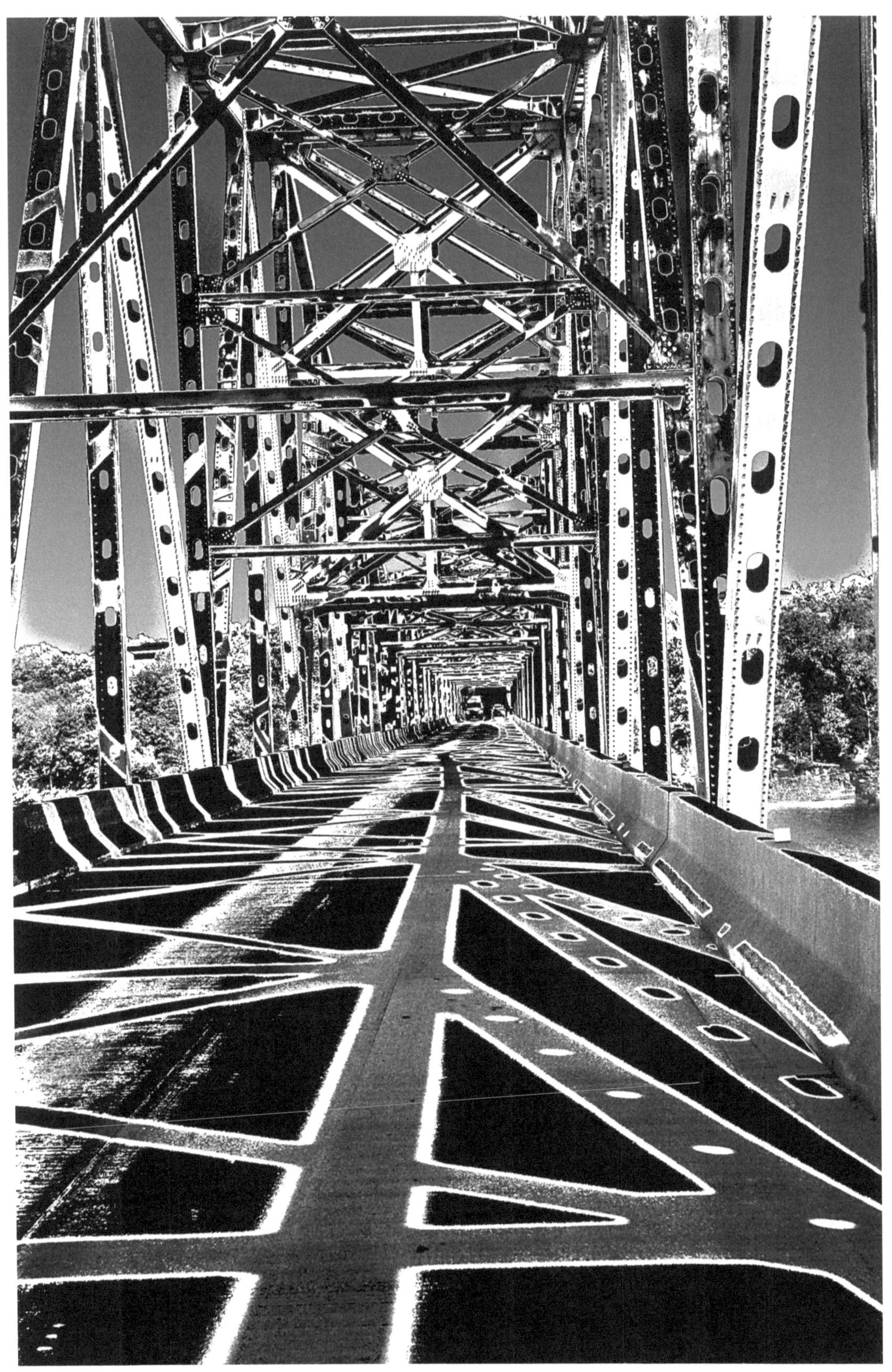

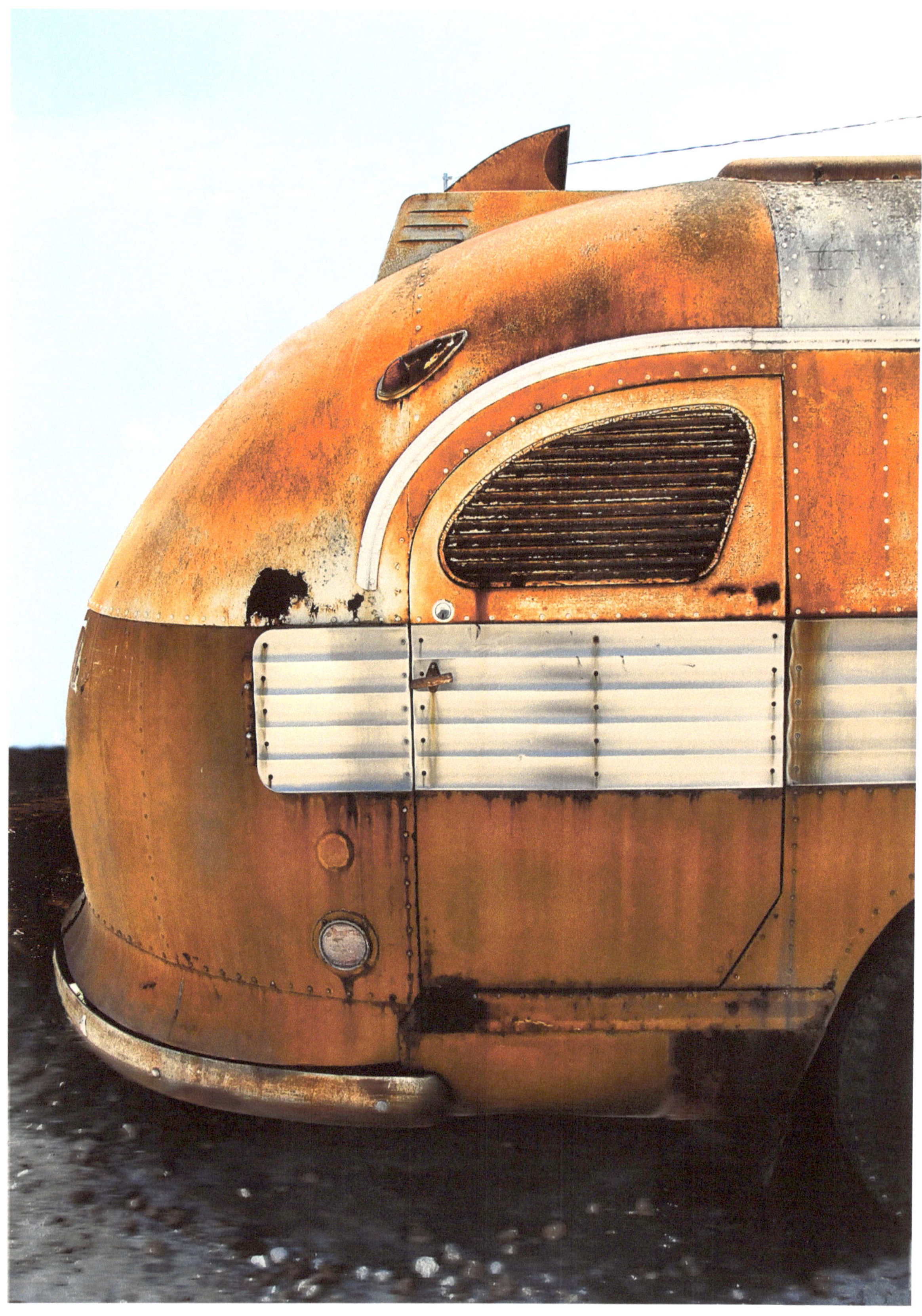

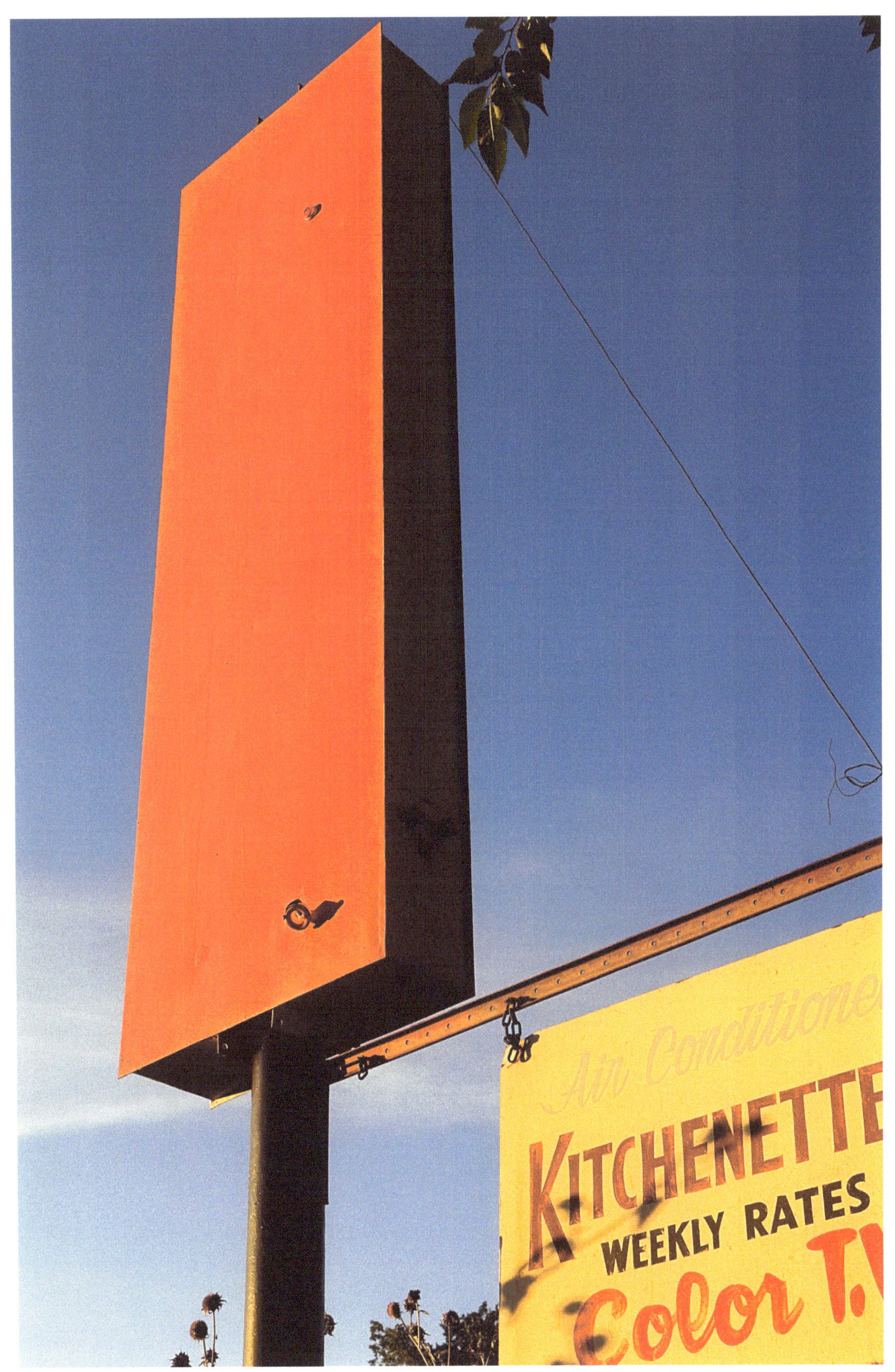
Air Conditioned
KITCHENETTE
WEEKLY RATES
Color T.V

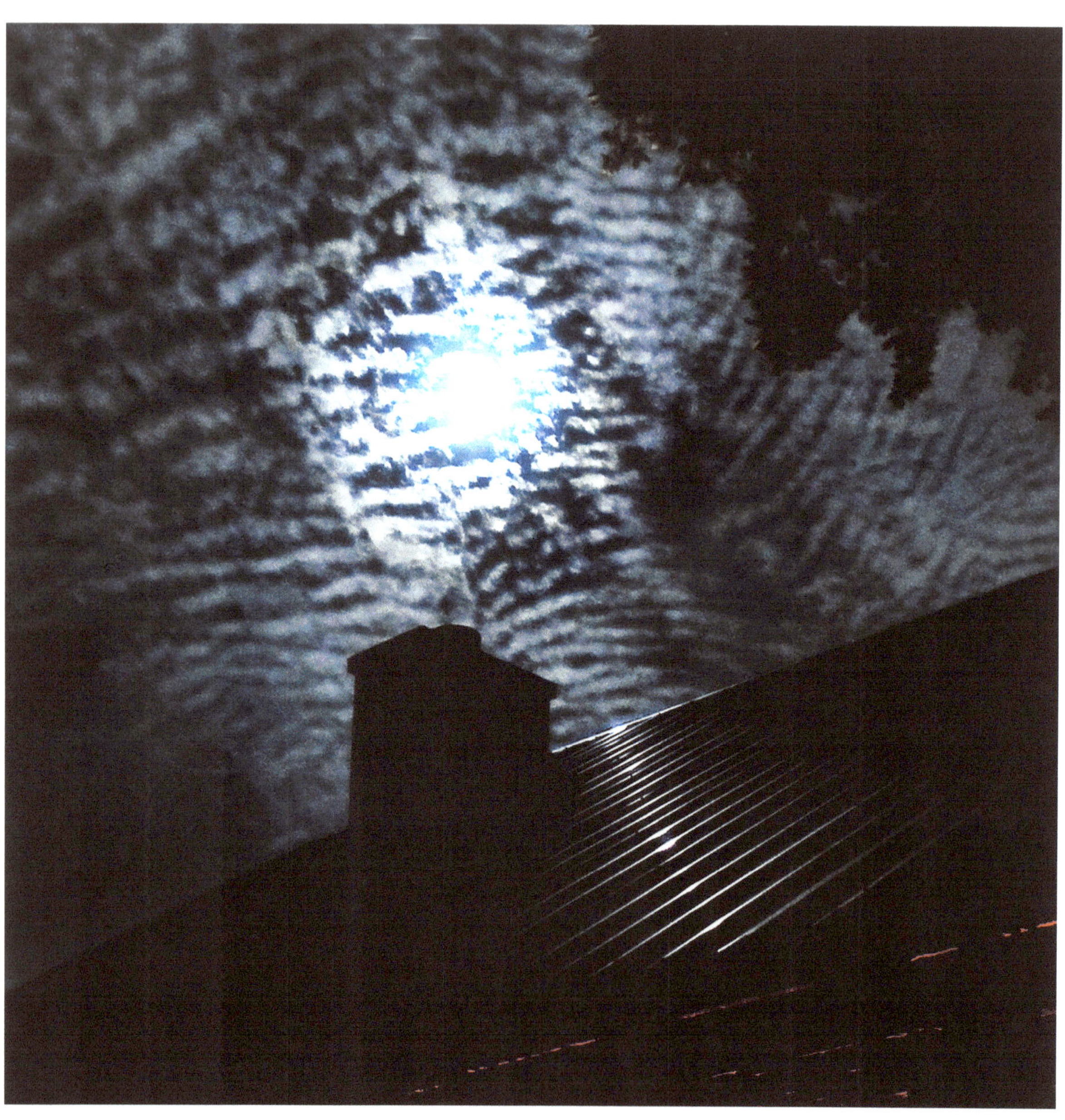

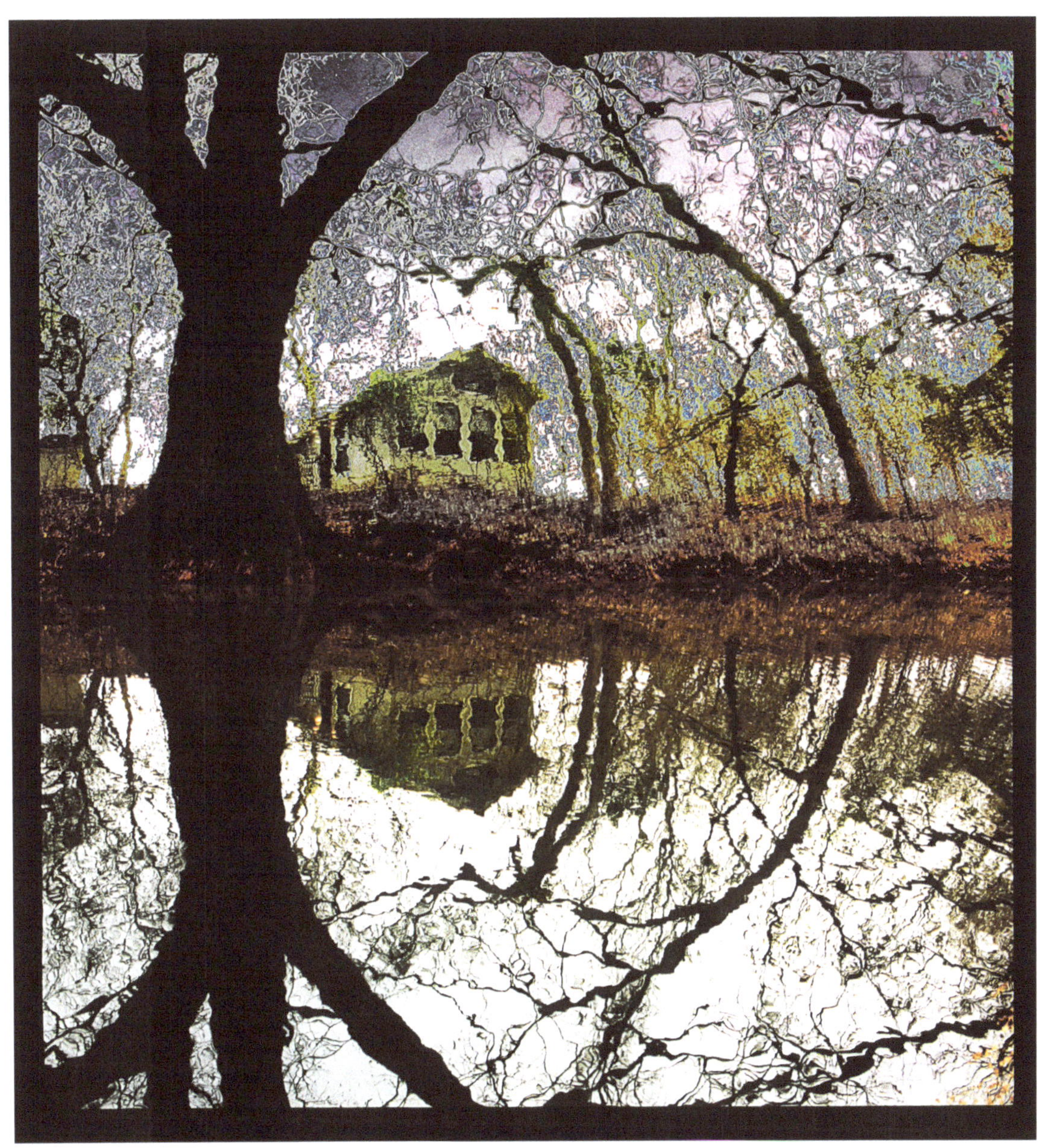

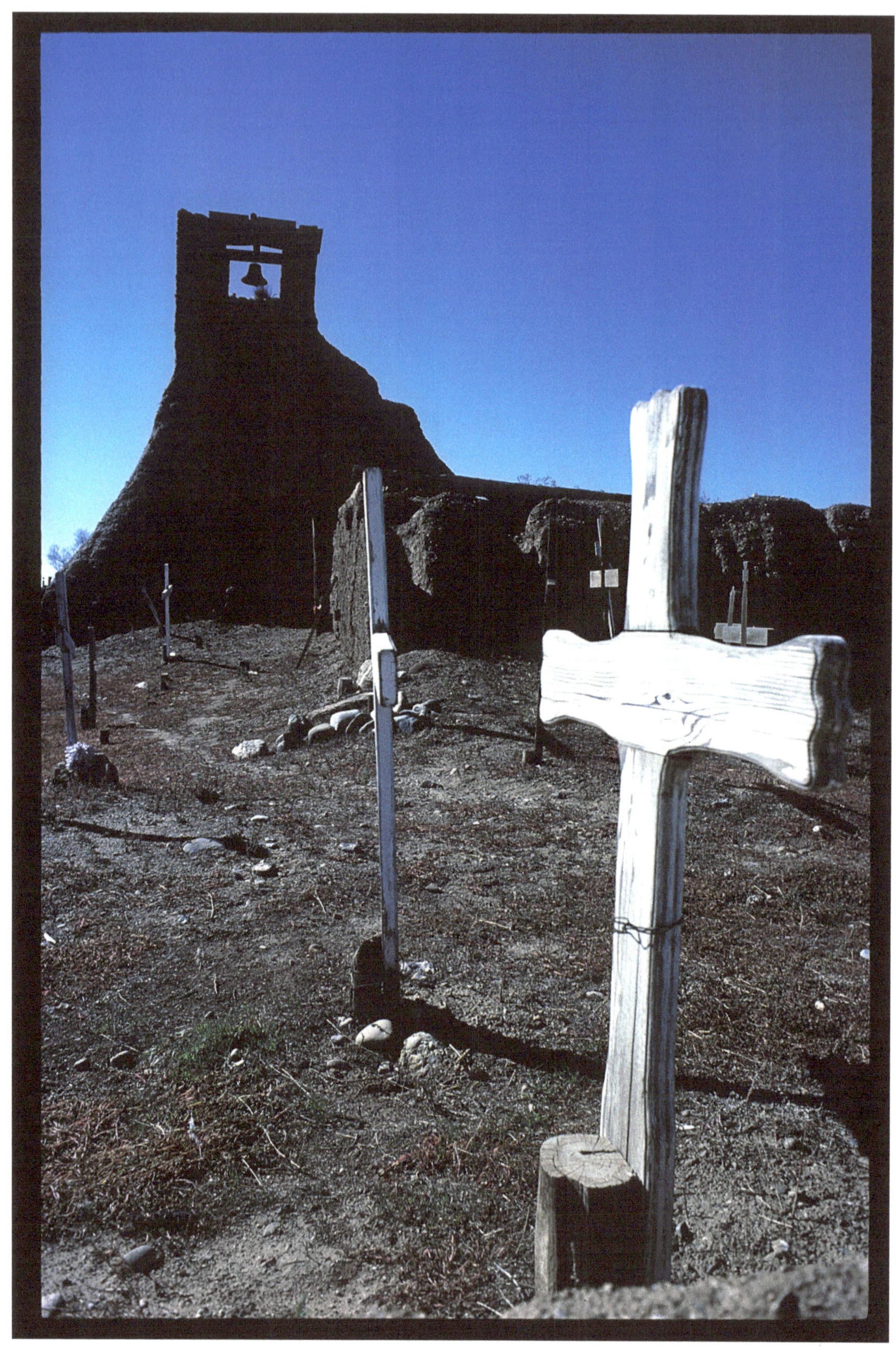

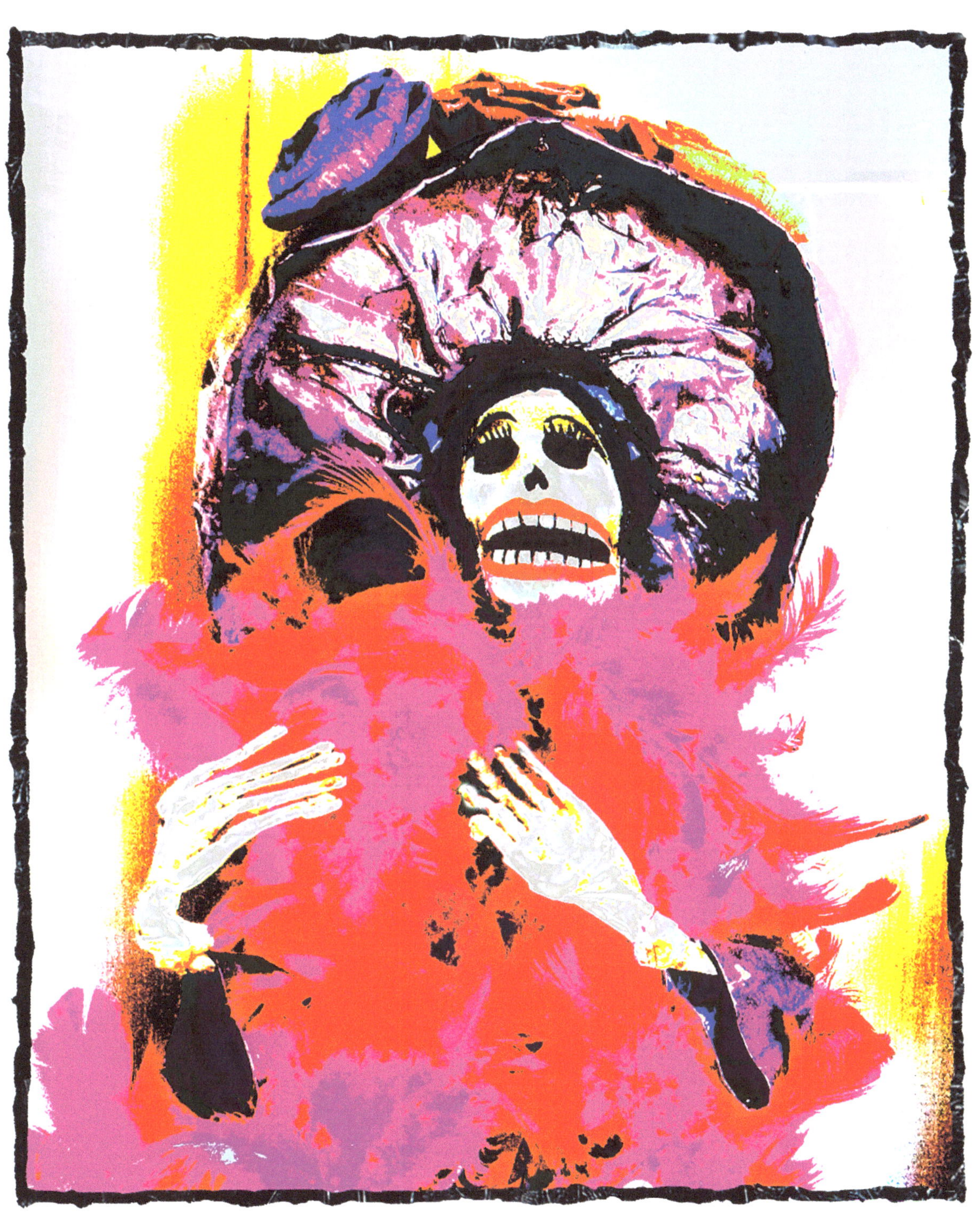

Enjoy life. There's plenty of time to be dead.

—Hans Christian Andersen

Moc Hoa

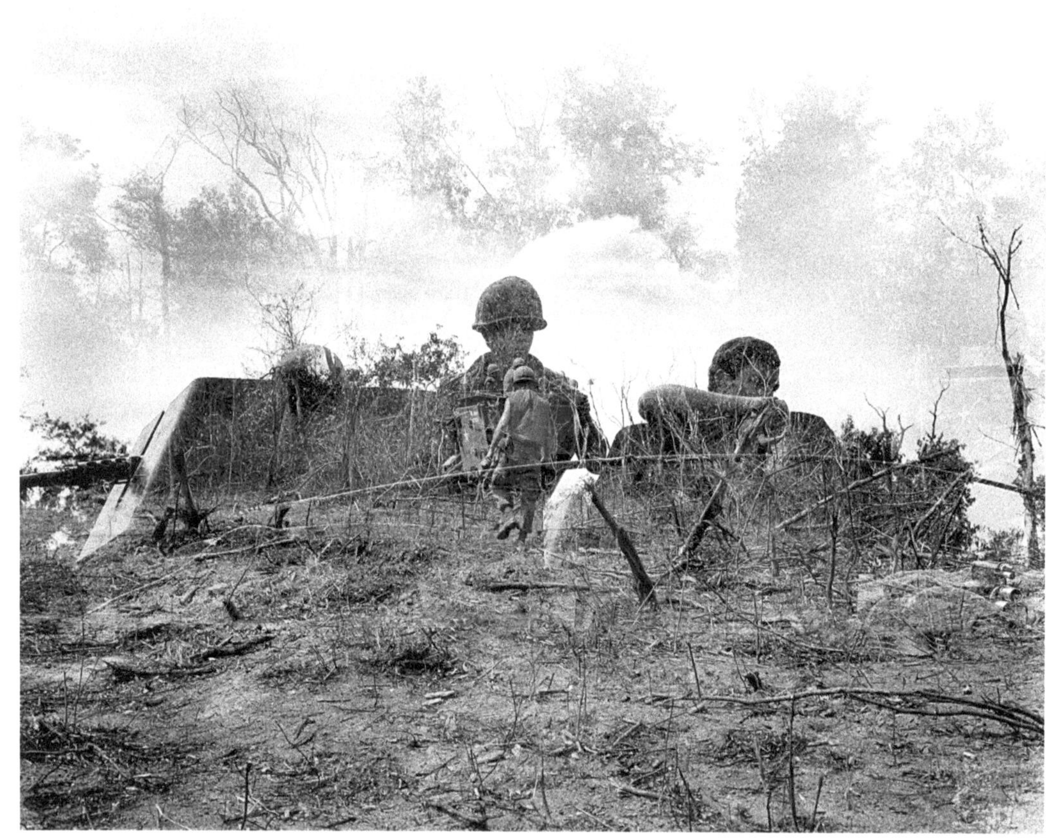

One of the largest and most expensive psychological operations of the Vietnam War was the Chieu Hoi (Open Arms) program, which was designed to entice and enable the enemy to defect. By the latter part of 1970, when Duncan McAllister and I were briefed on the small part we were to play in the program, over 150,000 enemy soldiers had surrendered their weapons. About 15,000 of those were NVA (North Vietnamese Army) regulars. The defectors were called Hoi Chans, and some of them became Kit Carson scouts for the US and South Vietnamese Armies, rooting out evil in the same patches of jungle where they had once committed evil.

It cost approximately five hundred dollars to turn each Viet Cong or NVA soldier into a good guy. In 1970, large operations were a thing of the past, and firefights were sporadic and due more to chance encounters than anything else. Consequently, the cost of killing a single enemy soldier had risen to thousands of dollars. The Chieu Hoi program was effective, but Psychological Operations officers still had to prove their case for budgetary reasons. They wanted pictures and a compelling story of a defection, preferably what they were calling a mass defection, meaning an entire Viet Cong cell of up to a half dozen bad guys. They had one in the works. It was going to happen soon, and that is why Duncan and I were in Moc Hoa district of Long An province, near the Cambodian border.

A young lieutenant who could not stop telling us how lucky we were to have scored this assignment picked us up at the airfield. The LT was what was referred to as a "shake and bake," fresh out of officers' training and set loose in the wild. He escorted us to Captain Adams' office, where we were given a brief history of the Open Arms Program and informed that we would be in the bush within a few days, documenting an actual Viet Cong defection. It would be a momentous occasion for the Open Arms Program and the war effort. Captain Adams said he had been assured by our Public Information Office in Long Binh that we were the perfect soldiers for the operation, and after meeting us he could tell that was correct. After our briefing we were given PSYOPS literature and leaflets, and a list of statistics for Duncan to write about.

The defection that we were supposed to document could happen tomorrow, or soon after. All we had to do was stay close and be ready. For some reason that probably had nothing to do with kindness, we were housed in a transient officers' quarters. Duncan and I were enlisted men, so the housing upgrade was unprecedented, and probably initiated to keep us in close contact. It was a single room with two cots and a desk, a couple of footlockers, chairs and electricity. It was the nicest military quarters either of us had seen "in country". There was another guesthouse nearby, but it was unoccupied. Showers and toilets were down a gravel path, closer to the real officers' quarters. The showers had a concrete floor with a drain. There were sinks and mirrors, and the toilets were real porcelain. It was resort living, or as Duncan put it, "like a really good meal before the execution."

That evening we took turns standing watch while the other guy smoked a joint, and then we played a game of chess and talked about the assignment. My concerns were the things that had not been said during the briefing, the questions we did not think of or were too timid to ask.

There could be as many as six VC, and they were bringing weapons (to turn in.) How many people did we have on our side? Our guys would be low profile, and not appear too heavily armed. We would strike a balance between non-threatening, and not vulnerable. I wasn't too concerned about entering a situation without enough firepower. The US Army did not operate that way.

The question I was wishing I had asked was what kind of soldiers were we following into the bush. Were they US or ARVN, or some mixture of American and South Vietnamese soldiers? No offense to the Armed Republic of Vietnam, but if there was a gunfight, I would rather have Americans around me.

Also, there was the possibility that boats would be involved. Did that mean Cambodia? Nobody had mentioned Cambodia, but the country was too close to not worry about it. And did the bad guys have sampans too, and if so, didn't that mean they could be hiding extra firepower?

"Check, and checkmate," Duncan said, ignoring all my questions. "You know something? I've been thinking we should go into town and score some Cambodian weed."

"What the fuck for? We've got enough pot between us to last a couple of weeks, and no place to smoke without bumping into brass."

"Cambodian weed is the best. It numba one GI. Make you feel vely good."

"The shit we got makes me comatose."

"You're an amateur."

That was not true, unless you compared my smoking habits with Duncan's. I tended to smoke when it was appropriate, and except for special occasions, comfortably numb was all I strived for. When possible, Duncan got stoned in the morning and stayed that way all day. He smoked OJs, high quality weed, doused in opium. They were tightly packed, and perfectly rolled to look like non-filtered cigarettes. I smoked Park Lanes, which were filtered because they used to be filtered cigarettes. That is the way the story goes, anyway. The rest of the story has a bunch of momasans in Saigon sitting around a big table where they remove the tobacco and replace it with weed. Then they stuff everything back in the pack and reseal the cellophane. You can buy them by the pack or the carton. They look just like regular cigarettes, and most of the guys I know carry a pack in their front pocket. The smell can still get you busted, but that hardly ever happens because if they busted everyone that did drugs they would have to crank up the draft again.

"I'll go to town with you when this thing is over, but if you go to Moc Hoa now, you're on your own."

"OK."

"Listen man. This is like vacation. It's the best job we ever had, even if it does turn to shit."

"When it turns to shit. Anyway, I said OK."

"You're not going?"

"Of course I'm going. I'm flying solo."

"That's stupid Duncan. It's fucking crazy."

"Yeah. Well what isn't?"

The next morning, Duncan walked around the compound looking official and taking notes, then wandered down to the main gate and caught a ride into town.

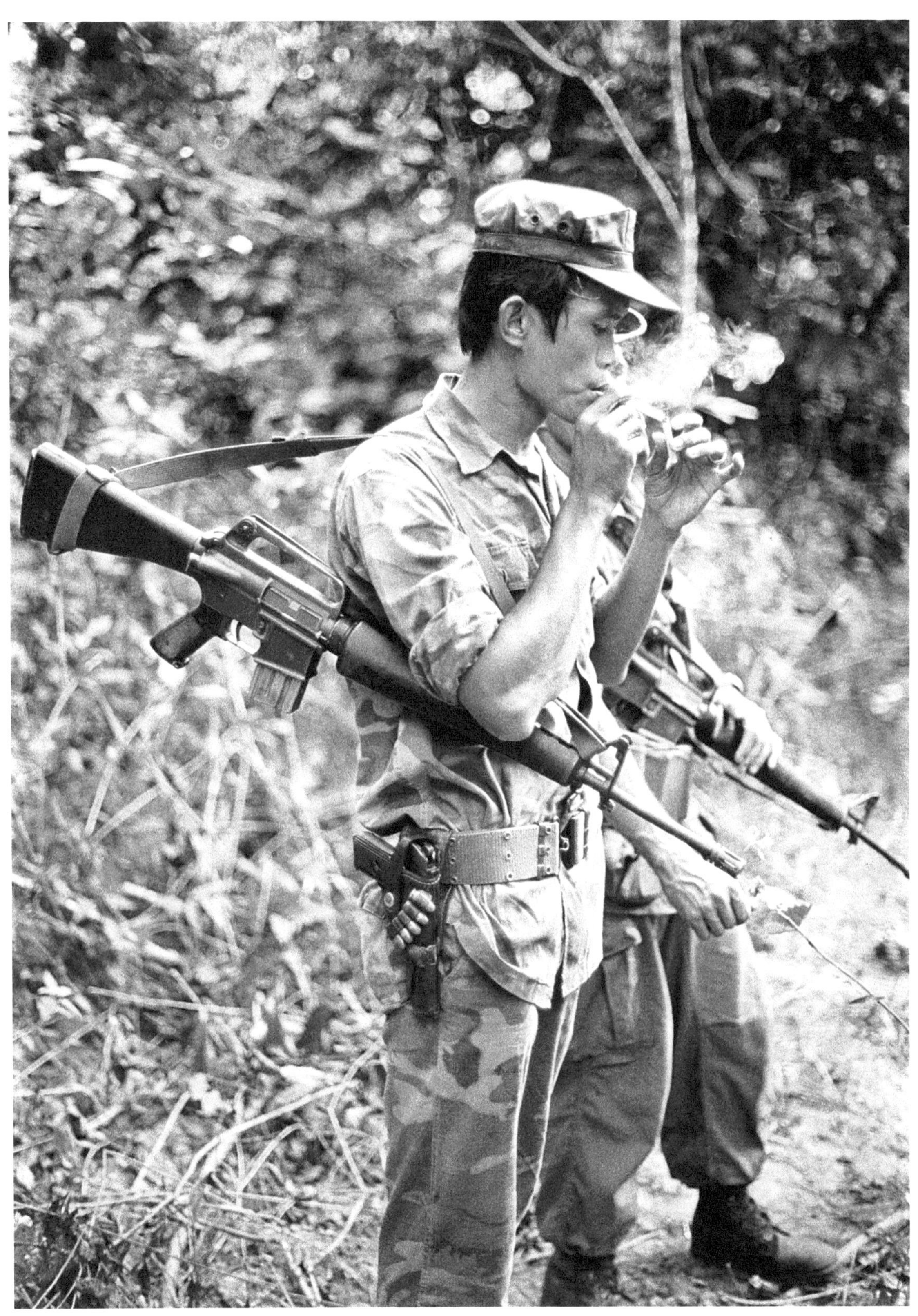

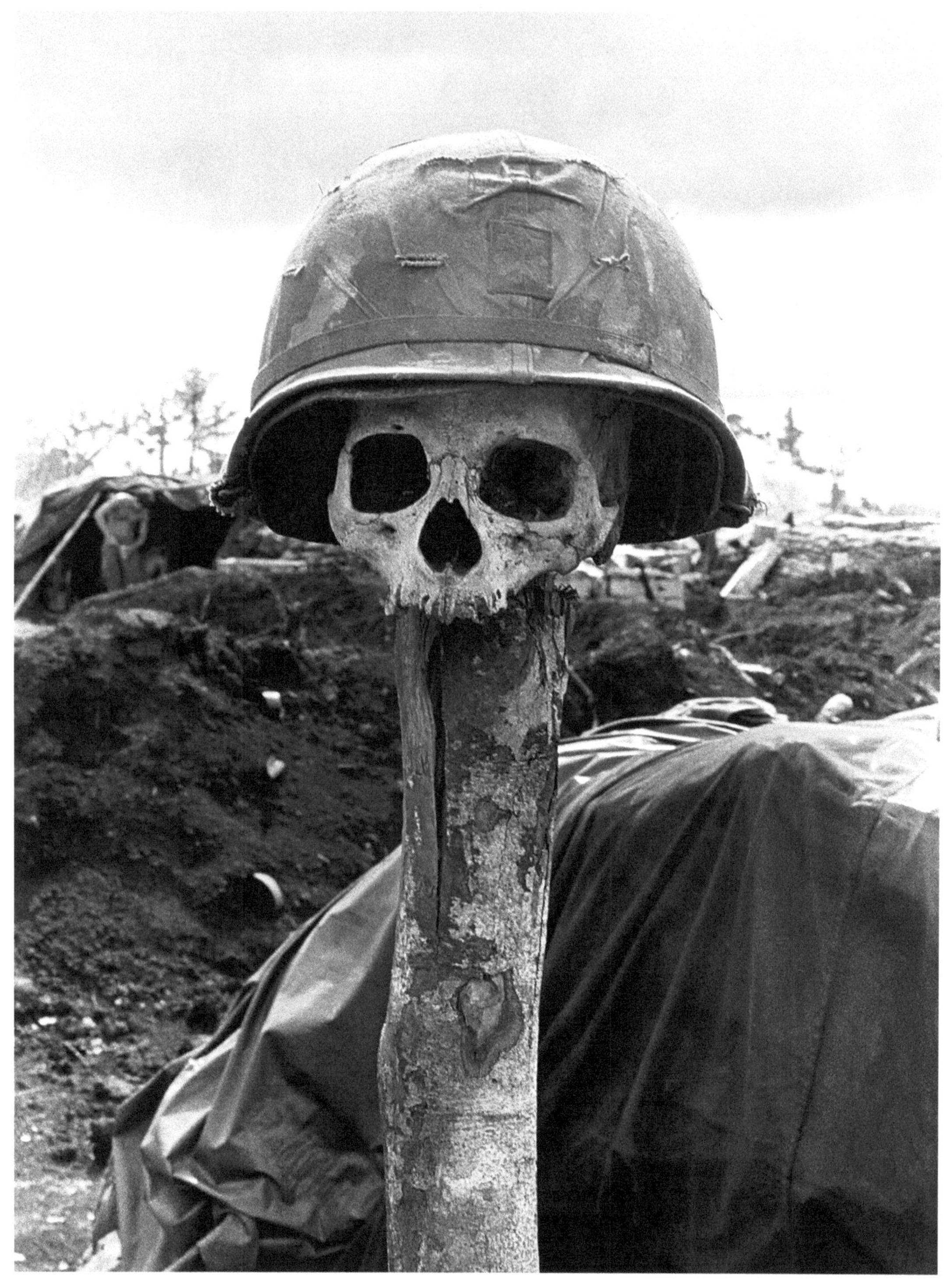

It never ceased to amaze me how easy it was to catch an unofficial ride in Vietnam. It was particularly easy for military journalists because we had press passes that had the correspondent's name, rank and picture on the front, and an official statement on the back that advised military police and other personnel to provide assistance to the bearer of the card. I seldom had to use my press card though, because going to town, or to the country, or even to another military installation for the hell of it was almost unheard of. Most military personnel had jobs that made their presence easily detectable. There was reveille, shift changes and all sorts of communal contact that made an absence stand out. It was difficult enough to take an unofficial nap. Joy rides were out of the question, even if there was some crazy desire to do so. South Vietnam was a war zone, after all.

The Moc Hoa Chieu Hoi center was a provincial operation, meaning it was small compared to the regional centers in Danang and Bien Hoa. Still, the compound was larger than I expected. It used to be a Special Forces camp, and there were still a lot of South Vietnamese soldiers walking around in tiger stripe uniforms. They were probably some of the guys Duncan and I would be following into the bush. Their uniforms designated a more dedicated and skilled soldier than the typical South Vietnamese fighter. It reminded me that we were where the action was. The elusive and ephemeral Ho Chi Minh trail wound its way through the jungle, in and around Long An province. For all we knew, Viet Cong stopped by the village we called Moc Hoa for rest and relaxation. The rice growing Delta area, where we were presently situated, was where VC troops and supplies snuck back into South Vietnam from Cambodia. It was the perfect place for a Chieu Hoi center.

I wandered down to the infirmary and snapped a few pictures of Vietnamese kids in the courtyard. They were sitting in the dirt, staring at a small television sitting on a window ledge. The TV was facing out towards the audience and sunlight glaring off the screen made it difficult to see the picture, but I could hear Bugs Bunny chewing carrots and asking, "What's up Doc?" The kids, who did not understand the language and could barely see the cartoon for the glare, were mesmerized. From behind they almost looked like American kids, glued to the tube. For me it was just another bizarre image in a country filled with confusing scenes.

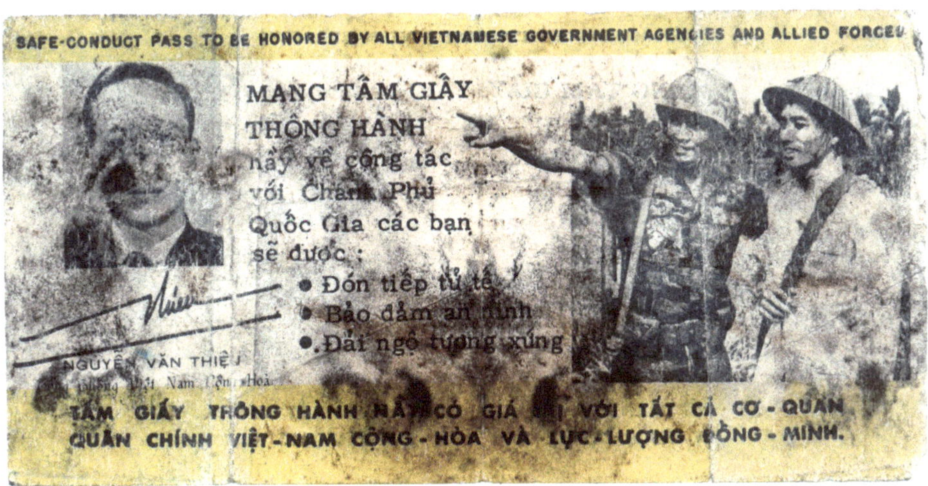

It was early afternoon when Duncan sauntered into the "resort," the name we had given our room, with about half a pound of Cambodian weed and a good story about some guy with a pock-marked face and a shantytown on stilts. "You should have been there. You could have captured the best pictures of all time." Duncan knew exactly where to place a barb of regret in my psyche.

I congratulated Duncan for obtaining more pot than he could possibly smoke or carry back to Long Binh, and he chided me about my lack of refinement. "If we were winos you'd be chugging a bottle of Mad Dog while I sipped a fine claret. I did not think Duncan knew exactly what claret was, but neither did I, so I let it pass. The wine analogy did lead to an interesting idea about brewing marijuana tea, which diminished the stash by about a quarter. The result was a pissy-looking substance that tasted like it looked, and packed a minimal amount of punch.

"This is too fucking stupid," Duncan said. "I'm rolling a joint."

"OK, but we should go outside to smoke it." I did not like sounding like a den mother, but sometimes Duncan required an authority figure. He twisted up a couple of joints and gave one to me. Joints were seldom passed around in Vietnam. Pot was so prevalent there was no need to share.

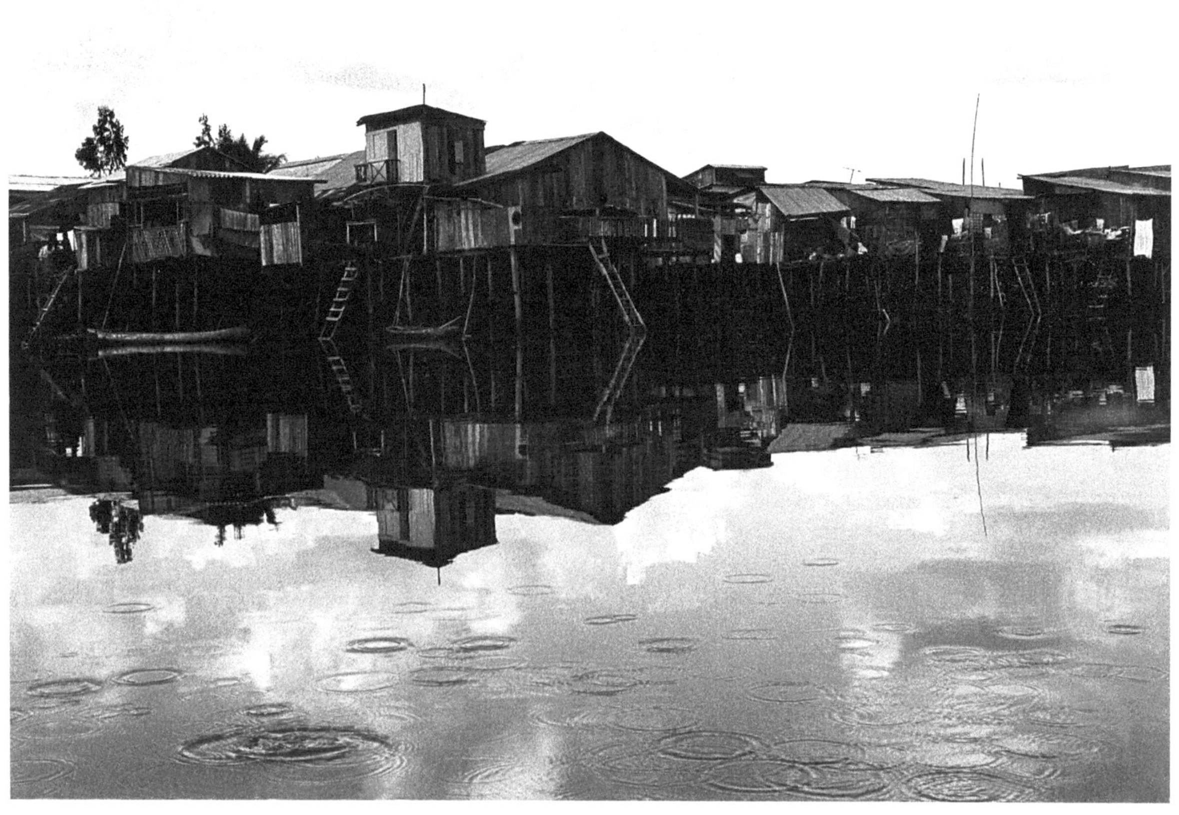

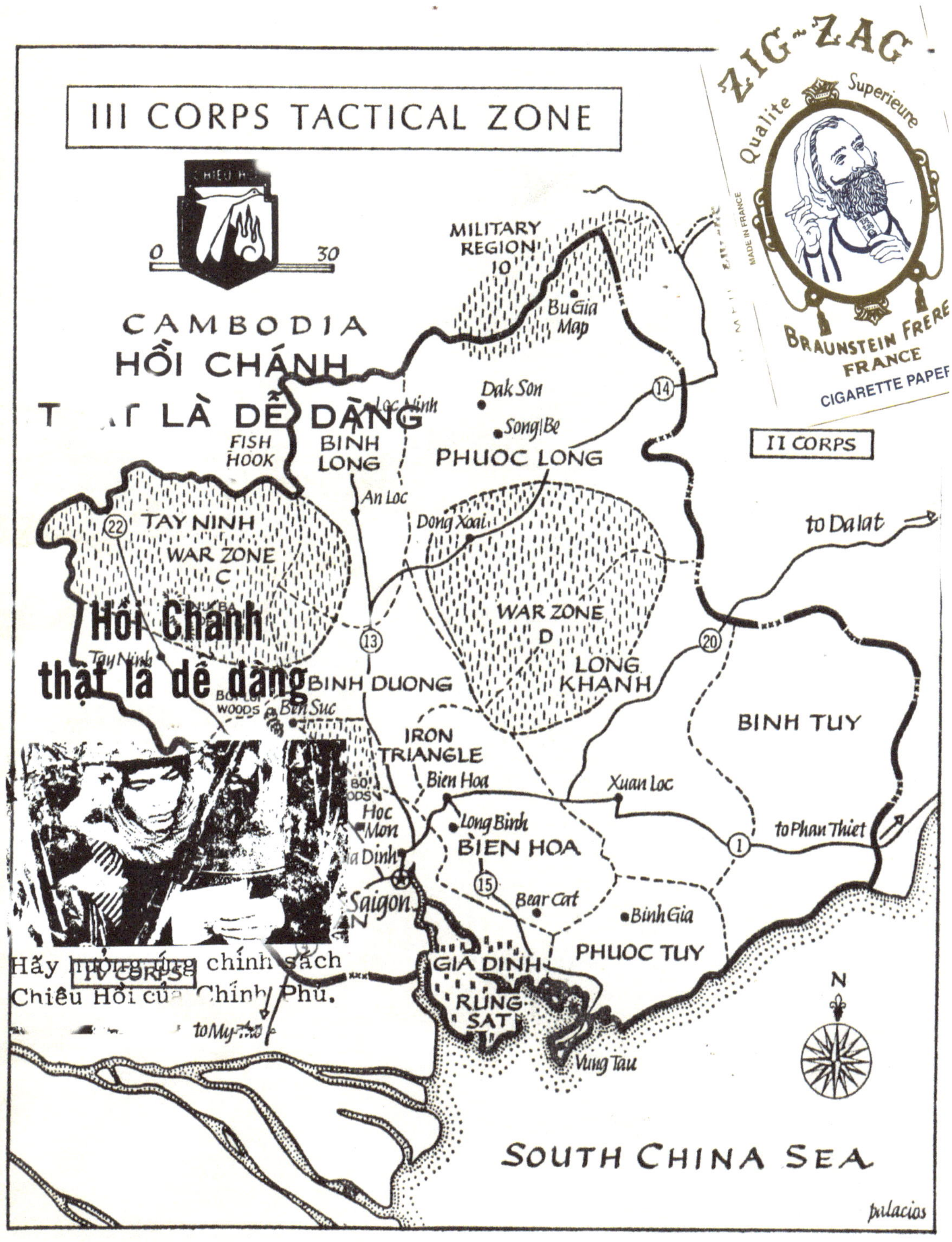

III Corps Tactical Zone

We decided it would be safer to stay inside and blow the smoke out the window. That lasted for a couple of tokes and then Duncan wandered over to the map table and began playing with his pile of weed. The fact that he was filling the room with smoke no longer seemed important, and in a short while I found myself sitting in a chair, rummaging through my camera bag for nothing in particular. We were both still puffing away.

Duncan was right about the potency of Cambodian marijuana. It produced a different sort of high. Park Lanes lowered my anxiety level. Cambodian pot gave me the giggles.

"This is some good shit," I said. I might have to move to Cambodia."

"Yeah. Maybe I'll move to the same neighborhood. I'll invite my friend Poc and he can bring his rickety old stilt house."

Cambodian weed seemed to have the same effect on Duncan, because we were both practically rolling on the floor when a loud drumbeat in the back of my mind came to the forefront of my consciousness, and I identified it as someone banging on the door.

Duncan came to his senses first, snatching his poncho liner off one of the beds and tossing it over the pile of marijuana. I continued staring at the door until a voice on the other side commanded, "Open up. I know you're in there." I got up and opened the door. It was Captain Adams.

Duncan and I came to attention and saluted. The Captain stepped inside just far enough to scan the interior. He did not return our salutes or bring us to the "at ease" position. Captain Adams looked grim, and the silence was overwhelming.

My brain was having trouble processing the situation. I felt as if I was watching myself in a movie, and was afraid the character that was playing me might blurt out something inappropriate. Thankfully, our military training overpowered the effects of Cambodian hemp, and Duncan and I remained at attention, staring silently ahead.

"I'm disappointed in you men."

"Yes sir," Duncan replied.

"Shut up." The Captain's voice seemed to echo around the room for an interminable length of time before fading away. I thought I could hear it slipping out the open window and fought the urge to turn my head to see what an echo looked like when exiting a building.

"I came here myself to tell you men to be at the parade ground at zero six hundred tomorrow morning. You have been briefed as to what to bring. Essentially, side arms, canteens and whatever equipment your jobs require."

The Captain's speech was angry but articulate, and everything he said stuck to my brainpan and leaked its contents and meaning into deep pools of random thought for me to peruse and assess at some later time.

I began to wonder what was going on behind me. Did I actually see Duncan cover the marijuana with a poncho liner, or did I just wish he had done that? Was Duncan still there? Was he making contorted faces?

The Captain's face was not exactly contorted, but it was becoming a bit animated. There was a place above his upper lip, in the indention where it is difficult to get to when shaving, and he had several hairs that looked as if they had been missed by the razor for at least a couple of days in a row.

He stared at us for what seemed like about two weeks before continuing. "Tonight you are confined to this room, the mess hall, and the head. Understood?"

"Yes sir!"

"Get rid of the marijuana."

"Yes sir!"

"At ease."

Captain Adams stepped back, spun around and closed the door behind him.

I slumped into the chair, and Duncan practically fell onto the bed. "Oh man. What a fucking drag", he sighed.

Duncan and I agreed that the only reason we were under house arrest instead of real arrest was because the Captain still needed us, and the only way to not be arrested after we came back from the bush was to give him exactly what he wanted. Special Operations needed a knockout piece of Hoi Chan propaganda, and that is exactly what we would produce. Hell, that was what we were going to do anyway. It was the only reason we had such cushy jobs. We gave the Army what it wanted, and we were good at what we did. The thought of having to trade my camera for a rifle and become a real grunt that lived in the bush for the rest of his tour scared the shit out of me.

Duncan and I had been in the bush plenty, with each other, and with other correspondents. I had ridden with the 11th Armored Cavalry and humped through jungles and swamps with the 25th Infantry. Duncan had been in Cambodia, almost all the way to Sihanoukville, during that big invasion almost eight months ago. That was where somebody told him Cambodian weed was so good. He never smoked any there because he never smoked pot in the bush, and neither did I. Almost never anyway, except on gunboats, or tanks, or firebases, where stealth and detection did not make much difference.

The fact was that Moc Hoa had seemed like such a safe haven, almost a miniature version of Long Binh where being high was close to the norm, that we had let our collective guard down.

We decided not to go to the mess hall that evening. Neither of us wanted to run into Captain Adams, so we chowed down on LRRPs, lightweight packages of freeze-dried food. The acronym stood for long-range reconnaissance patrol, which is who the meals were originally intended for, and they were actually very tasty. They were also easy to prepare. Open the top of the foil container, pour in some boiling water, mix and eat. In the field we boiled water by lighting a small chunk of C-4 (plastic explosive – the volatile material used in claymore mines). C-4 combusts immediately and burns intensely, so a canteen cup of water comes to a boil in a matter of seconds. It only explodes when contained, or somewhat pressurized, so it is a good idea not to stomp the fire out when finished cooking. There are numerous unofficial stories about neophyte grunts that did not get the message, and lost a foot by stamping out the fire. Duncan and I did not have any C-4, but one of the previous lodgers in our room had left a couple of cans of sterno in one of the footlockers. Very convenient.

We double-checked our gear and went outside to watch the sun set behind the latrines. It was not much of a show since clouds obscured most of the color, and the latrines blocked the point where the sun sank behind the earth. "I'm going to go write a novel", Duncan said. He made the same announcement almost every evening before scribbling in his notebook and passing out.

"Think I'll take a shower. I'd like to be clean for the Hoi Chans."

"They're going to love you, man. Especially after they capture you and take you home."

I stripped down to my underwear and grabbed a towel. I was not sure what the protocol was in brassville, but back in the enlisted mans' section of Long Binh, underwear, or just a towel wrap was considered proper attire when going to and from the showers.

As usual, there was nobody in the showers, and the latrine section of the structure was also empty. The large expanse of concrete floor, with its drains, and the showerheads and faucets and soap dishes made me feel like I was at a YMCA instead of an army installation. Almost as soon as I turned on the water there was a muffled boom. It was so distant that it might not have happened at all, but I stepped away from the shower and listened anyway. Nothing. I was about to step back under the water when I heard it again, still distant but louder. Incoming. I knew the sound. The mortars were landing too far away to panic, but caution was one of my better qualities so I turned off the water and grabbed my towel. I was about to hightail it back to the resort to grab my clothes and gear when another shell landed close enough to spray a shower of dust down from the rafters. I ran for the closest sandbagged dugout I could think of. It was on the other side of the transient officer's quarters, near the main road through camp. As I was about to round the barracks, another mortar landed close enough to spray the far side of the building with shrapnel and debris. I sprawled face down in the dirt and listened. Another shell landed in the distance, and then another, much closer, but farther down the road than the explosion that had sent me running from the latrine.

I felt a cool breeze across my backside, and something wet trickled between my shoulder blades and slid down my side. I reached back and was relieved not to feel any gaping holes. I inspected my hands. They were wet and caked with mud. It was difficult to tell in the dark, but I was fairly certain there was no blood involved. I systematically moved my extremities and everything seemed to function properly.

There was another distant explosion, and then another closer one, but farther away than the last two. They seemed to be heading in the same direction, through the compound, following the main road and another parallel avenue.

I knew I was close to the bunker and my first impulse was to dash around the corner and dive in. It was dug into the ground and fortified with enough sand bags to withstand anything but a direct hit. It was more than likely also filled with grunts and ARVNs who were expecting to be overrun by NVA. I decided to call out first.

"Hello in the bunker. I'm coming in. I'm friendly. Don't shoot." There were voices, English and Vietnamese, and then I heard Duncan yell, "Get your ass in here." As I rounded the corner I could hear Duncan telling the Vietnamese, "He numba one. No shoot".

I slid down the earthen ramp, still clutching my towel, and crawled away from the entrance. There were about eight other soldiers inside, pressed against the side walls. All except Duncan were wearing flak jackets and helmets. Most of them had weapons pointing out the firing slits. Everybody was wide eyed, staring at me. Duncan was the only one smiling. Aware that I was the only naked man in the bunker, I casually wrapped the towel around my waist.

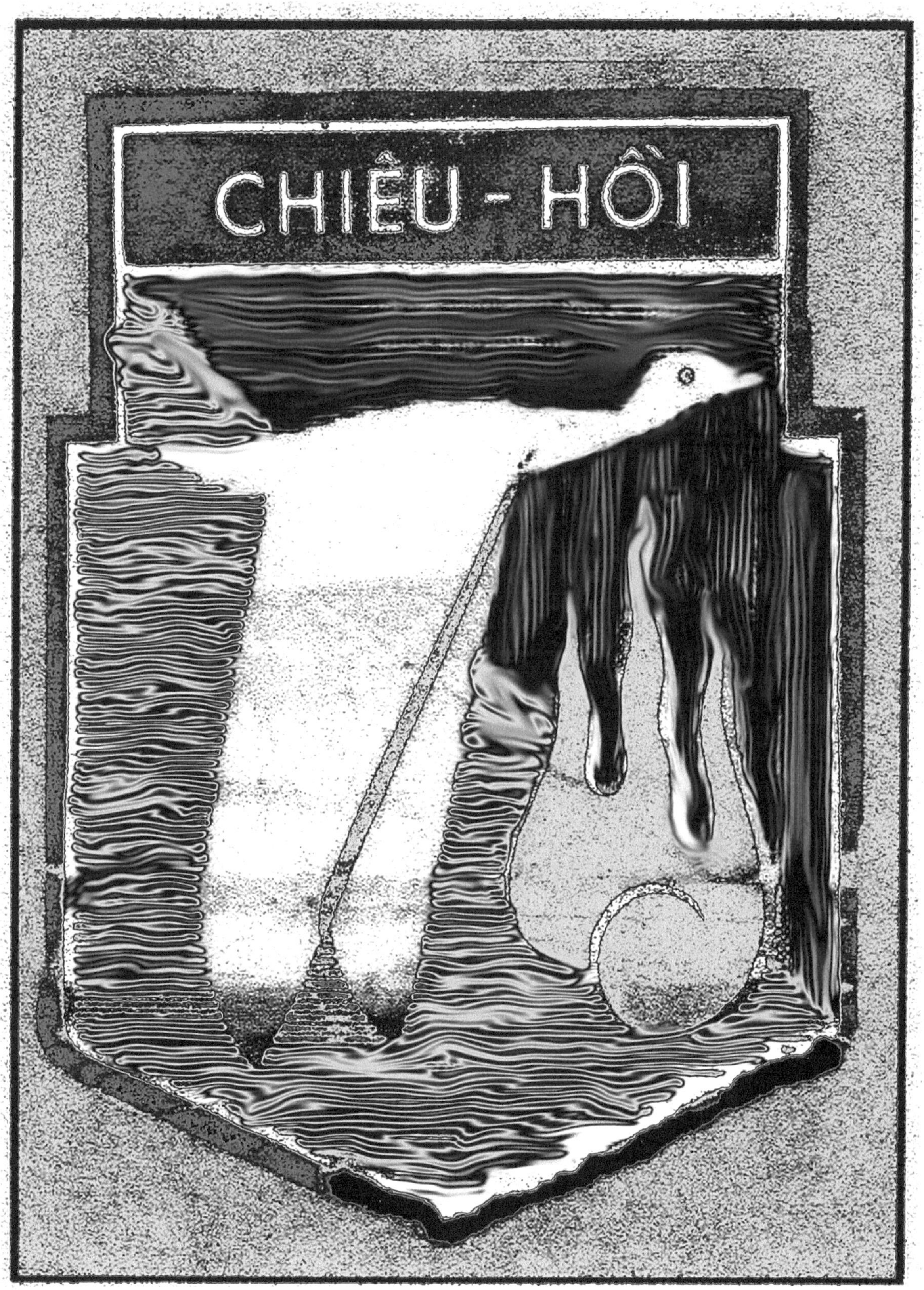
CHIÊU - HỒI

"You don't seem very prepared for this." Duncan was the only one who spoke, and I could tell he was stoned. For some reason that pissed me off more than it should have, given our present situation. There was another American pressed against the sandbags and I asked him if anyone had seen any VC inside the compound.

"No sir," he replied, and I realized everyone but Duncan thought I was brass because I had come from the officer's transient quarters.

"He ain't a sir," Duncan said. "It's just that officers and enlisted men look kind of similar when they're naked. The only way to be sure is compare their nuts. Officers are smaller."

Nobody said much after that. There were a few more explosions, each one landing farther from our position and deeper into the compound. There were sirens and lights, parachute flares and automatic weapons fire along the perimeter, but the incoming barrage was over. The VC had packed up their mortar tubes and slithered back into the jungle.

Later that evening Duncan said he and the other American in the bunker had talked about how someone inside the compound must have been directing the mortar fire. "It was just too fucking obvious," he said. "They just walked those mortars down the street until they got to the hospital. The ones down by the perimeter probably had some other objective."

"What makes you think they hit the hospital?"

"That's what the grunt said, while we were watching your lily white ass scurry back to the resort. He wanted to know why we were staying in the officer's quarters if we weren't brass. I told him we were special."

"We are, aren't we? Sacrifices are special."

"Yeah. He also seemed to think the mortars were just a show for the Hoi Chan, to let them know they aren't safe here."

We never got a chance to find out. The shake and bake lieutenant that had escorted us to the Captain's briefing knocked on our door before sunup.

"The operation is canceled," he said. "Grab your gear. I'm taking you to the flight line."

"The flight line didn't get hit last night?" I asked.

"The runway is operational. Grab your shit. We're leaving."

The LT's jeep was parked in the street, not far from the bunker we had crouched in the night before. As we threw our packs in the back, Duncan asked if the hospital had been hit and the "shake and bake" turned on him like his mother had been insulted. "Listen up. Your part in this operation is over. Last night never happened. I'm going to drop you two at the runway and you are going to stay there until the next plane comes through heading for Tan Son Nhut. If you have to go to Nha Trang first then do it. You are done here. Understood?"

"Yes sir."

The lieutenant left us among the rubble of what used to be the flight line waiting room. The communications building was pockmarked, but intact. There was a backhoe pushing debris off the runway, and about two dozen ARVN soldiers standing guard and assisting with the clean up.

There were two American technicians in the communication building, and one of them told us to go somewhere else to wait. "Try the waiting area," he said. Then, as if to amend for his lack of hospitality, "There's an Air America prop coming in from Nha Trang, and going back the same way. Should be here in a couple of hours."

Duncan and I pulled a couple of wooden benches out of the rubble and dragged them away from the activity. "You think they don't want anybody to know the Hoi Chan program took a hit?" I asked.

"I think they were just embarrassed about you running around naked in a fire fight. What if you did that out in the field? They'd never get any VC converts."

"Fuck you," I said, unable to think of a better reply. "Let's go to Nha Trang. We can catch a ride to Tan Son Nhut from there."

"Yeah. I got some friends in the photo lab there. We can trade some of this Cambodian weed for some real drugs."

We never heard anything else about what happened in Moc Hoa, but I suspect that was because the PSYOPS people never advertised their failures. Duncan and I caught the prop to Nha Trang where he traded most of his weed for some acid. I never got to do any of it, but Duncan told me later that it was the best drug deal he ever made. Maybe it was, but Duncan wasn't the kind of guy to admit failure either, so what else was he going to say?

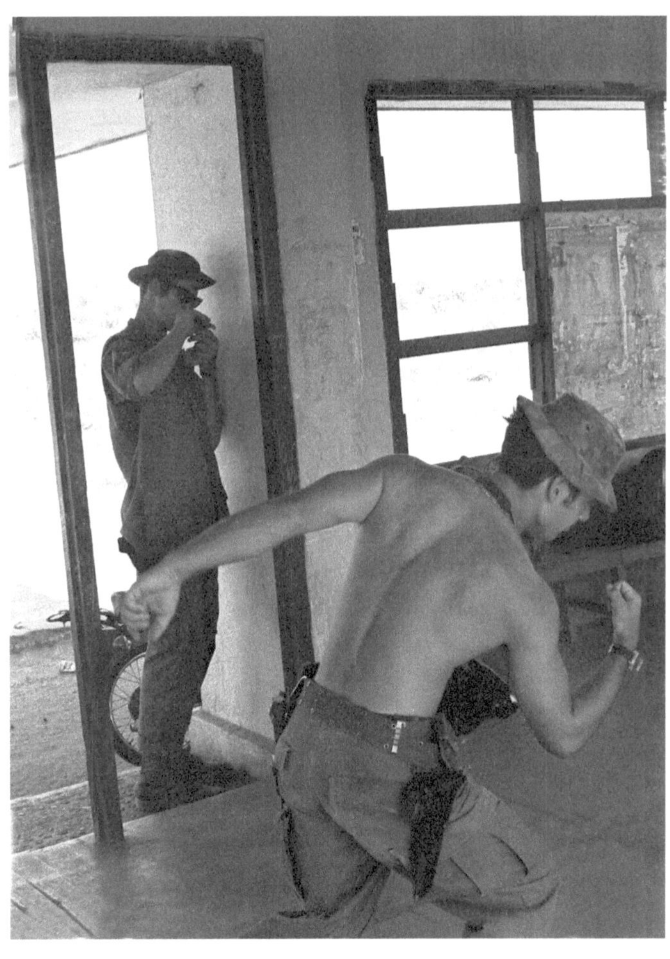

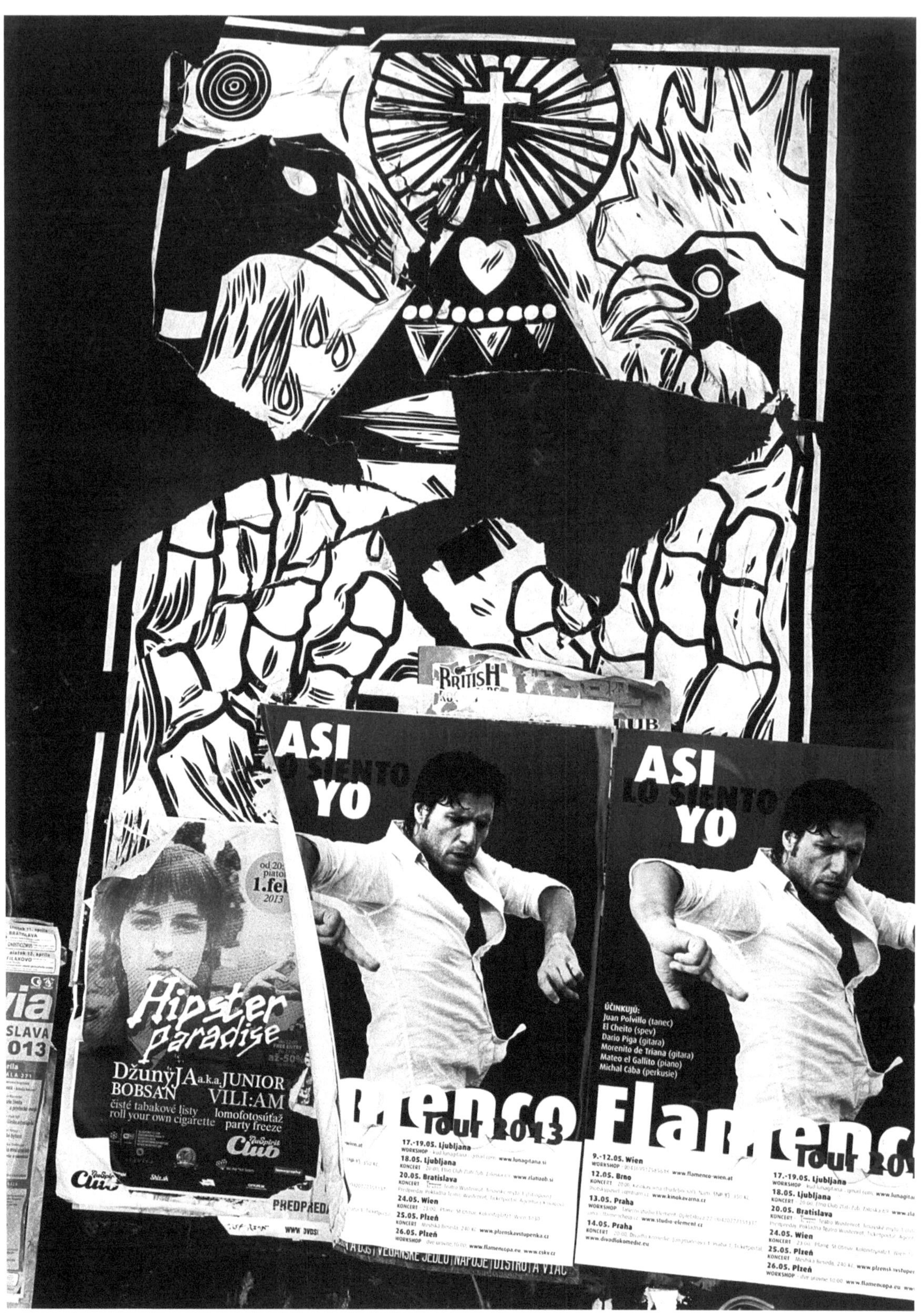

ASI
YO
ASI
LO SIENTO
YO
BRITISH
Hipster paradise
1.feb
2013
DžunýJA a.k.a. JUNIOR
BOBSAN
VILI:AM
čisté tabakové listy
roll your own cigarette
lomofotosúťaž
party freeze
Club
ÚČINKUJÚ:
Juan Polvillo (tanec)
El Cheito (spev)
Dario Piga (gitara)
Morenito de Triana (gitara)
Mateo el Gallito (piano)
Michal Cába (perkusie)
Flamenco
Tour 2013
9.-12.05. Wien
12.05. Brno
13.05. Praha
14.05. Praha
17.-19.05. Ljubljana
18.05. Ljubljana
20.05. Bratislava
24.05. Wien
25.05. Plzeň
26.05. Plzeň

Unorthodox Behavior

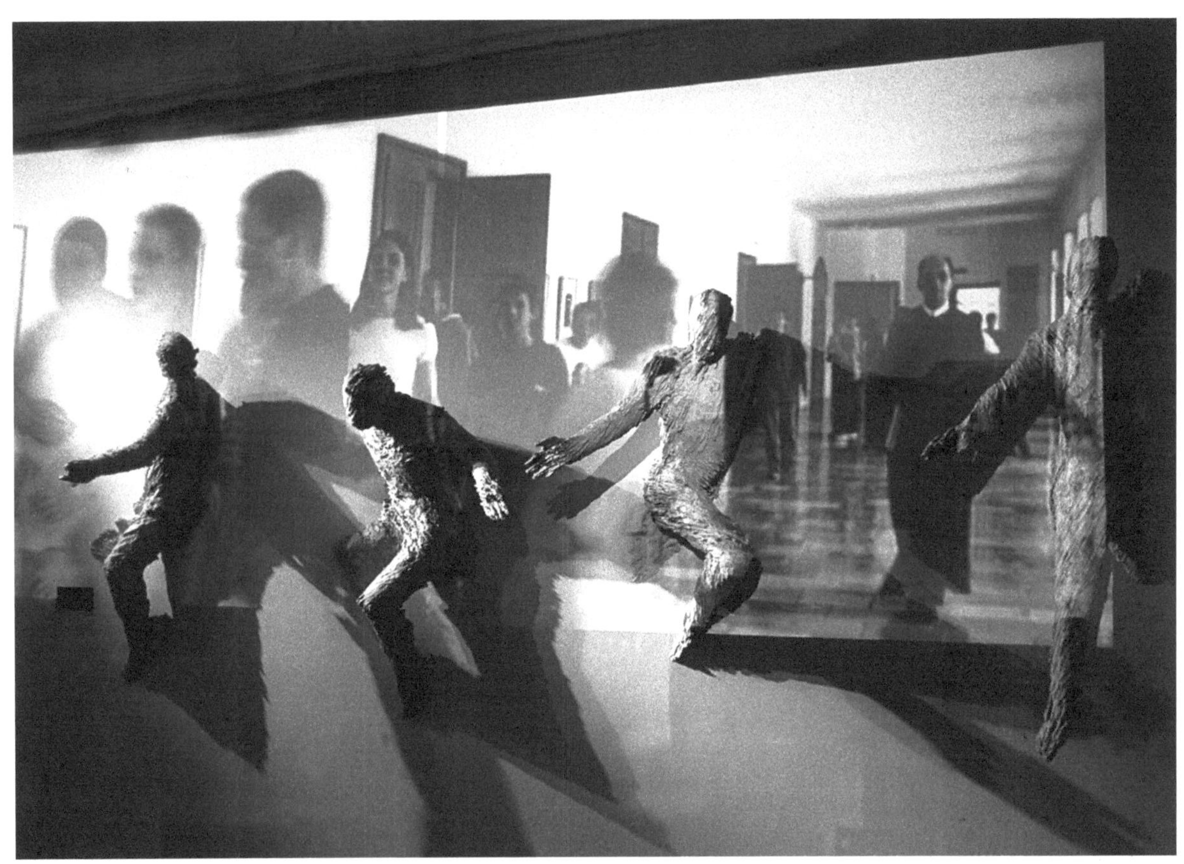

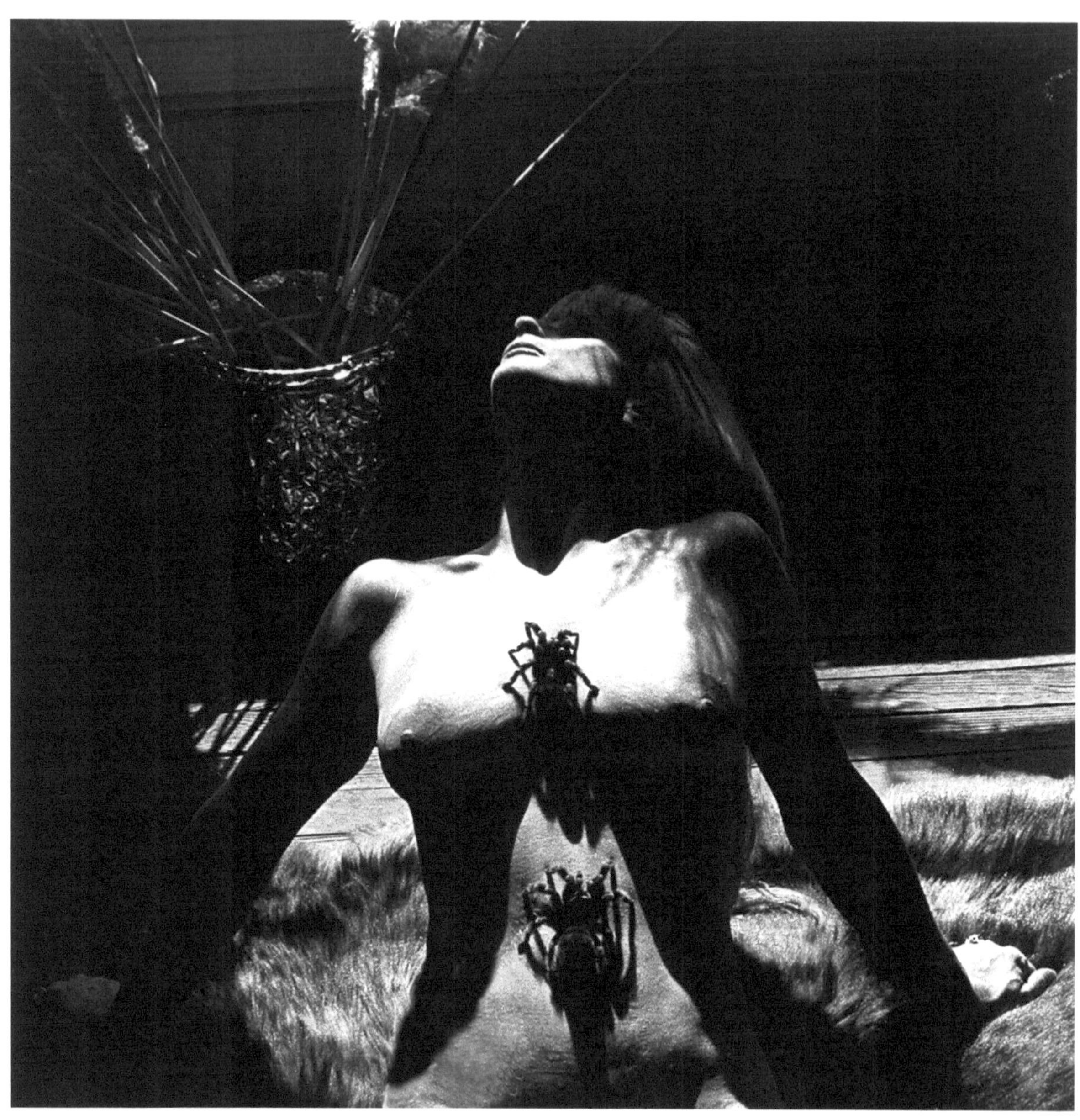

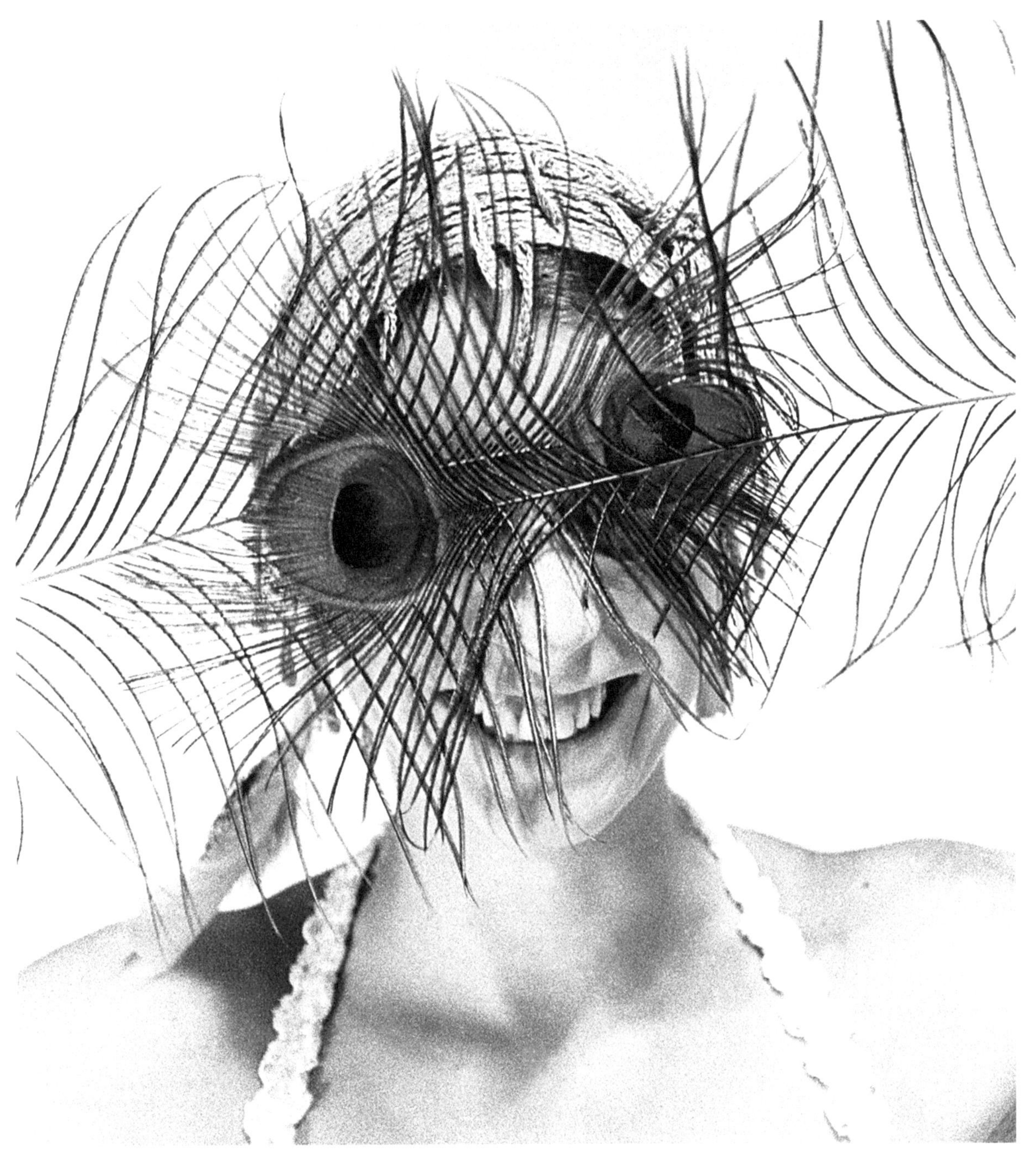

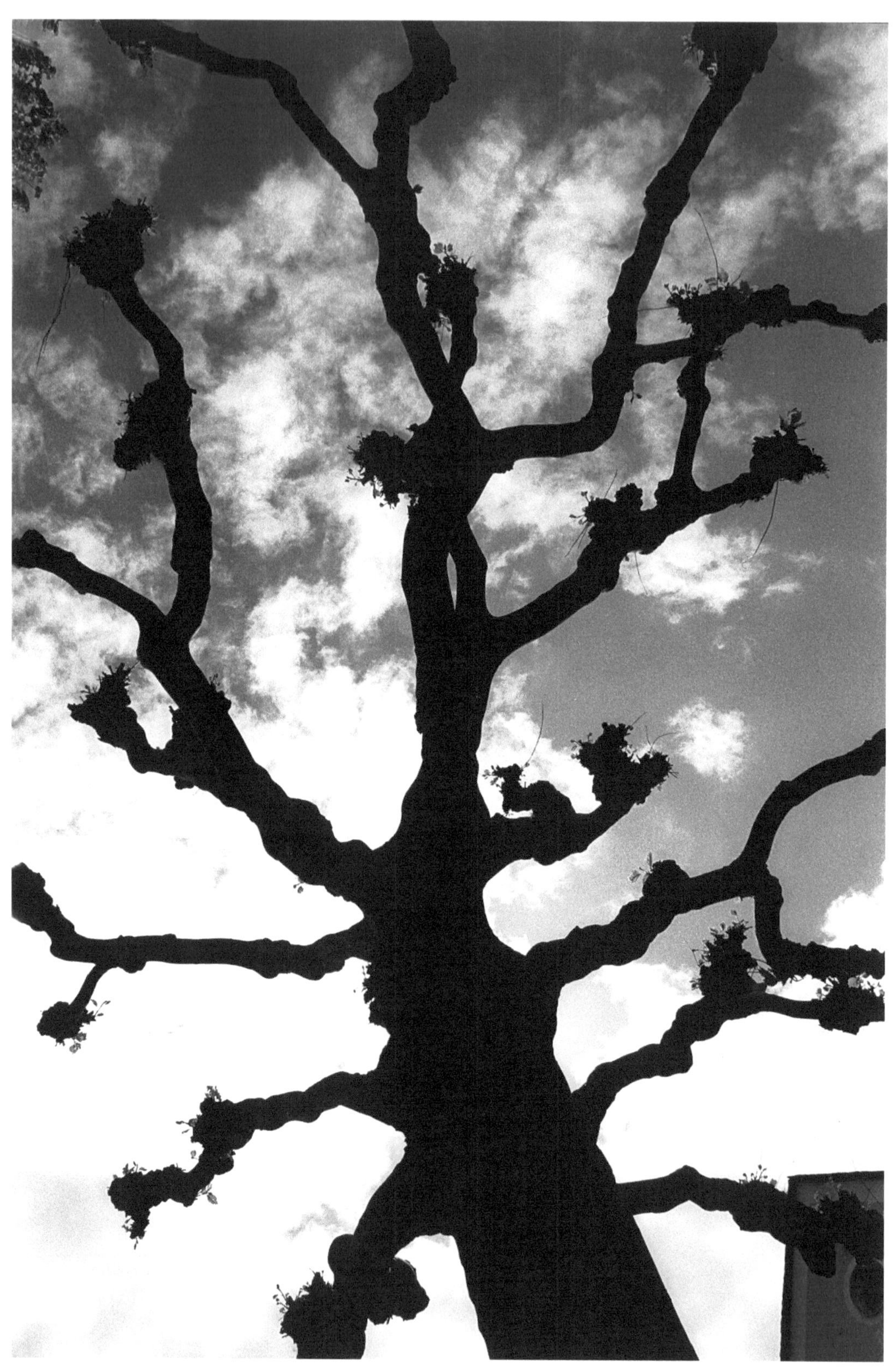

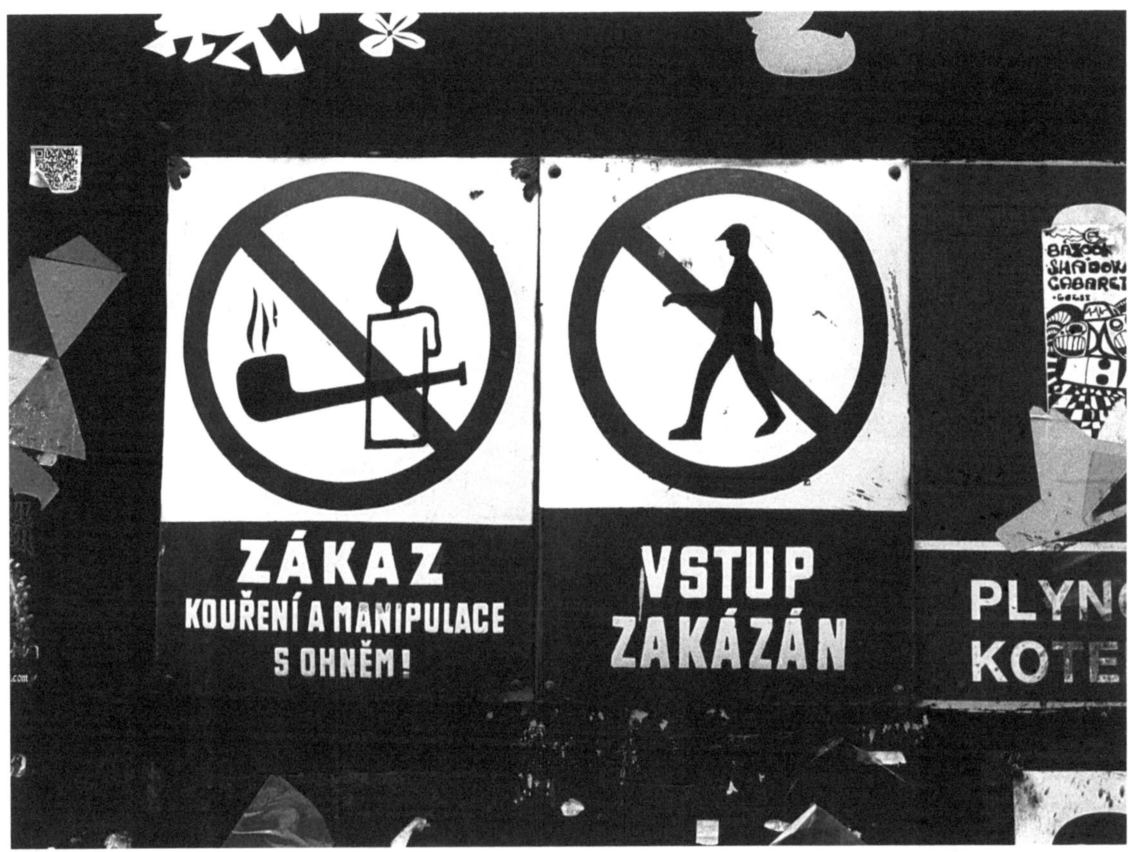

"Zakaz! ZAKAZ!" the man yelled. "Vstup Zakazan"! Unsure of my offense, I made a hasty departure, secure in the knowledge that it would happen again, farther into the course of my life.

Minefields of similar scenarios litter the road that everybody travels. Protocols of conduct do not have solid boundaries. It is not necessary to leave home in order to create a faux pas, but traveling through strange cultures does seem to accentuate the problem.

Human nature created the necessity for, and overabundance of rules and regulations. Protocol keeps anarchy at bay, and customs create feelings of cohesiveness. We are more comfortable when people conduct themselves in an "acceptable" manner, but nonconformity keeps things interesting and gives us something to talk about. Prejudice and extremism take the concept to another level.

Have you ever wandered into the wrong neighborhood, or made an irreversibly bad decision? Don't worry. It was bound to happen sooner or later.

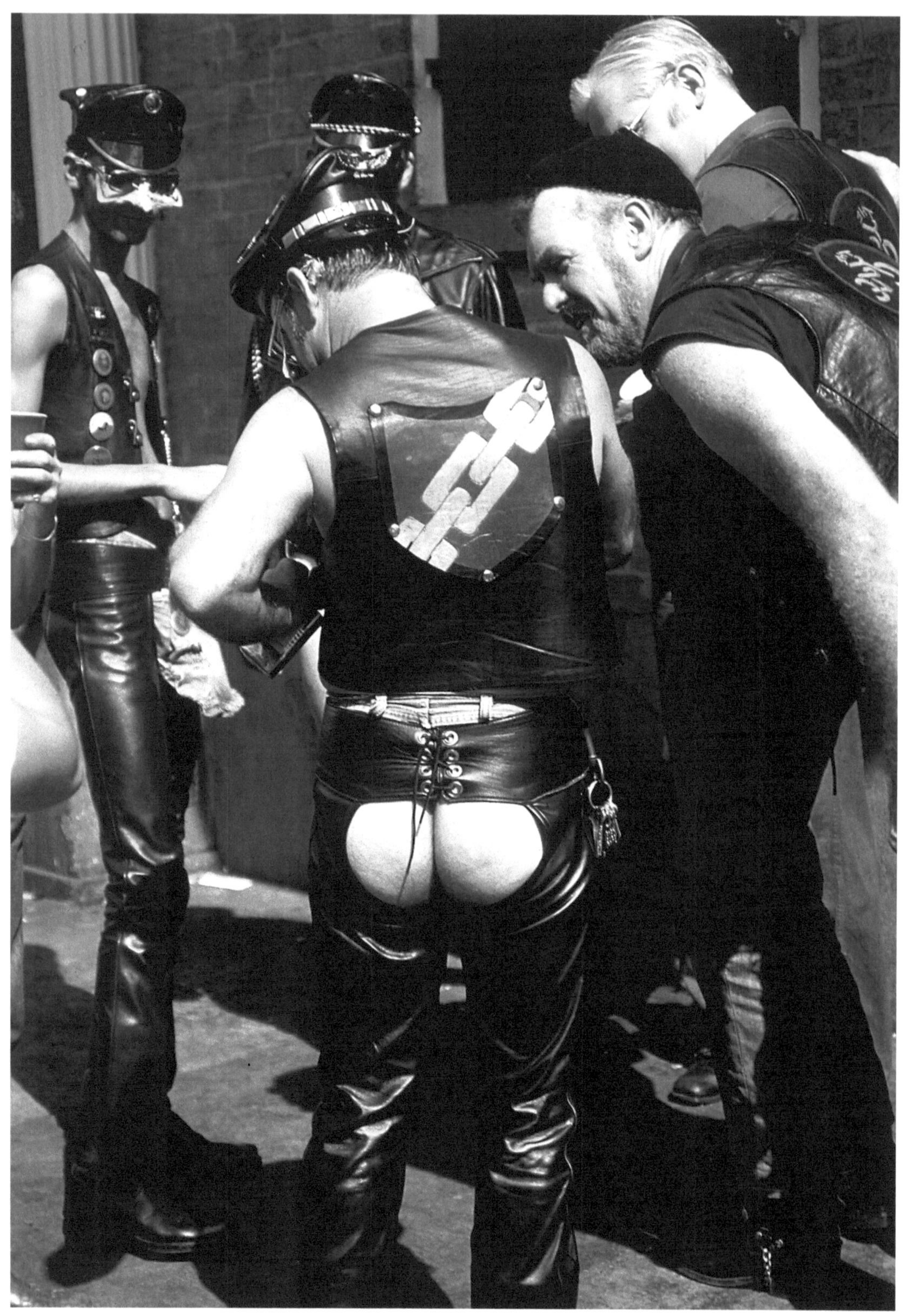

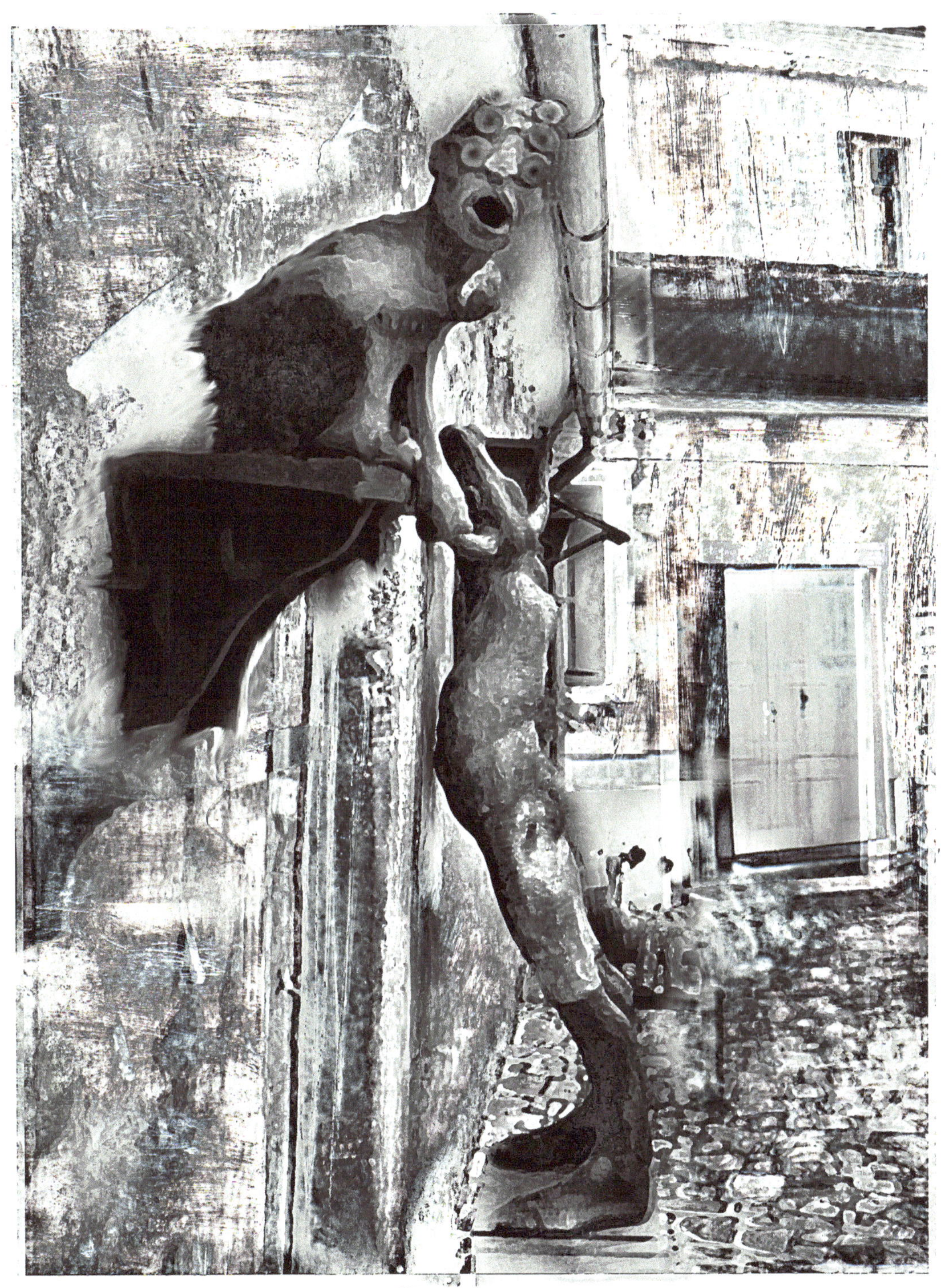

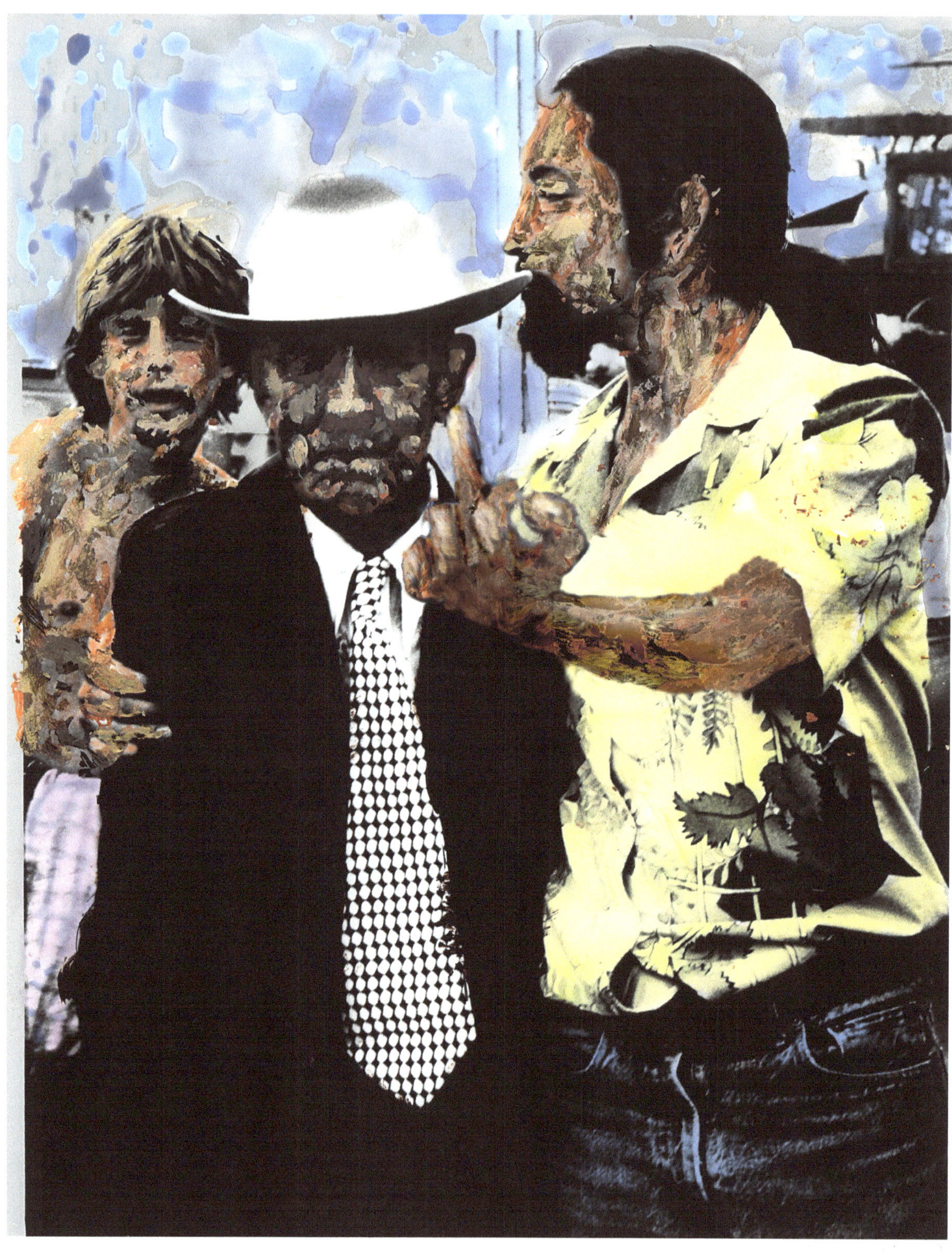

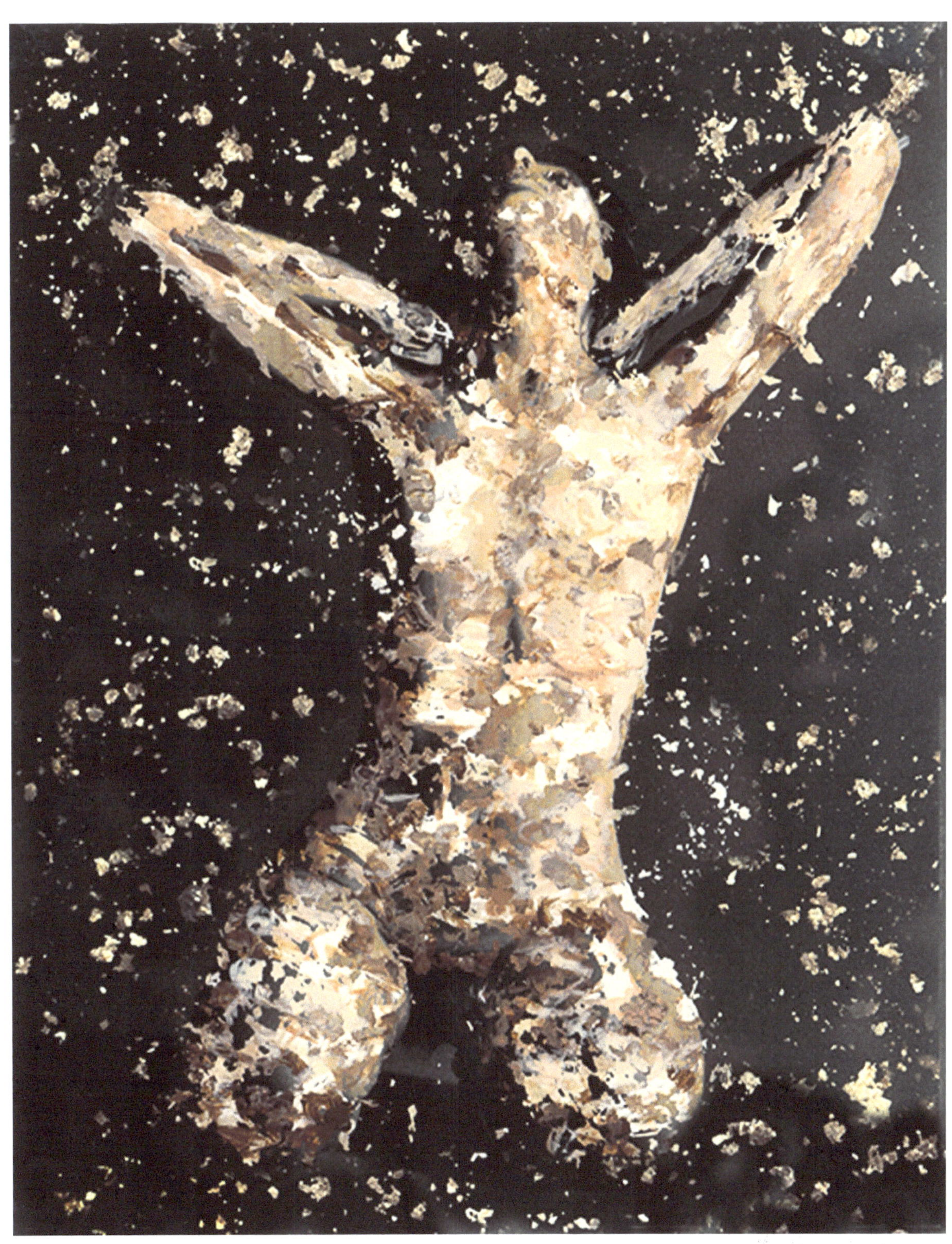

Conclusion

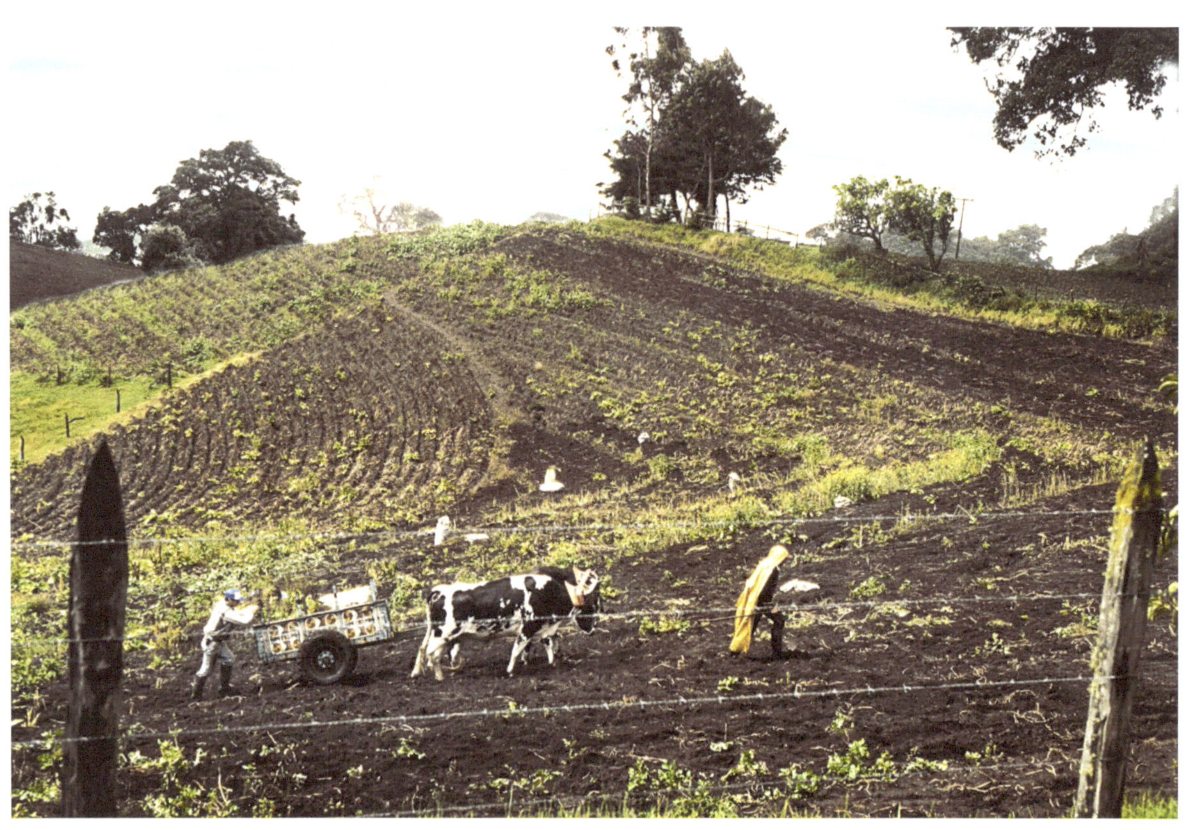

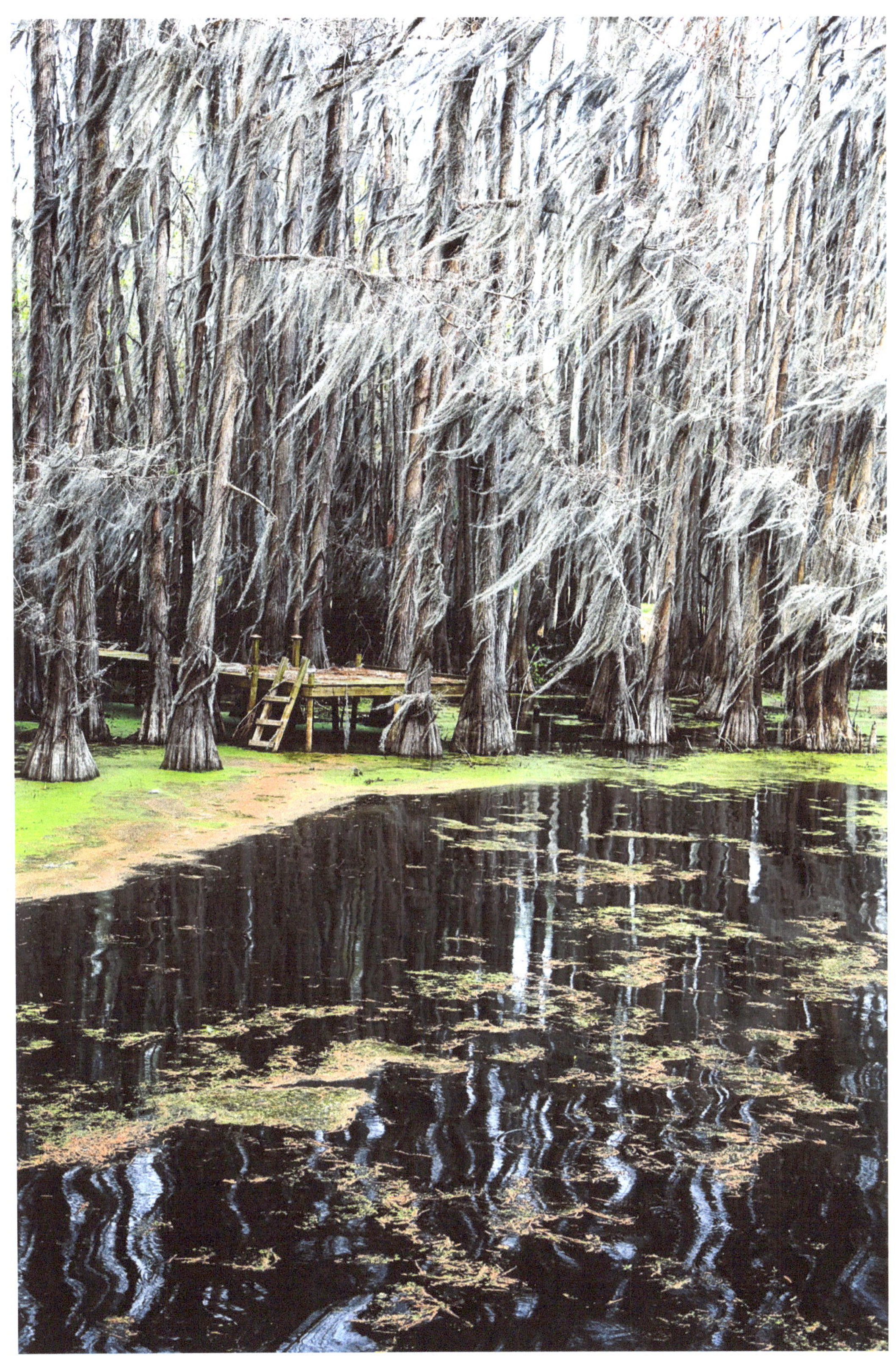

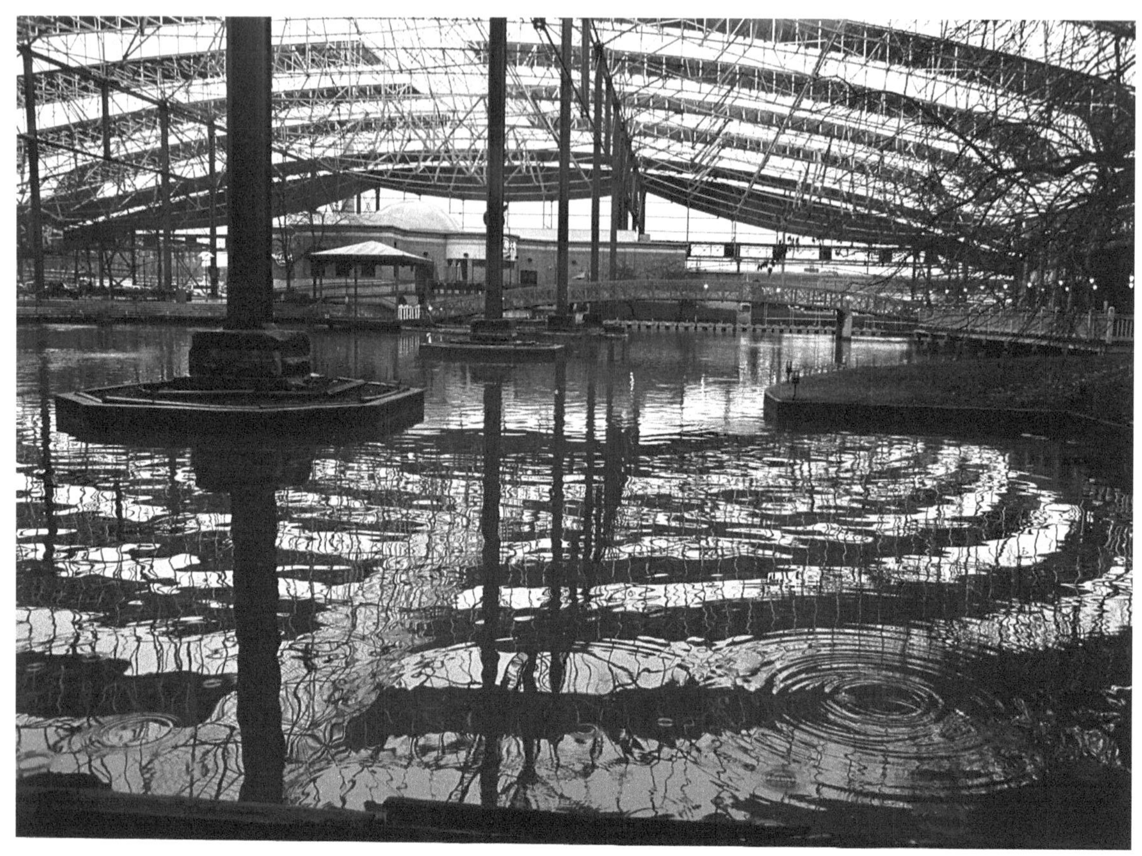

Mankind created much of what is to be encountered in life. We added to what was already there in order to avoid or coexist with nature, and we added to that because to do so is our nature. Earth is big, but there is only so much room, so sometimes we have to destroy in order to build. We create and propagate because we can, and until Mother Nature or some greater force decides otherwise, we rule the earth.

Some of Earth's most spectacular sights have no real substance. Mist and fog and rainbows dissipate into nothing. Lightning is there and gone in a flash of brilliance. Smoke rides the breeze to nowhere, and even ice and rain are ephemeral.

The reflection of an object is not solid. It is an image, and when it is out of sight it is still an image of memory, just like the thing it reflects. Objects without mass can inspire fear and wonder. They are elements of life, and deserve to be inventoried along with all earthly things.

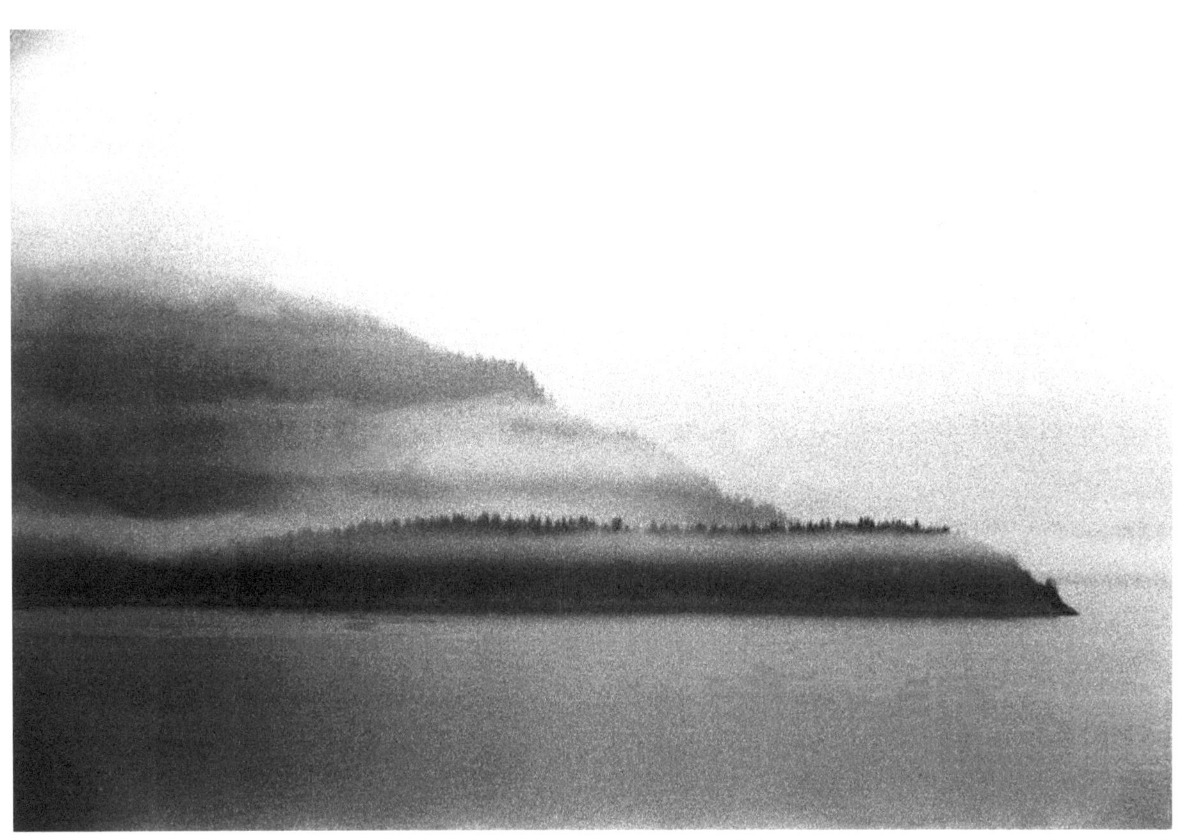

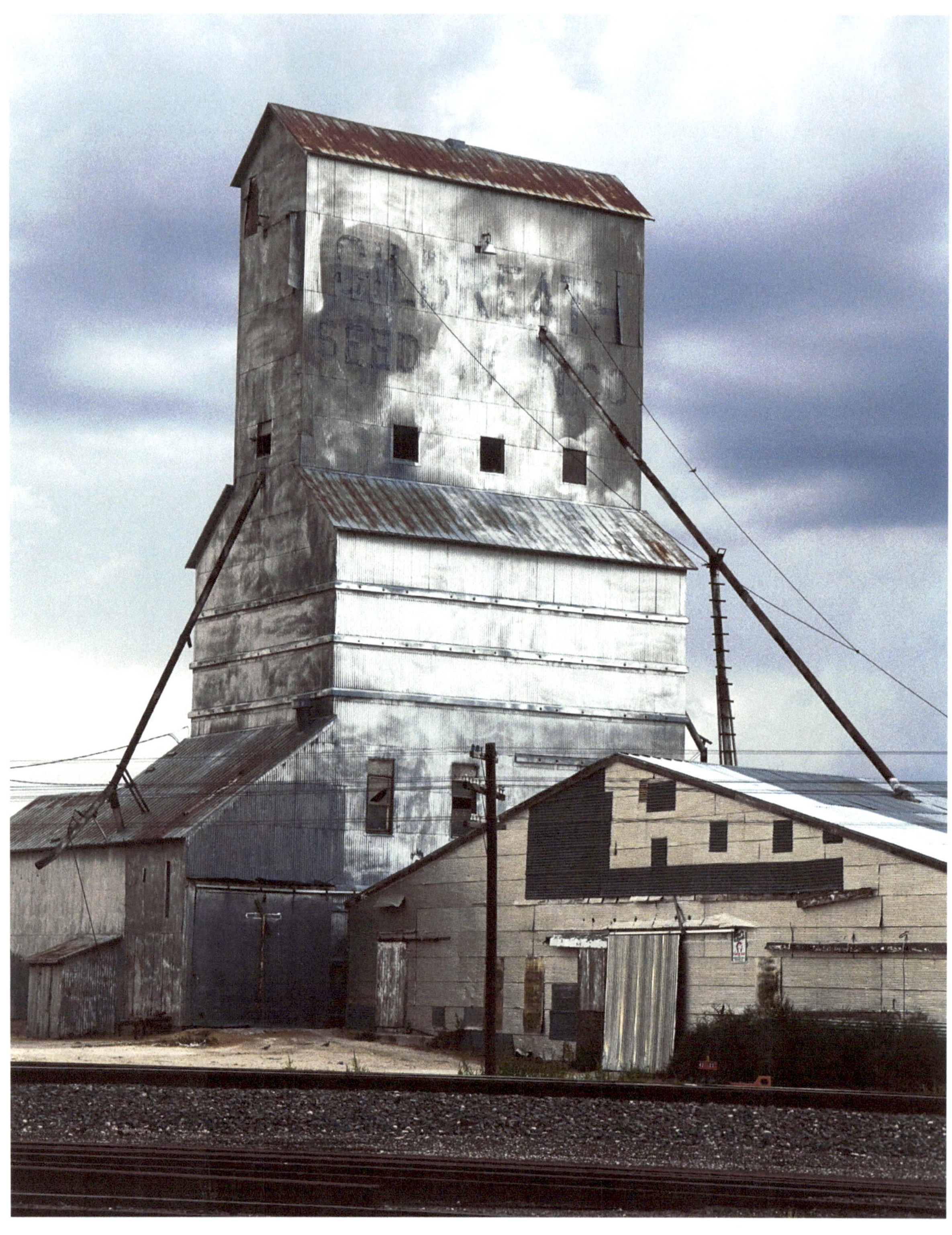

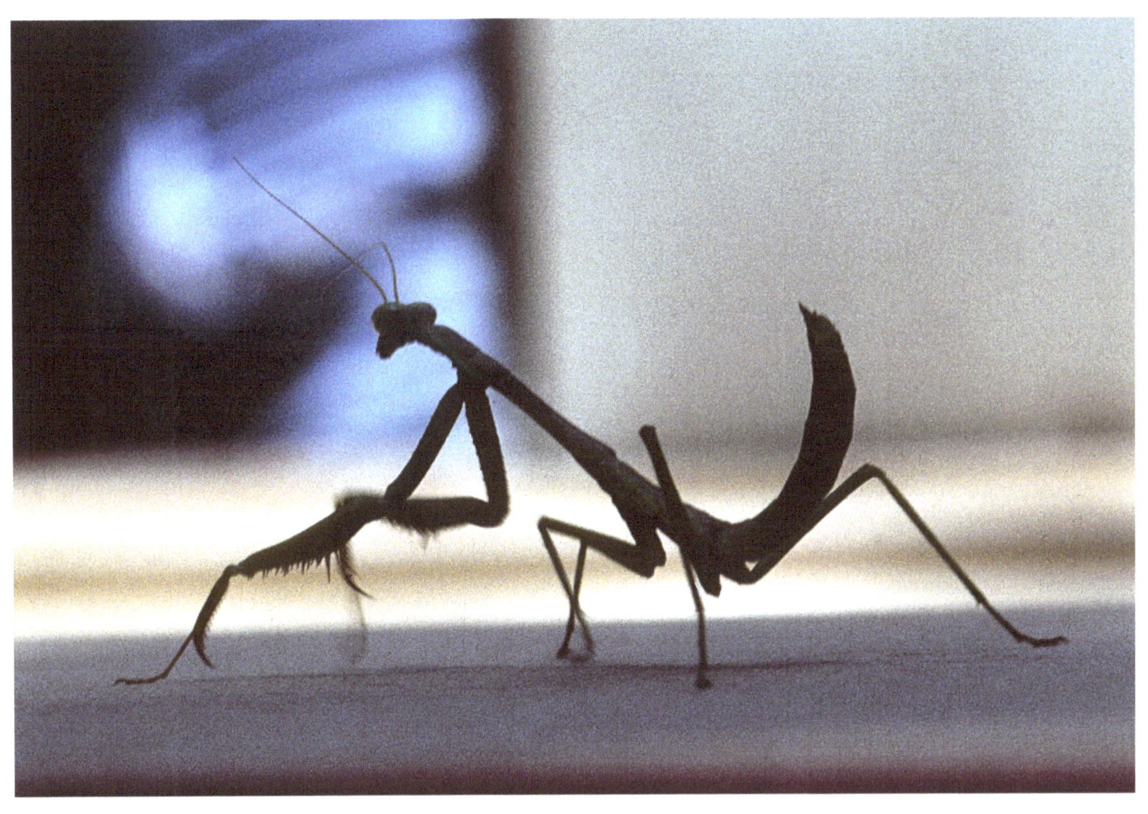

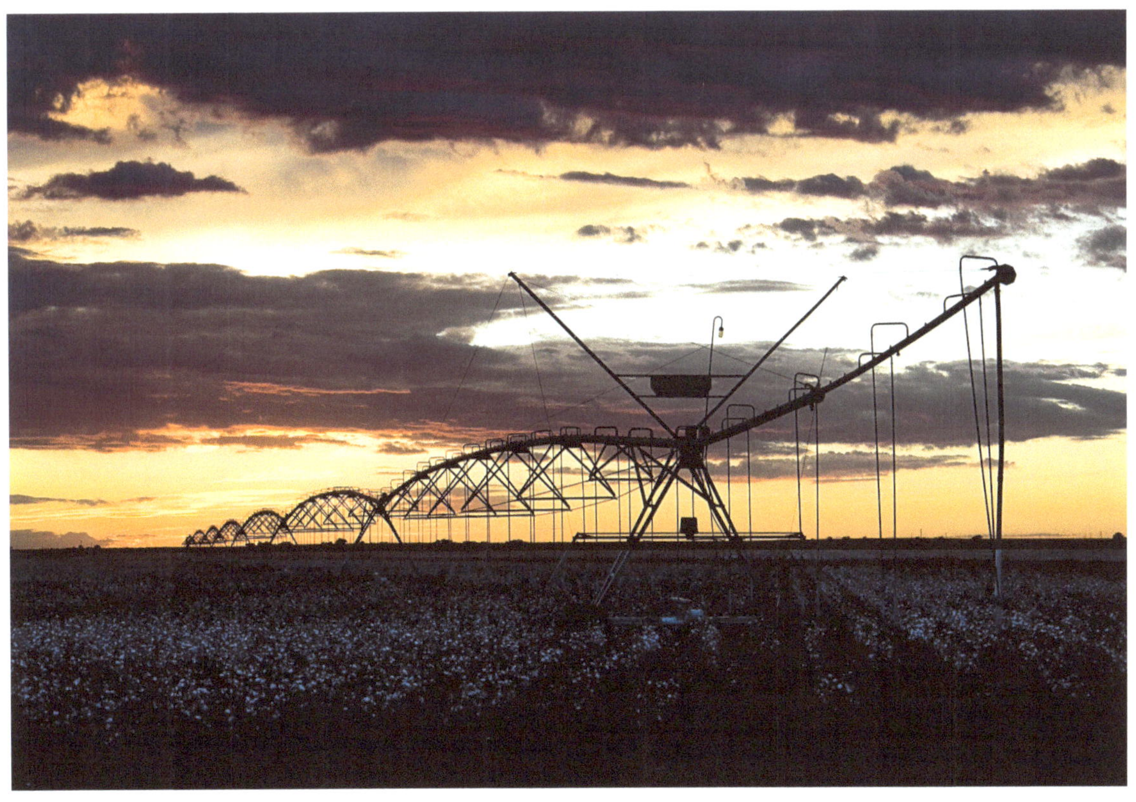

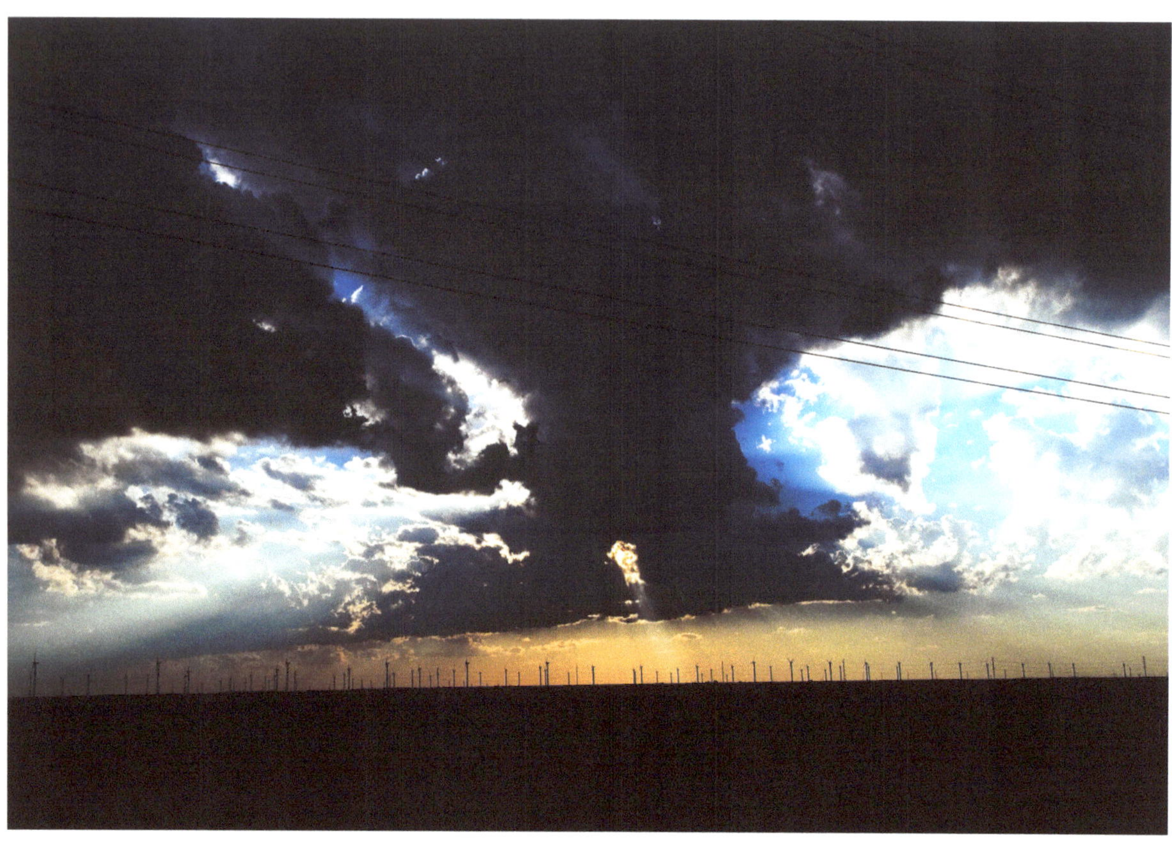

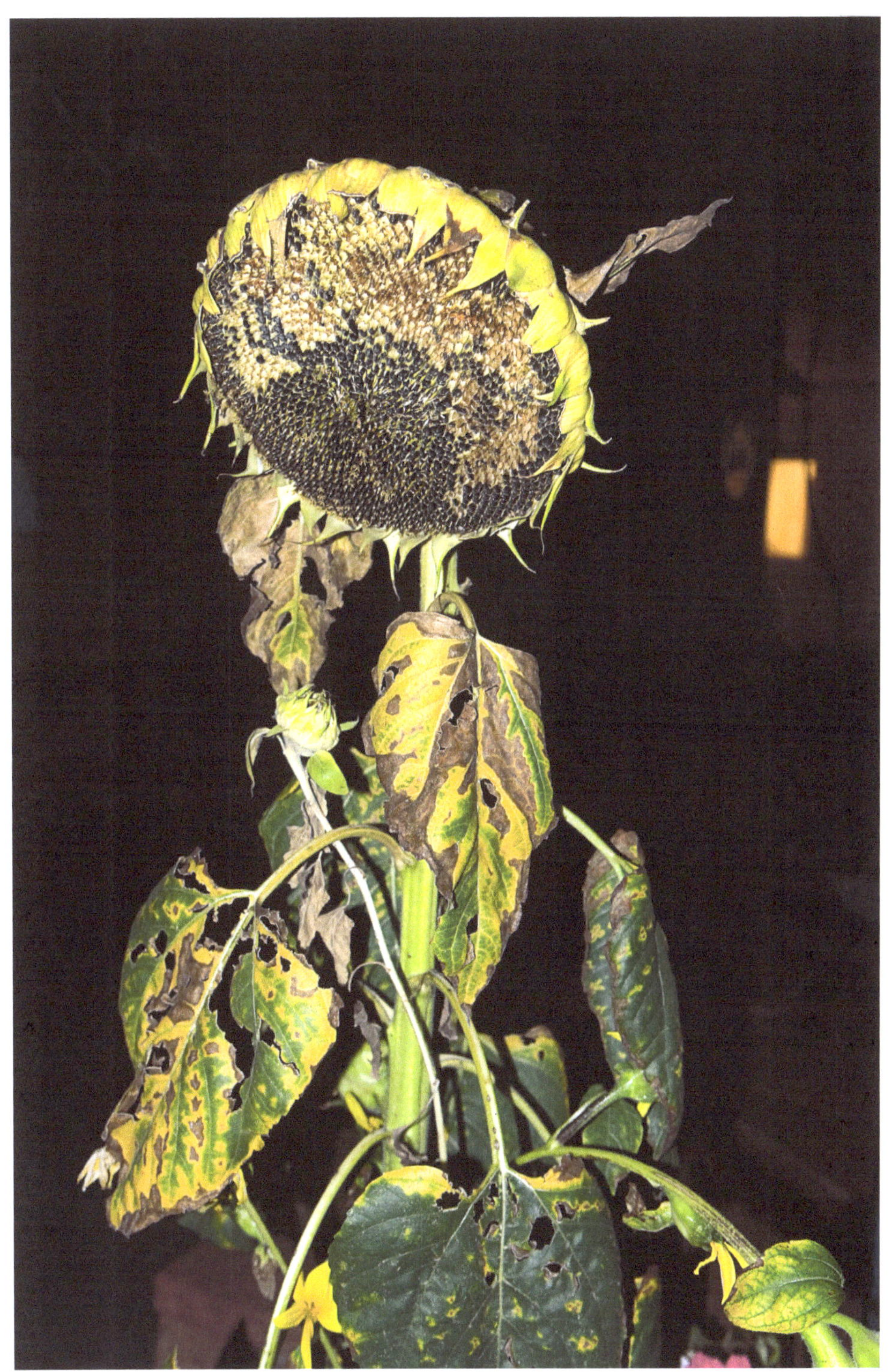

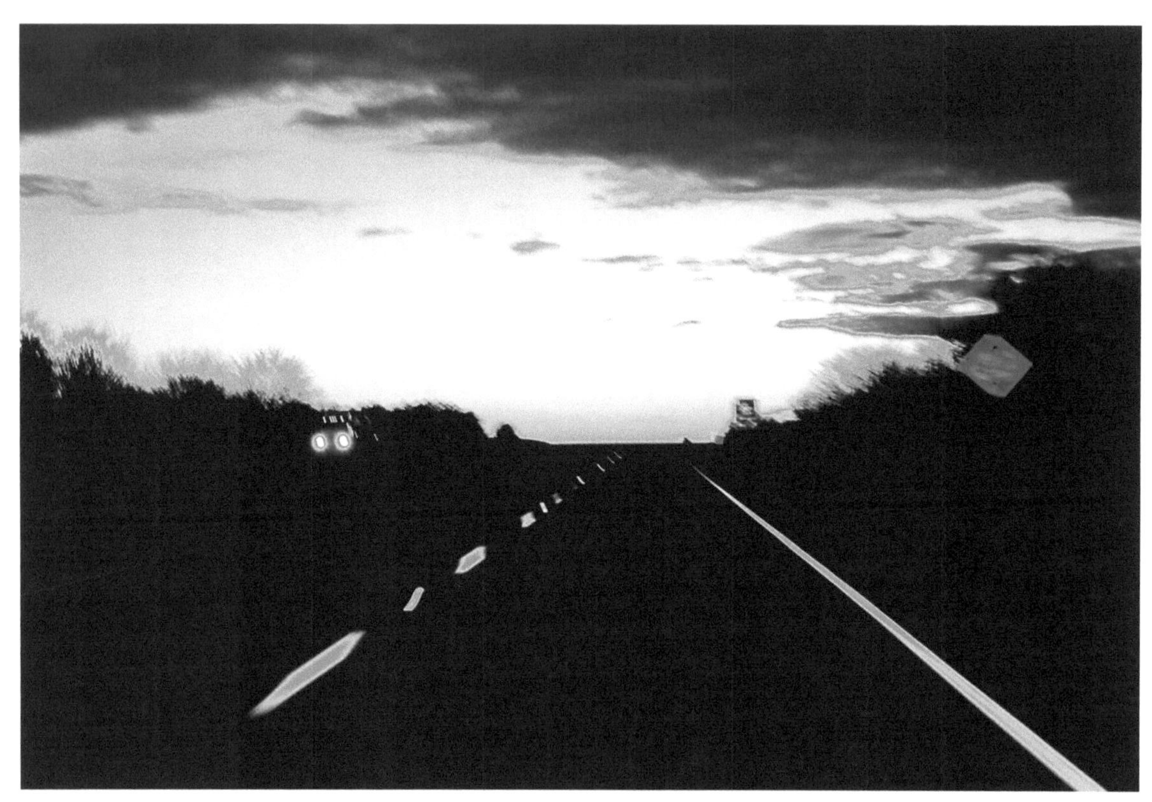

Life is a shipwreck, but we must not forget to sing in the lifeboats.
—Voltaire

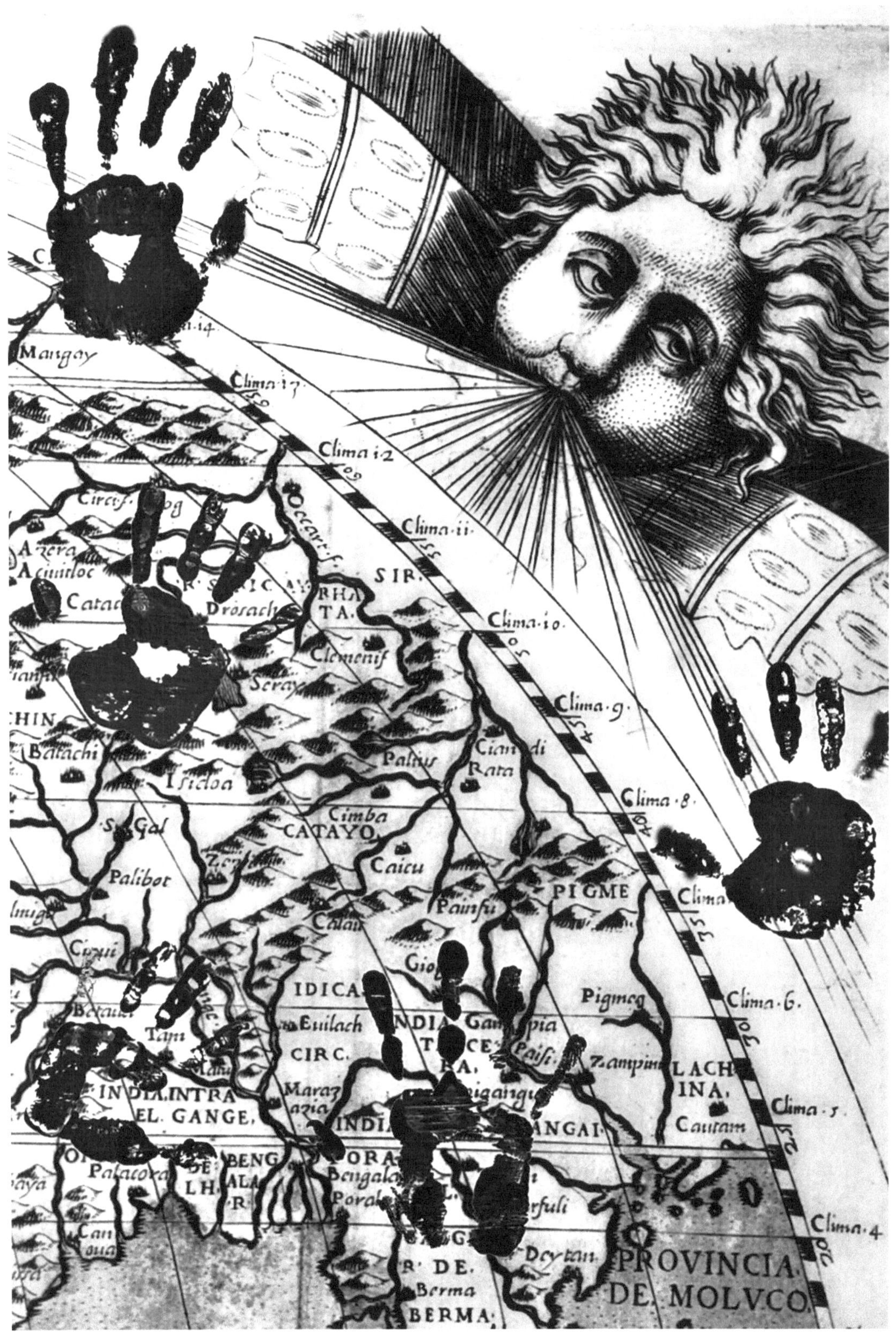
Mangay
Clima 17
Clima 12
Clima 11
SIR
RHA TA
Clima 10
Clima 9
Clima 8
Clima 6
Clima 5
Clima 4
Catai
Drosach
Clemenis
Seray
CHIN
Balachi
Paltus
Ciam di Rata
Cimba
CATAYO
Caicu
Palibot
Painfu
PIGME
IDICA
Euilach
INDIA
CIRC.
Pigmeg
LACH INA
Cautam
INDIA INTRA EL. GANGE
BENG ALA
Bengala
Palacora
Deytan
PROVINCIA DE MOLVCO
Berma
BERMA

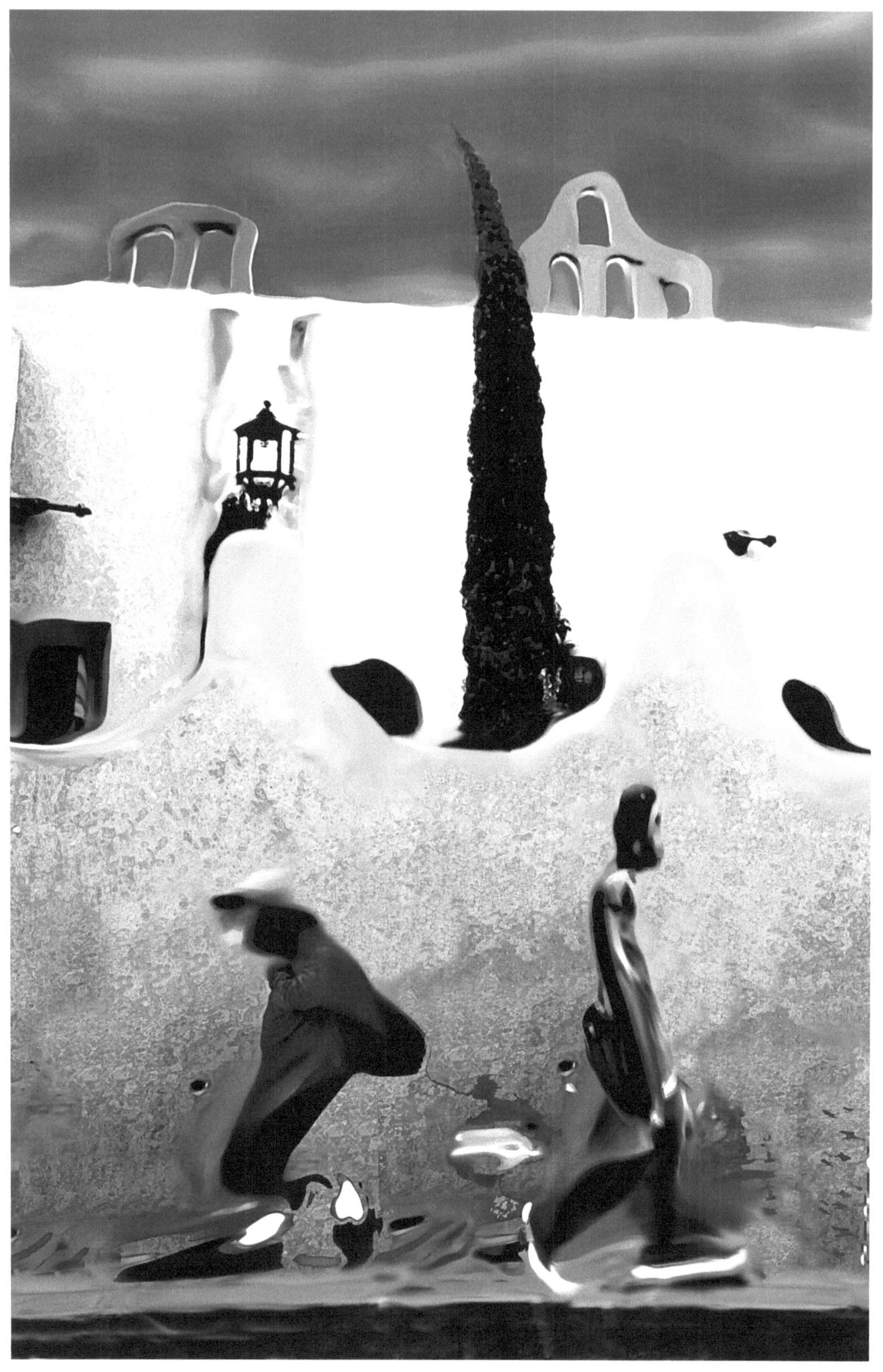

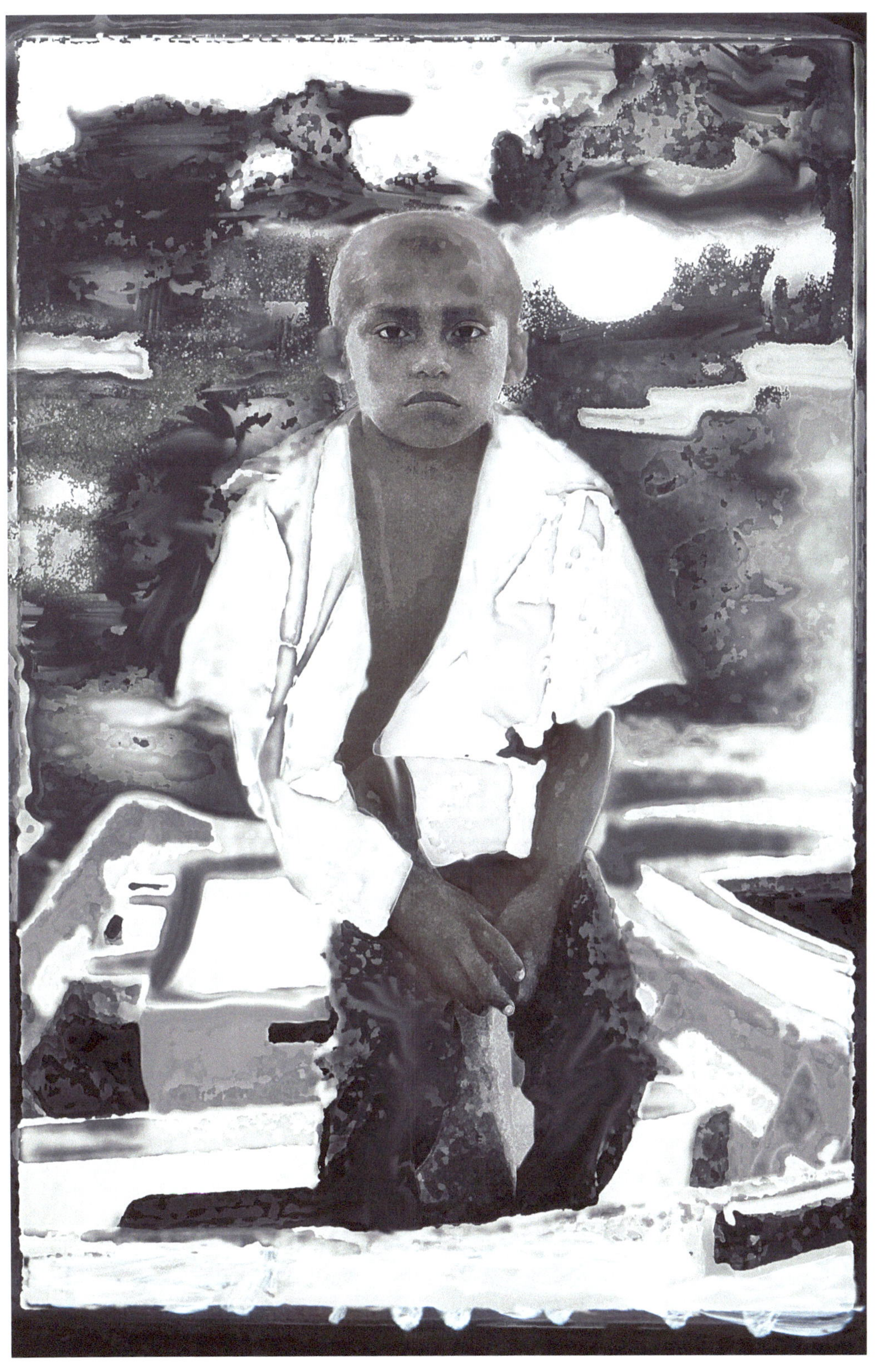

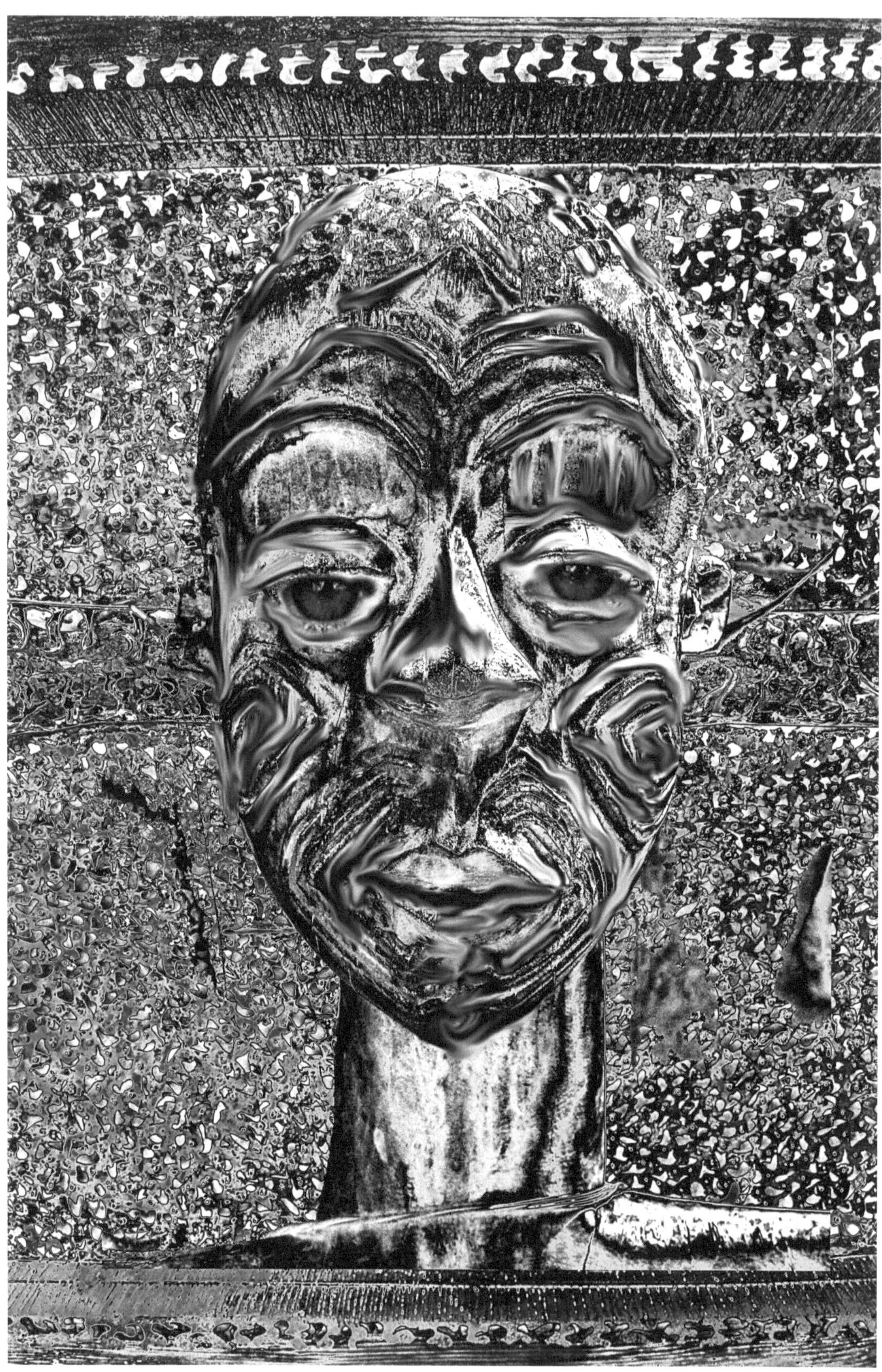

Vacant eyes and belly hair, and
musty rooms with dust in the air.
African masks and sleeping dogs.
Scriptures and porn and low-lying fog.

So much to do, so much to see.
Ingredients in a recipe.
People and things in so many places,
crammed into cramped and open spaces.

Leaves in the pool, stars in the sky
How did it happen, and why?
Man made, natural, and in between.
So many things overlooked and unseen.

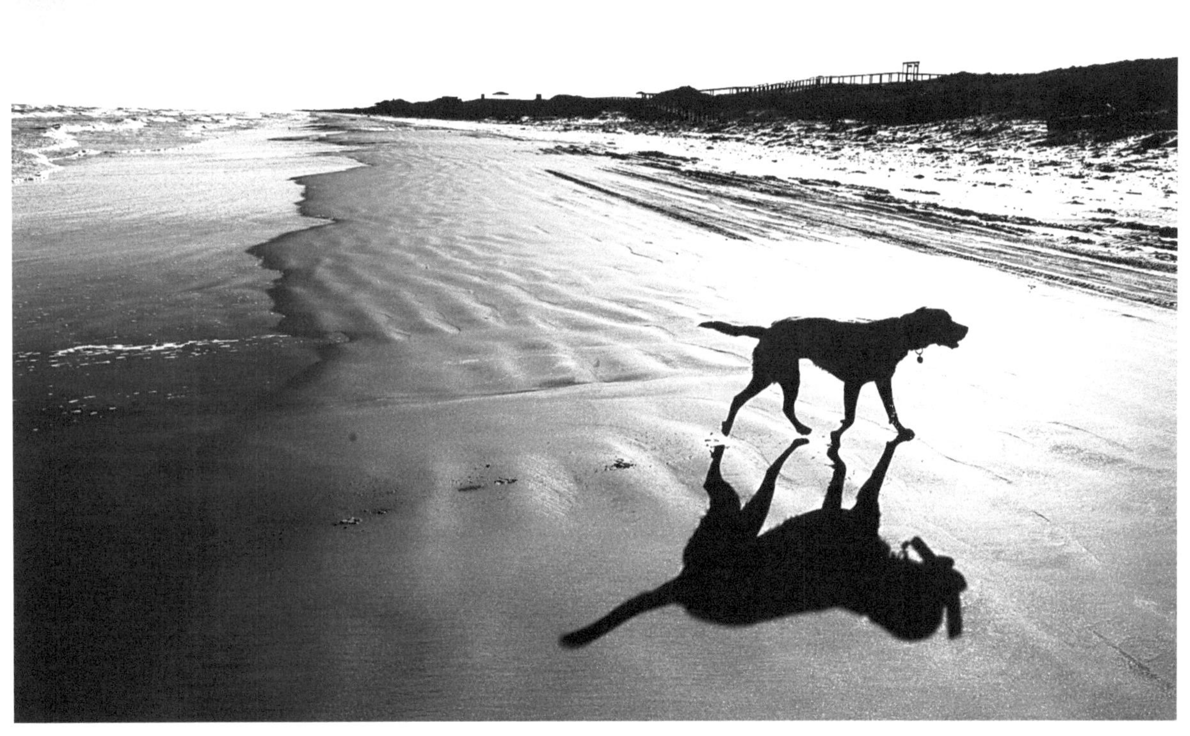

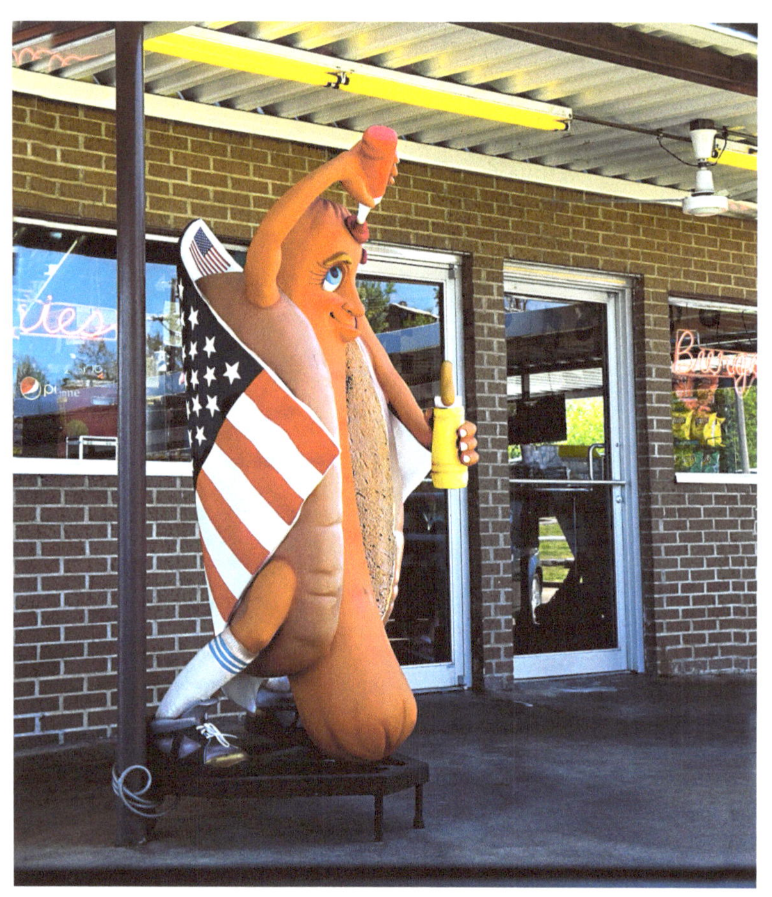

List of Images

Most of the photographs depict an event that actually happened. They are listed here with a somewhat descriptive title, and the place the picture was taken. Some of the images are multiple exposures or mixed media, identified below as composite. Those visual metaphors are as fictitious as the text.

Acknowledgments

Thanks to Beth McJunkin, Dan Gauthier, Shiila Safer, and Jason Scalise for making this book possible, and to the rest of the Scalise family for their advice and support.

www.ingramcontent.com/pod-product-compliance
Lightning Source LLC
LaVergne TN
LVHW070129110826
845147LV00002B/215

* 9 7 8 0 6 9 2 8 8 0 9 5 1 *